POWER AND SOCIETY

A Framework for Political Inquiry

HAROLD D. LASSWELL
and
ABRAHAM KAPLAN

It is not names that constitute governments, but the use and exercise of those powers that were intended to accompany them.

JOHN LOCKE

NEW HAVEN AND LONDON
Yale University Press

Ninth printing, 1976.
ISBN: 0–300–00675–6

Printed in the United States of America
by The Murray Printing Company,
Westford, Massachusetts.

Originally published with assistance
from the fund established in mem-
ory of Ganson Goodyear Depew.

PREFACE

A BRIEF BIOGRAPHY of this collaboration between a political scientist and a philosopher may be of interest to anyone concerned with increasing the amount of inter-disciplinary teamwork. The present book is a by-product of the Research Project on Wartime Communication which was organized within the framework of the Library of Congress shortly before World War II on the basis of a grant from the Rockefeller Foundation. The Library project had several responsibilities: to perfect tools of research on mass communication; to recruit and train personnel for service in the agencies of propaganda, information, and intelligence; to advise on matters of strategy, tactics, and organization; to describe and analyze certain phases of the history of the war crisis.

As a guide to research and analysis, it was necessary to review the then current state of knowledge of political communication, particularly of war communication. A review of this kind must obviously be conducted with full regard to the theories, procedures, and findings of the disciplines concerned with the institutions of power and the process of communication. Such a review was handicapped by the relatively unsystematic and fragmentary nature of the literature in all pertinent fields. The situation prevailing at the time was part of the cost of the extraordinarily rapid expansion of empirical research, which had experienced an epoch of unparalleled richness in inventing and applying new methods of observing and processing data. The methods used in the "empirical revolution" covered a wide range of intensive and extensive procedures: for example, the prolonged psychoanalytic interview; the solicitation of life histories; participant observation of the life of a community; tests of aptitude, attitude, and attainment; brief polling interviews.

The research review was designed to give prominence to propositions amenable to further investigation. The degree of vagueness and ambiguity of the terms usually employed in the field required a considerable exercise in definition. And the orientation toward the ongoing of political inquiry demanded sufficient logical analysis to guarantee empirical significance in the propositions formulated. Hence the desirability of collaboration between a subject-matter specialist and a student of the philosophy of language and of scientific methodology. Teamwork was made easier because the role of symbols was central to both interests, the political scientist having been occupied with the theory of propaganda for many years and the philosopher having worked in the theory of signs and semantics with Charles Morris, Rudolph Carnap, and Bertrand Russell at the University of Chicago.

The manuscript was finished by the end of 1945, when Mr. Kaplan joined the Department of Philosophy at the University of California at Los Angeles, and Mr. Lasswell became a professor at the Yale Law School. In the past five years there have been many changes, both in the state of research in the field and in our own thinking about these problems. But the task of developing a framework for inquiry contemporaneous with the state of research is an unending one. Practical considerations have made it seem preferable to offer the material in its present form rather than attempt once more to reformulate it in accord with our continuing changes in viewpoint on this or that detail.

The text has been read in connection with seminars, especially at Yale, where it has been preliminary to more detailed study of certain legal problems. It is feasible to name but a few of our helpful critics, some of whose constructive points can be taken advantage of only in future work. At the formative stage we were particularly aware of the valuable aid of Nathan Leites, now of the RAND Corporation, and of Joseph M. Goldsen, research director of the project at the Library of Congress, now likewise of RAND. At Yale we name especially Professors William T. R. Fox (now of Columbia) and Myres S. McDougal. Dr. Harald Ofstad of the University of Oslo did a particularly thorough commentary during his stay in this country. As the references show, the published work of several recent and contemporary scholars has been most useful. In the United States we can name Charles E. Merriam, Robert M. MacIver, W. W. Willoughby, Carl J. Friedrich; in Great Britain, Harold J. Laski, George E. G. Catlin, Richard H. Tawney, and James Bryce; in Western Europe, Robert Michels, Gaetano Mosca, Vilfredo Pareto, and J. K. Bluntschli.

Finally we wish to acknowledge the facilities of the Yale Law School, made available by Dean Wesley A. Sturges, and of the Library of Congress under the librarianships of Archibald MacLeish and Luther H. Evans.

H. D. L.
A. K.

June 1950

CONTENTS

TABLES

INTRODUCTION

§0.1 *Political Science, Philosophy, and Policy*

THIS IS A BOOK of political theory, not an analysis of the contemporary or impending political situation. The following pages contain no compilations of data, statistical or anecdotal, purporting to describe the significant political trends of our day, and urging the adoption of this or that policy or practice to thwart or encourage these trends.

Yet awareness of these trends has given direction to the views to be put forth. In an era of war, famine, and atomic destruction, safety and physical well-being are at the focus of world attention, and the control of violence the primary world problem. We have selected "well-being" in this specific sense as one of the major societal values entering into political analysis, and given special consideration to the role of violence in interpersonal relations. The global perspectives imposed by the alternative of "one world or none" are expressed in the following pages in the striving for cultural generality, for formulations that are not limited to the special conditions of our own society. Again, political forces in our day seem to be approximating a bi-polar pattern, around the last two centers of world revolution—the liberal-democratic and the bolshevist. Hence we treat revolution as an organic part of the political process, elaborate the role of ideology in political affairs, and call attention to the integrative (rather than divisive) use of power in preventive politics. The present-day importance of class, both as social fact and social symbol, is reflected in our own class analysis, and in our emphasis on merit rather than rank, skill rather than status, as keystones of democratic rule.

The list could be extended; but no end is served here by elaborating a point-to-point correspondence between the theoretical structure and the situational pattern. For our purpose is not to provide a guide for political action. Such guides and manuals have a long and impressive history, from Kautilya's *Arthaśāstra*—contemporaneous with Aristotle—through Machiavelli's *Prince*, to the writings of Lenin.[1] Our aim, however, is not to rewrite such manuals,

1. Compare G. P. Gooch, *Studies in Diplomacy and Statecraft*, Longmans, Green, 1942, 350–1: Machiavelli "wrote primarily for rulers, Hobbes primarily for subjects. *The Prince* is a manual of statecraft, *De Cive* a grammar of obedience."

but rather to elaborate a conceptual framework within which inquiry into the political process may fruitfully proceed. For, at bottom, it is only on the basis of such inquiry that political policy can be intelligently selected and applied.

If our purpose is primarily to advance political theory rather than the techniques of political practice, it does not follow, however, that we have no concern with such practice in its concrete particularity. Theorizing, even about politics, is not to be confused with metaphysical speculation in terms of abstractions hopelessly removed from empirical observation and control. Such speculation characterized the German *Staatslehre* tradition so influential at the turn of the century.[2] The present work is much closer to the straightforward empirical standpoint of Machiavelli's *Discourses* or Michels' *Political Parties*. But this standpoint is not to be confused, on the other hand, with "brute empiricism"—the gathering of "facts" without a corresponding elaboration of hypotheses—a position to which the descriptive politics of De Tocqueville and Bryce sometimes appears to come dangerously close. "It is Facts that are needed," Bryce exclaims, "Facts, Facts, Facts" (1924, I, 12).[3] Of themselves, of course, "facts" are mere collections of details; they are significant only as data for hypotheses.

The elaboration of hypotheses presupposes, logically, a conceptual framework in terms of which clear hypotheses may be formulated. In the history of political thought, a number of books have aimed to provide a suitable vocabulary. Of these, the most famous in English is Sir George Cornwall Lewis' *The Use and Abuse of Political Terms*, published in 1832. Lewis hoped to bring the languages of political theory and of practical politics into closer harmony. Such expectations are, of course, doomed to disappointment: uniformity of usage cannot be brought about by either fiat or exhortation. Nor is this uniformity of any transcending importance. What does matter is self-consistency, and clarity sufficient to make translation and empirical reference always possible.

2. See, for instance, J. K. Bluntschli, 1921. Bluntschli defines political science (p. 1) as "the science which is concerned with the State, which endeavours to understand and comprehend the State in its conditions, in its essential nature, its various forms or manifestations, its development." The "essential nature" of the state, on his view, turns out to be that of a "masculine personality"! Such writing gives point to Pareto's remark about a neighboring social science, political economy, that it "has been and largely continues to be a branch of literature."

3. Frequent citations, listed on pp. 285–286, will be referred to by date of publication.

Our concern, moreover, is not with words but with concepts. The problems involved are no more "merely terminological" than the physicist's problem of the meaning of "simultaneity" or the biologist's of the analysis of "species." [4]

Many of the most influential political writings—those of Plato, Locke, Rousseau, the *Federalist*, and others—have not been concerned with political inquiry at all, but with the justification of existent or proposed political structures. We say such works formulate *political doctrine* rather than propositions of *political science*. *Political philosophy* includes not only doctrine, but also logical analysis of both doctrine and science; the term *political theory* may be used as a comprehensive designation for all these types of sentences.

In these terms, the present work is an attempt to formulate the basic concepts and hypotheses of political science. It contains no elaborations of political doctrine, of what the state and society *ought* to be. Historically, as Laski has pointed out (1935, 31), such doctrines have served chiefly to justify the political philosopher's own preferences (and, of course, those of the groups with which he identifies himself). Witness, for instance, Hegel's appraisal of the Prussian state as the highest embodiment of universal Reason. As has been remarked elsewhere, "The task of political thought may be far more to clear away the prejudices which prevent men from seeing the state as they have made it than to offer doctrines of what the state ought to be" (MacIver, 1926, 426).

It must be emphasized, however, that a scientific interest in political inquiry need not exclude a political interest in its outcome and applications. Inquiry has not only a creative role in the formation of policy—serving as a means of self-orientation in a flow of events of changing significance—but also an instrumental role in implementing policy. Thus the purport of inquiry is not necessarily "theoretical" rather than "practical": both manipulative and contemplative standpoints may be adopted.

From the *manipulative standpoint*, the problematic situation with which inquiry begins is resolved into alternative goals possible in the situation, and the problem is formulated in terms of courses of action leading to the goal. The elements of the situation are analyzed and appraised in terms of their bearing on the formation of policy.

4. The analysis of political concepts also involves problems of methods of observation and verification. This methodological concern in political thought is exemplified in recent times in the writings of Charles E. Merriam, 1945.

The result of inquiry is a warranted statement of the way in which an actor in the situation can increase the probability of occurrence of a specified state of affairs: "To produce Y (or: To make Y most likely to occur), do X!"

The *contemplative standpoint* is not concerned with the isolation of goal variables, and discovery of the operations required for them to assume specified magnitudes. Rather, relations of interdependence are formulated in terms of their significance for the ongoing of inquiry itself. Here, propositions state the existence of functional co-relations (in the form Y is a function of X). It is evident that these formulations may be translated into those of the manipulative standpoint, and conversely: one must do X to produce Y if and only if Y is a function of X.

Yet to say that the results of inquiry from these different standpoints are intertranslatable is not to say that the difference in standpoint makes no difference. To rely exclusively on the manipulative approach—thus limiting inquiry to a consideration of ways and means—is to court the danger of interfering with inquiry if it has implications contrary to antecedently fixed policy (ends). The purely contemplative standpoint, on the other hand, fails to maximize the relevance of inquiry to the richest potentialities and most pressing needs of society in the given situation. This is what is sound about the emphasis on "unity of theory and practice" in pragmatism and the traditional literature of Marxism.[5]

From a manipulative standpoint, the social sciences are better designated as *policy sciences*—their function is to provide intelligence pertinent to the integration of values realized by and embodied in interpersonal relations. We conceive of political science as one of the policy sciences—that which studies influence and power as instruments of such integration. The problem of social policy is that of creating conditions under which power can and does act integratively in relation to the major values of society as a whole.

This definition of political science is in many ways in accord

5. Integration of the manipulative and contemplative standpoints implies, among other things, that political science research must give due weight to the emerging future, rather than dealing only with the more or less casual and haphazard data from the past. Compare Dewey, *German Philosophy and Politics*, Henry Holt, 1915, 5: "Historians should be engaged in construing the past in terms of the problems and interests of an impending future, instead of reporting a past in order to discover some mathematical curve which future events are bound to describe."

with the grand tradition of political thought. No one of the great political thinkers of tradition has conceived of political science in terms of "power politics," if by "power politics" is meant the pursuit of power as the supreme value of society. All of them, to be sure, have been aware of the coercive aspect of power, and they have noted that all people, to some degree, use coercion and submit to coercion. All of them, however, have also taken cognizance of the possibility of using power as an instrument by means of which other values might be maximized, and the "good life" brought into being.

The present conception conforms, therefore, to the philosophical tradition in which politics and ethics have always been closely associated. But it deviates from the tradition in giving full recognition to the existence of two distinct components in political theory —the empirical propositions of political science and the value judgments of political doctrine. Only statements of the first kind are explicitly formulated in the present work.

The adoption of both the manipulative and contemplative standpoints in inquiry we designate the *principle of configurative analysis.*[6] The deliberate use of both standpoints is of value for both theory and practice. The functions of the scientist overlap and interact with those of the policy maker. As a citizen, a moral person, the scientist has his own preferences, goals, values; all his acts, including his acts of scientific inquiry, are subject to self-discipline by moral aims. And these aims, in turn, stimulate and fructify his science.

Thus, that the purpose of this book is to provide a framework for political science does not imply that the authors are unconcerned with political policy. Our own values are those of the citizen of a society that aspires toward freedom. Hence we have given special attention to the formulation of conditions favorable to the establishment and continuance of a free society. Such formulations, to the degree that they are warranted and fruitful, themselves foster freedom by communicating insight into the kind of institutions by which freedom is realized. But we are not concerned with the justification of democratic values, their derivation from some metaphysical or moral base. This is the province of political doctrine,

6. Later in this introduction we shall formulate other "principles" followed in this work. We use the term in the sense of Charles S. Peirce's *leading principles:* formulations, not of metaphysical truths, but of logical instruments operative in inquiry.

not political science. Confusion between the two provinces, rather than configurative analysis in which they are distinguished yet brought into relation with one another, only does injury to both.

§0.2 *The Power Process*

In recent decades a thoroughgoing empiricist philosophy of the sciences has been elaborated in a number of approaches—logical positivism, operationalism, instrumentalism—concurring in an insistence on the importance of relating scientific ideas to materials ultimately accessible to direct observation.[7] Adopting this standpoint, the present work analyzes such political abstractions as "state" and "sovereignty" in terms of concrete interpersonal relationships of influence and control. The experiential data of political science are acts considered as affecting or determining other acts, a relation embodied in the key concept of power. Political science, as an empirical discipline, is the study of the shaping and sharing of power.

This empirical grounding of political abstractions may be expressed by formulating the subject matter of political science in terms of a certain class of *events* (including "subjective" events), rather than timeless institutions or political patterns. We deal with power as a process in time, constituted by experientially localized and observable acts. Both structures and functions are construed as abstractions from what is empirically given as process. This orientation in political inquiry may be designated the *principle of temporality*.

The principle of temporality does not imply a concern with only *changes* in situations rather than with *states* of affairs. Inquiry deals with both sorts of problems, and may be designated as *equilibrium* or *developmental analysis* accordingly.

In some cases a set of variables interact "systemically"—they constitute a system in that they tend toward the maintenance of a particular pattern of interaction. The organism is a system in this sense. The standpoint of equilibrium analysis directs inquiry to the isolation of such systems and investigation of the conditions of their maintenance: disturbances may lead to a reestablishment of equilibrium or the disruption of the system. This standpoint has

7. Unfortunately, empiricists like Carnap and Reichenbach have devoted little attention to social thought; and philosophers like Russell and the pragmatists have been more concerned with social policy than with a logical analysis of the social sciences.

been fruitful not only in physiology (to say nothing of the "closed systems" of physics), but in various of the social sciences as well, for instance in economic analysis. And it is equally available for the study of power, respect, or other value processes. A structure of power relationships may be such that interference with the pattern sets in motion tendencies to reinstate the original structure ("balance of power" process).[8]

The developmental standpoint is concerned, not with systems in equilibrium, but with patterns of succession of events. Inquiry into these patterns is directed to the specification of terminal phases—the "from what" and "toward what" of developmental sequences.[9] Hence the key concepts are likely to be less generalized than those of equilibrium analysis. We may speak of the world as moving from "19th century private capitalism" to "20th century socialism," for example—terms lacking the universality of, say, "economic system" and "economic crisis." But the lesser generality of the developmental standpoint gives it a correspondingly more direct purport for action. Decision making is forward looking, formu-

8. Emphasis on equilibrium analysis occurs throughout Pareto's *Mind and Society,* whence it was given further impetus by the physiologists L. J. Henderson and W. B. Cannon, influencing such work as Elton Mayo's *Human Problems of an Industrial Civilization,* Macmillan, 1933. The application of equilibrium analysis to social phenomena does not necessarily involve the classical "organism" metaphor of society (unless, indeed, the concept of "organism" is taken in some such generalized sense as it has, say, in Whitehead). What it implies methodologically is an insistence on the futility of efforts to conduct social inquiry by pairing of single variables rather than dealing with multiple correlations (see the discussion of this point in Lasswell, 1939, 541–2). An explicit formulation of the standpoint of equilibrium analysis in the social sciences is given by A. R. Radcliffe-Brown in his preface to *African Political Systems,* edited by M. Fortes and E. E. Evans-Pritchard, Oxford University Press, 1940, xxii–xxiii: "Social structure is not to be thought of as static, but as a condition of equilibrium that only persists by being continually renewed, like the chemical-physiological homostasis of a living organism. Events occur which disturb the equilibrium in some way, and a social reaction follows which tends to restore it." See also Gunnar Myrdal, *An American Dilemma,* Harper, 1944, Appendix 3: "A Methodological Note on the Principle of Cumulation."

9. Developmental analysis is often combined with an equilibrium component—laws of change in addition to characterizations of the process of change. Confusion between these components may interfere with sound appraisal of both. Thus Darwin's developmental analysis of the evolutionary process is distinguished by the biologist from "Darwinism" as a statement of conditions and mechanisms supposedly operative in the process. In Marxist theory, however, "laws" of social change are seldom explicitly distinguished from the description of a specific historical process; data confirming the account of that process is often mistakenly construed as evidence for the supposed laws according to which the changes occur, and conversely.

lating alternative courses of action extending into the future, and selecting among the alternatives by expectations of how things will turn out. And "the way things will turn out" is the type problem for the developmental standpoint.[10]

One of the implications of the principle of temporality is an emphasis on the gradations—both actual and possible—among the kinds of events distinguished. Political science does not deal with essential natures, eternally distinct from one another and separable into fixed species. There is as much continuity between political categories as is in fact characteristic of the shifting events which the categories comprise. Hence, wherever possible, distinctions are formulated here in terms of polarities rather than dichotomies; a political characteristic is not designated simply as an "A" to be distinguished from the "non-A," but "A" and "Z" are taken to mark the extremes of a continuous range of the character in question. Rather than isolating democracy, for instance, as an absolutely distinct political form, we specify a range of democratic-despotic characteristics. Technically, absolute predicates have been replaced by functors, that is, terms signifying functions having many "values," and thereby admitting of variation in degree.[11]

It is not presupposed that these degrees are capable of quantitative comparison; the introduction of a metric does not precede but follows the ordering of the elements in a series. From a logical viewpoint, it is the substitution of ordering for absolute classification which underlies the difference between Greek and modern science—a difference between a science of species and a science of functional

10. Nineteenth-century thought was especially rich in developmental concepts. Many of these were vitiated by being construed in terms of a rigid causal determination between a succession of "stages," rather than in terms of a pattern of continuing variables assuming different magnitudes under different conditions. Grandiose "evolutionary" thinkers after Darwin dealt with social institutions as developmental sequences, affirming a progression from the "mystical" to the "metaphysical" to the "scientific," or from "Despotism" to "Freedom." These ambiguous designations often gave to the formulations in which they appeared a high propaganda resonance, making a sure thing of the shape of the world to come, and adding scientific authority to the appeal of prophecy. Analysis readily discloses the confusions, distortions, and unwarranted assumptions on which such formulations rested. Yet, open as it is to abuse, the developmental standpoint can nevertheless be of value in bringing the process of inquiry into closer accord with the needs of policy, when this standpoint is deliberately taken as a technique of self-stimulation in the envisioning of alternative futures.

11. R. Carnap, *The Logical Syntax of Language,* Kegan Paul, Trench, Trubner, 1937, §53.

co-relations. Once concepts are formulated in terms of order, of variation in degree, scales and methods of measurement can be developed to suit the needs of the particular problem.[12]

The principle of temporality also has an important bearing on the scope of political science. Since the subject matter of political science is constituted by power as a process, its scope cannot be sharply differentiated from that of the other social sciences. For events, unlike the classical species, merge into and react with one another. The power process is not a distinct and separable part of the social process, but only the political aspect of an interactive whole. It is, in fact, only the political aspect of the social process in its entirety.[13] Hence much of what follows is appropriate, from other standpoints, to psychology, economics, or sociology, rather than "political science proper." For we are concerned with all variables entering significantly into the situations and acts dealt with, not merely with the variables belonging to certain categories in an antecedent classification of the sciences.

In particular, full emphasis is given to the multiplicity of factors involved in any given political event—an emphasis that may be designated as a *principle of interdetermination.* This standpoint is sometimes formulated as a principle of "multiple causation." But more is involved than multiple causes; there are multiple effects as well, and more important, there are patterns of interaction in which it is impossible to distinguish between cause and effect. Hence we speak of the interdetermination of a set of variables—each is corelated with the others. Thus no attempt is made here to confine political analysis to the consideration of some one particular kind

12. The matter is worth emphasizing because of the prevalence of the conception among social scientists that their disciplines cannot be "scientific" without exact measurements. (Graven in stone on the social science research building at the University of Chicago are the words of the physicist, Lord Kelvin: "Only that is knowledge which can be weighed and measured.") Hence quantitative considerations are introduced at all costs; and when the difficulties in the way of numerical determinations become apparent, inquiry is blocked. In fact, nonmetrical orders may suffice for the recognition of functional co-relations. (On this point see Kurt Lewin, *Principles of Topological Psychology,* McGraw-Hill, 1936.) Social inquiry may profit from a relaxation of the demand for precise quantitative determinations *at the very outset;* numerical determination marks the successful close of inquiry, not its indispensable prerequisite.

13. Compare W. C. MacLeod, 1931, 15: "The political is merely the social examined from the purposely narrowed view of the political scientist. . . . We might even speak of a political process which is the social process politically considered."

of variable; political science is autonomous, and not merely applied psychology or applied economics. But its autonomy does not mean that it is independent of all the other social sciences, but rather that it cannot be circumscribed as a part of any one of them.[14]

Among the multiple determinants of the political process to which we give particular emphasis are various cultural and personality factors often neglected by specialized conceptions of politics (for instance, the economic). Such factors are analyzable in terms of the symbols in which they are expressed and operative. In recent decades rapid advances have been made in symbolic logic, semantics, and the general theory of signs. These disciplines have emphasized and clarified the important part played by symbols in various ranges of activity, and have also brought to the focus of attention important confusions concerning the nature and function of symbols. The role of symbols in the political process will be elaborated to a considerable degree in the following chapters, particularly as expressions of expectations, demands, and identifications. This emphasis in political science we may designate as a *principle of symbolization.*

This principle involves not only a recognition of the part played in politics by symbols (and the subjective events of which they are an expression), but also an acute awareness of the difference between symbol and symbolized, language and reference. In particular, formal power must often be distinguished from the effective control with which it purports to be identical. The attribute of authority may be analyzed, we shall suggest, in terms of the operation of certain sorts of symbols; and these symbols may in fact

14. The interdetermination of social variables is sometimes taken as ground for denying the possibility of any social science: human affairs, it is urged, are too complex to lend themselves to theoretical simplifications. But the complex factors determining voting behavior, for instance, do not prevent us from making reliable election forecasts. And as Hume somewhere observes, we can be as certain that a bag of gold placed on Picadilly Circus at noon will have disappeared at 1 P.M. as if it had been a block of ice. Sometimes, not the overdetermination but the "underdetermination" of human affairs—the great role of "chance"—is made the basis of pessimism as to the fruitfulness of social inquiry. But as has been often pointed out (see for instance Mosca, 1939, 283), at least we can predict what will *not* happen: "chance" operates only within certain limits. Inquiry is most fruitful where there are either a very few determinants, or sufficiently many to allow for statistical treatment. But whether these conditions are satisfied cannot be settled by a priori speculation. The task is not to develop or refute dialectical "proofs" of the impossibility of political science, but to push as far as we can specific inquiries into the political process.

conceal a structure of control quite distinct from the pattern of authority of which they are constitutive.[15]

§0.3 *Political Inquiry*

Attention must be given not only to the symbols functioning in the political process, but to the symbols used in inquiry into that process as well. Semantic confusions, in political theory as elsewhere, have markedly interfered with fruitful research; certainly such confusions enter into the common disparagement of the political insights of the past and the widespread despair of what might be attained in this area in the future. But obscurity, vagueness, and ambiguity are not inherent in the subject matter of political science; they are inescapable only when no effort is made to escape them.[16]

Hence in the following chapters we introduce the major terms of political science by explicit definition. In many instances, the differentiation of concepts and terms is proliferated into complex taxonomic structures. *Such a taxonomy is not a substitute for but an instrument of political inquiry.* The definitions will encourage only a sterile verbalization unless they are taken as tools for the systematic observation and interpretation of the political process. The epigraph on the title page from John Locke is doubly apropos: names constitute neither government nor the science of government. They are limited to providing only instruments and a framework in the one case as in the other. But the instruments must be *used,* in the framework, if the names and their definitions are to have more than a merely verbal significance.

In some cases the definitions are purely "nominal": they introduce words not previously in use (in such contexts, at any rate),

15. In modern political theory, the principle of symbolization emerges with the Marxist critique of ideology, and has been developed by Pareto, among others, in his theory of "derivations" and by Mannheim in his sociology of knowledge.

16. Compare the *Federalist*, No. XXXI: "Though it cannot be pretended that the principles of moral and political knowledge have, in general, the same degree of certainty with those of mathematics, yet they have much better claims in this respect than, to judge from the conduct of men in particular situations, we should be disposed to allow them. The obscurity is much oftener in the passions and prejudices of the reasoner than in the subject. Men, upon too many occasions, do not give their own understandings fair play; but, yielding to some untoward bias, they entangle themselves in words and confound themselves in subtleties."

for the sake of notational convenience. But for the most part, the definitions are of the kind designated in traditional logic as "real definitions." They are intended to make clear and explicit the content embodied in more or less established usage, and thus to constitute analyses of the concepts signified.

But usage is only one of the considerations taken into account in formulating the definitions; it is not by itself determinative. This is true not only because usage may be inconsistent, but, more important, because explicit formulation of definitions is here instrumental to political, not linguistic, inquiry. Successful fulfillment of this kind of function often requires restricting or extending common usage. Where usage is too firmly established, however, for the term to be dissociated from its special or "emotive" signification, we have replaced it by other designations.[17] In any case, our aim is not that of standardizing usage. It is, rather, to provide a framework for political theory which can be understood by all in the same way, and which is serviceable—whether directly or in translation—in the carrying on of inquiry into the problems of politics.[18]

To fulfill this function the definitions must provide for empirical indices which ultimately connect the terms introduced with experiential situations. Stable indices of this kind are not so readily available in the social as in the physical sciences. The chemist using the term "carbon" knows that his spectroscope will record certain wave bands whether he uses the instrument in New England or Mexico. But the social scientist studying anger cannot specify for it a simple index applicable in both places. Not only are the patterns on the basis of which anger is inferable different in the two cultures; there are also variations among income groups and other social stratifications. Moreover, the indices may acquire different significance with time—Mexico, for example, may progressively assimilate "Anglo-Saxon" standards of reticence.

Such *index instability*, as it may be called, contributes signifi-

17. "It may perhaps be censured an impertinent criticism in a discourse of this nature to find fault with words and names that have obtained in the world. And yet possibly it may not be amiss to offer new ones when the old are apt to lead men into mistakes" (Locke, *Civil Government,* chap. viii, 52).

18. Of course, all definitions are in part terminological proposals, but this is not always their most important function. Moreover, in the case of words having a strong "attitudinal" or "emotive" component, what appears to be a terminological proposal may in fact be—as C. L. Stevenson has suggested in his analysis of "persuasive definitions"—a proposal for the attachment of those attitudes and emotions to the new object specified in the definitions. This is true of definitions of such words as "democracy," for example.

cantly to the futility in the present state of research of many attempts at metricizing (quantifying) political hypotheses. As a further consequence, generalizations of social theory, to be of service in the continuing process of social research, must be restricted to specified social conditions. We may speak here of a *principle of situational reference.* Empirical significance requires that the propositions of social science, rather than affirming unqualifiedly universal invariances, state relations between variables assuming different magnitudes in different social contexts.[19]

To omit this context is not to universalize the proposition, but rather to hide its particularized reference to the situations characteristic of our own culture. The principle is of particular importance in political science, where interest reinforces inclination to regard the given societal patterns as the only ones conceivable. Recent work has increased insight into the parochial and ethnocentric elements in the political theory of both the classical and modern periods—as illustrated by the conception of women, "barbarians," and slaves in Aristotle, and of "human nature" in Hobbes and Rousseau.[20]

These considerations bring into prominence the part played by the observer in adding to the unreliability of indices. The social scientist may affect the phenomena he observes to a much more significant degree than is true of the physical scientist. The observer is part of society, and the reporting of his results part of the social process. Members of society may deliberately modify their responses in taking account of being observed or of the observations reported. If this possibility is to be subjected to control, the impact of the observer on the field of observation must itself be observed, and procedures elaborated to make possible stable indices of the effect. Hence the many inquiries now being carried on into the various observational standpoints of social inquiry: interviewing, participant observation, the standpoint of the spectator, and so on.

Clearly defined terms, even when given empirical content by stable

19. This implies, therefore, not that the social sciences cannot formulate "universal" propositions, but rather that such formulations require terms sufficiently general to provide for the data of cultural and social variation.

20. The instability of social indices also suggests the great importance of trend research in the social sciences. Provision must be made for continuous calibration of indices subject to transformation in the process of social change. Knowledge of trends is necessary to determine the degree to which new indices are inter-changeable with the old.

indices, are not themselves sufficient to provide a framework for inquiry. Propositions must be formulated, as hypotheses to be confirmed or disconfirmed in the process of inquiry. But, it may be asked, are there propositions of political science worth formulating at all? Is not the "science" an agglomeration of vague commonsense beliefs about certain aspects of human conduct? Certainly, many of the "base-line hypotheses" are derived from common sense, as C. J. Friedrich observes (1937, 7 and 19). But this does not entail either that they are worthless or that they are most fruitful in the formulations which common sense gives them.

These formulations, from the manipulative standpoint, are an expression of what Merriam (1931, 210) calls "political prudence." They enjoin certain courses of action to attain various political ends. In doing so they embody practical wisdom in the same sense as do, say, the maxims of chess. Statements like "Seize the open file" or "In a closed game the knight is preferable to the bishop" are fruits of knowledge and experience even though they are not parts of a theory of chess in a strict sense. But the practitioners of politics as of chess need a "positional sense"; the maxims of prudence require "good judgment" for successful application. Prudential statements, to be of maximum utility from the contemplative standpoint, must be supplemented by a specification of the conditions under which they hold, and these specifications must be related to observation by empirical indices. That the materials for a political science are available is thus shown by the existence in various persons and groups of a working knowledge of politics. But this working knowledge must be recast in theoretical terms to serve the ends of political inquiry rather than political practice.

The propositions formulated in the following chapters, therefore, are not putative "laws" of an already established science, but largely reformulations, as hypotheses to be subjected to inquiry, of the content of political prudence. More strictly, they are not hypotheses but *hypotheses-schema:* statements which formulate hypotheses when specific indices relate them to the conditions of a given problem.[21] (It is these conditions which determine, for

21. Many *ceteris paribus* propositions are of this kind. Literally interpreted, such propositions are empty because they cannot be falsified: contrary instances may be explained by holding that "other things were not equal." But these statements may fruitfully be taken as rules for formulating hypotheses in specific cases: there are to be made explicit certain factors whose constancy is a necessary and sufficient condition for the co-relation originally asserted. See the discussion of this point in F. Kaufmann's *Methodology of the Social Sciences,* Oxford University Press, 1944, 84 ff.

example, "where to draw the line" in the application of concepts admitting of degrees.)

Since the propositions are taken as regulative hypotheses, not formulations of established laws, we are not concerned with marshaling evidence supposed to establish them. They are intended to serve the functions of directing the search for significant data, not of predicting what the data will be found to disclose. From this standpoint, they may be regarded as helping provide a "speculative model," which is useful in calling attention to *deviations* from the type as in characterizing the few cases that exactly conform to it.[22]

Thus there is nothing here of the quest for "universal laws" in the grand style. Such quests—rendered fruitless by the index instability previously mentioned, if for no other reason—serve in the present state of political science chiefly to distract attention and energies from partial inquiries that can illuminate situationally localized problems in empirical ways. The conceptual framework and theoretical structure is elaborated in the following chapters to fructify such specific inquiries, and not for its own sake.[23]

The brief discussions of the propositions are therefore intended not to take the place of proofs but to clarify the content of the hypotheses and to indicate the considerations for supposing them a useful framework for inquiry. The numerous citations from the main body of political thought are to be construed in the light of these purposes, not as forensic appeals to authority. And the citations serve as well to disclose, behind the array of new terms and usages, the continuity of our standpoint with the major currents of the political thought of both past and present.[24]

22. Among sociologists, Max Weber was especially interested in speculative models, which he discussed as the concept of an "ideal type." See the introduction to *From Max Weber: Essays in Sociology,* by H. H. Gerth and C. Wright Mills, Oxford University Press, 1946.

23. Thus no attempt is made here to develop a simplified notation or postulational system permitting formal or quasi-mathematical manipulations of the basic concepts. The construction of such a system would not, it appears, be too difficult; but whether anything is to be gained in the present state of political inquiry from such formalization is quite another problem. For an example of what purports to be a fully mathematical theory of international relations and war crises, see Lewis F. Richardson, "Generalized Foreign Politics," *British Journal of Psychology,* Mon. Suppl., Vol. XXIII, 1939. New interest in mathematics and social relations has been stirred by John von Neumann and Oskar Morgenstern, *Theory of Games and Economic Behavior,* Princeton University Press, 1944.

24. For the senior author, this work is an inventory and self-appraisal; citations from his earlier writings are to be taken as contributory to this end.

This standpoint may be designated, if a term is wanted, as *hominocentric politics.* As science, it finds its subject matter in interpersonal relations, not abstract institutions or organizations; and it sees the person as a whole, in all his aspects, not as the embodiment of this or that limited set of needs or interests. As policy, it prizes not the glory of a depersonalized state or the efficiency of a social mechanism, but human dignity and the realization of human capacities.

It is here, the authors would like to think, that this volume has a contribution to make to contemporary political thought. There is in our culture a vast and increasingly intense concern with *respect* (both from self and others) as a major human value—the Kantian treatment of human beings as ends, never merely as means. This concern has, however, been comparatively inarticulate; certainly social scientists have grossly neglected this value in contrast to the extensive treatment accorded power and wealth. Concepts derived from these latter areas, especially economics, have been used with reference to the value process as a whole. In consequence, attention has been diverted from those aspects of inter-personal relations in which human dignity is central; and where they have been taken into account it has been in a nonnaturalistic framework that removes them from empirical control. One of the great tasks of the value sciences (social sciences) in our day is to develop a naturalistic treatment of the distinctively human values potential in the social process.

Such a treatment is required for a progressive realization, not only of the democratic ideal, but of the scientific ideal as well. For power is only one of the values and instruments manifested in interpersonal relations; and it cannot be adequately understood in abstraction from the other values operative. "Power politics," in the sense of concern with "power for the sake of power," is as limited a standpoint for inquiry as for policy. In the following chapters power analysis is related to analysis of respect and other values. Our own values call for the replacement of "power politics," both in theory and in practice, by a conception in which attention is focused on the human consequences of power as the major concern of both political thought and political action. Such a standpoint provides a basis for a program of preventive and integrative action appropriate to a many-valued hominocentric politics.

But they may be construed as well as an invitation to others to collaborate in the continuing task of summarizing and clarifying the present status and orientation of political thought.

PART ONE

The subject matter of political science is constituted by the conduct of *persons* with various *perspectives* of action, and organized into *groups* of varying complexity.

I

PERSONS

This chapter introduces the fundamental units of the political process—acts performed by individuals who are not merely biological entities but persons who have an individual "ego" and a social "self."

§1.1 *Response, Environment, and Predisposition*

UNDEFINED.[1] *Actor, Act*

THE CHOICE of these terms as a starting point results from the conception of political science as a branch of the study of human behavior. Central throughout are persons and their acts, not "governments" and "states." Terms like "state," "government," "law," "power"—all the traditional vocabulary of political science—are words of ambiguous reference until it is clear how they are to be used in describing what people say and do.[2] Of course, human behavior includes "subjectivity" as well as physical motions. "Thinking," "feeling," "willing" and the like are open to direct observation by the self, and may be inferred in others on the basis of words and gestures.

That we begin with the concepts of an act and a single person acting is not to be taken as minimizing the importance of groups rather than individuals in the political process. The significance of this starting point is purely logical: the group act is construed as a pattern of individual acts. An act is always that of

1. In any set of definitions some terms must be left undefined on pain of circularity. The chain of definitions must have a starting point, but no terms are indefinable in principle. There is in general a range of choice as to which terms will be taken as undefined, subject only to the requirements that the terms chosen provide a sufficient basis for the others to be introduced, and that they be sufficiently intelligible without definition. Only two or three terms used in this book without definition will be explicitly introduced as undefined. In most cases, of course, we assume that undefined terms will be understood in the sense intended, without calling attention to this assumption by labeling them "undefined."

2. "The subject matter of politics is the acts of individuals, not of states; the individual will is the political unit" (George E. G. Catlin, 1927, 141–2).

a single person, and when we speak of "group acts" a pattern formed by individual acts is to be understood. With this qualification, the terms "act" and "actor" are to be taken in the broadest possible sense as comprising all deeds and doers.[3]

DEFINITION.[4] The *environment* of an act consists of the events other than the act itself within which the act is included. A *situation* is a pattern of actors-in-an-environment.

The line between act and environment, and between environment and encompassing universe, is determined by the specific problem under consideration. Marking the ballot is part of the act of voting if we are concerned with the fraudulent tabulation of returns; the weather may be specified as part of the environment if we are concerned with the problem of nonvoting. Both might perhaps be disregarded if we are concerned with the effect on an election of various campaign practices. Act and environment are as limited or inclusive as is required by the initial data and hypotheses. In particular, the environment may include other actors and the kind of events known as symbols.

Environment being defined in relation to specified acts, the concept of a situation involves reference to acts completed or about to be undertaken. A situation is thus a state of affairs characterized as to (1) a number of actors, a set of whose acts, in their initial or terminal phases, are comprised in the state of affairs; and (2) the environment of the acts in question. The same state of affairs may therefore constitute different situa-

3. We characterize a completed act—and note that acts can terminate short of completion—as a sequence of events passing through the phases of *impulse, subjectivity,* and *expression;* subjective and expressive events may occur simultaneously as well as in sequence. In a more general perspective the act arises in *tension* and concludes in *gratification,* which is the abolition of tension (the restoration of an initial pattern of relationships taken as the base of comparison). The scientific observer of the acts of another person relies upon indices which are symbols (words, or word equivalents) or nonsymbols (movements of striated or smooth muscle, etc.). It is inconsequential whether he uses "behavioristic" or "non-behavioristic" terminology, if his definitions and operational rules are explicit. On the general theory of the act, see the writings of George Herbert Mead, especially his *Philosophy of the Act,* University of Chicago Press, 1938.

4. It may be emphasized that the definitions are not intended to be fully precise and rigorous from a strict logical viewpoint, but only to make more explicit than is usually done the framework relating the various concepts employed. Each concept may be given independent empirical content by specification of indices appropriate to various observational standpoints.

tions, according to the observational standpoint from which actors, acts, and environment are selected.

DF. *A response* [5] is an act, act-phase, or pattern of acts characterized in relation to its covariants (factors that explain or may explain its occurrence). The *predisposition* is the nonenvironmental determinant of response.

Inquiry into the conditions of occurrence of politically significant acts can proceed in two directions: we can look for possible determining factors in the environment of the acts or in the traits of the actors. There is little doubt that arrogant behavior by a despotic ruler may account, in part, for an act of assassination. The ruler is plainly a part of the assassin's environment. But more than environmental factors are often necessary to provide an adequate explanation of politics: there have been despotic rulers who have not been assassinated. It may be necessary to inquire also into the personality or other characteristics of the rebellious person or group. Previous experiences, including exposure to certain types of symbols, may have created in the group predispositions favorable to assassination of the despot. Both types of factors—environing and predispositional—determine response.

So important are environmental circumstances in political behavior that it is hopeless to attempt the construction of an adequate science of politics on the basis of alleged permanent factors in "human nature." It is true that men have social, affectionate impulses; it is also true that they all display aggressive-destructive tendencies. But it does not follow that we can explain solely on this basis the enormous variations in political conduct found from area to area, time to time, and class to class.

At the other extreme, it is hopeless to compress all into the environment. Even the strong emphasis on environment characteristic of Marxist analysis has, quite wisely, not prevented recognition—"in principle"—of nonenvironmental determinants of behavior. Trotsky writes:

5. The concept of response is not to be misconstrued in terms of a metaphysical determinism: "Man does nothing of his own free-will but merely responds to the stimuli impinging on him." Throughout we speak only of conditions under which various sorts of acts take place. Whatever is empirical in the concept of free will is comprised in the statement that certain subjective events are included among these conditions.

We do not at all pretend to deny the significance of the personal in the mechanics of the historical process, nor the significance of the personal in the accidental. We only demand that a historic personality, with all its peculiarities, should not be taken as a bare list of psychological traits, but as a living reality grown out of definite social conditions and reacting upon them.[6]

It is evident that factors figuring as predisposing or environing in one inquiry may have a reverse significance in another. The despotic ruler who is comprised in the environment when acts of assassination are being investigated becomes an actor whose predispositions are relevant if the inquiry is a study of factors affecting despotism. But it is a consequence of the definitions that variations in response where either environment or predisposition is constant is a function of variation in the other. In convenient abbreviations, R is by definition a function of E and P.[7]

§1.2 *Externalization and Integration*

DF. An *externalized response* is one by which the actor brings about changes in the environment; an *internalized response*, one in which such changes are minimal.

Since it is clear that no one who participates in an interpersonal situation is ever wholly without effect upon it, externalization and internalization must be taken as directions on a continuous scale. The man who assassinates another has an obvious impact on his environment; at the other extreme is the spectator who joins thousands of others in performing a routine affirmation of loyalty. Expression of hostility to the head of a

6. Trotsky, 1936, I, 35. Compare also the *Federalist,* No. VI: "To multiply examples of the agency of personal considerations in the production of great national events, either foreign or domestic, according to their direction, would be an unnecessary waste of time. Those who have but a superficial acquaintance with the sources from which they are to be drawn, will themselves recollect a variety of instances; and those who have a tolerable knowledge of human nature will not stand in need of such lights, to form their opinion either of the reality or extent of that agency."

7. Compare Timasheff, 1939, 6: "Every uniformity in human behavior can be reduced to the basic proposition: similar conditions acting on men of essentially similar nature produce similar effects." The statement itself has a logical rather than empirical significance. What is empirical is the specification of the E, P, and R in the concrete case and, in particular, the determination of what exactly is the function relating them.

state exemplifies the intermediate ranges: it is an externalized response if the symbols occur in a harangue to a mob; internalized, if they occur only in a diary.

DF. *Facilitation* is support among acts; *conflict*, interference; *compatibility* is the relationship of acts neither integrated nor in conflict.

Acts are facilitated when each aids the progress to completion of the others, and in conflict when completion is interfered with.[8] These are not the only possible alternatives; we call acts "compatible" when, though not in conflict with one another, none supports the others. Acts of political parties are in conflict in campaigning for rival candidates; the acts are facilitative in efforts to "get out the vote" or in coalition; and compatible in the selection of party officials. Similar relations may obtain among the acts of a single individual. Of course, which relations hold between acts depends on the environment as well as on the acts themselves: conflicts may be created or resolved by changes in the environment as well as in patterns of action.[9]

DF. The *intensity* of an actor in a situation is his stress toward action in that situation. The *tension level* is the intensity of all the actors.

The level of intensity is the strength of the tendency toward completion of acts projected or already initiated. The higher the intensity, the larger is the share of the actor's energies involved in the action and the greater the stress toward carrying the acts into the phase of expression. Hence we measure intensity by the persistence with which the act is continued regardless

8. It is important that "conflict" and "integration" are defined in terms of acts, rather than purposes conceived as distinct from the actual doing. The motive must be taken into account as a predisposition determinative of later acts, not as nullifying a conflict or integration which actually exists in the given case. Two groups may both have genuine interests in preserving peace, the one advocating and the other opposing universal military training. The acts of these groups are in fact in conflict with one another, in spite of shared aims. The significance of the shared aim is in the basis it provides for modifications in action leading ultimately to integration.

9. An act may be facilitated or obstructed by other acts at any of its phases of completion. Interference constitutes *resistance, repression, suppression,* or *rejection* according to whether the conflict occurs at the phase of impulse, or at an early, mid-, or late phase of subjectivity (and expression). Approximate definitions are in the *Dictionary of Psychology,* edited by Howard C. Warren, Houghton Mifflin, 1934.

of interference. The specific indices may be physical energy expended or economic cost or in terms of any value the sacrifice of which is entailed by carrying the act to completion.

Intensity is defined for an actor; the intensity of a situation is to be determined by some measure of the intensities of the actors in the situation. For political situations, intensity has been defined by C. J. Friedrich (1937, 15) as "the absolute amount of both consent and constraint." As indices for the former he suggests voluntary donations, relative infrequency and lightness of punishments, public manifestations of great enthusiasm, willing sacrifice of life by the governed; and as indices of constraint, frequency of killings, suicides, large-scale confiscations and corporal punishments. These indices may be construed as measures of stress toward action, involving as they do completion of acts against interference or in spite of cost. In effect, therefore, his definition and that given here roughly coincide.

DF. A *family of alternatives* is a set of acts expected to have the same initial and final phase. An actor exhibits *rigidity* in relation to the family in the degree to which he is differentially predisposed toward the alternatives; otherwise, *flexibility*.

Speaking generally, a specified goal may be reached in a variety of ways from a given starting point. The coup d'état is a course of action belonging to the family of alternatives leading from a given political situation to the establishment of a new government. Another alternative is agitation and propaganda work among the masses. Leaders who are contemptuous of the masses may adhere rigidly to the path of conspiracy, while others are more flexible in their choice of political tactics.

Conflicts are by no means always between whole families of alternatives, but often occur only between particular courses of action. Conflicts of the former kind may be called *primary* and the latter *secondary*. Clearly, secondary conflicts may be resolved by selection of other courses of action in the same family. The likelihood of integration in these cases is thus a direct function of the flexibility of the actors. In situations of high intensity, rigidity may lead to complete breakdown of the patterns of action.

DF. *Catharsis* is a reduction of intensity with a minimum of change in the factors determining intensity.

Some political movements die away without affecting political life in any abiding fashion. Neither the environment nor the basic political orientation of those who participate in the movement is permanently modified. Catharisis has taken place: a weakening of the stress toward action without completion of the act, or completion only of an act failing to alter significant factors. The former case is exemplified by the mob reduced to passivity by appeals to loyalty or exposure to symbols of authority.[10] In the latter case, though the action is externalized, it fails to affect the features of the environment evoking the intense response. Catharsis of this kind is a "substitutive response," often carried out by ceremonialization or aggression against a scapegoat.

PROPOSITION.[11] The probability of catharsis varies directly with the extent of conflict and inversely with the intensity of the situation.

Catharsis is the more probable the more it is facilitated by interference with the acts projected, and the less the intensity of those acts in the situation. A protest movement is most likely to subside without reaching its goal when there is (1) maximum interference with that goal, as indicated by imprisonment of leaders, calling out of troops, renewed emphasis on symbols of loyalty; and (2) minimal initial intensity, shown by failure to attend demonstrations or make contributions, limited use of the protest symbols, high turnover in membership. (In situations of initially *high* intensity, interference may have the effect of heightening intensity still further rather than facilitating catharsis.) Those against whom the protest movement is directed further facilitate catharsis by providing channels for substitutive response: bread and circuses, face-saving symbols of acquiescence, alternative targets. Guided catharsis is a major means of political control.

10. Instances are given in Machiavelli's *Discourses*, Bk. I, chap. 54, entitled "How Much Influence a Great Man Has in Restraining a Multitude."

11. Statements designated as "propositions" are to be construed as hypotheses or hypotheses-schema only, not as "laws" asserted to be true—see Introduction, pp. xxiii–iv. The designation is to distinguish them from definitions. Only two or three such propositions will be formulated in the early chapters, since the concepts to occur in them must first be introduced.

§1.3 *Symbols, Identification, and Personality*

UNDEFINED. *Symbol, Statement*

A symbol is whatever has meaning or significance in any sense. Though the most important kinds of symbols are linguistic, not all are such. In politics in particular nonlinguistic symbols play a considerable role (flags, insignia, monuments).[12] A statement is a complete unit of significance: an assertion, command, question, and so on. Functionally, the statement is primary and the individual symbol derivative: we classify statements by their functions, symbols by the kinds of statements in which they characteristically occur. (The word "symbol" will be used in some contexts for both single symbols and whole statements, and even for sets of statements.)

Subjective factors entering into political phenomena, whether or not they are fully expressed in symbols, are most easily studied by an examination of symbol outputs. Hence the techniques of symbol analysis can serve as instruments of inquiry into the varying relations between the "material" and "ideal" elements in any situation.[13]

DF. An *operation* is the nonsymbol event in an act.

An act is usually characterized in terms of its significance (for the actor, or from the standpoint of some other observer): it is "voting," "saluting," "bribing." For some purposes it is convenient to describe the act apart from such significance. We may characterize voting by the operations of dropping a ball into an urn, or bribing by a transfer of documents. The act in its significance we call a "practice" (§2.3) rather than "operation."

DF. An *ego* is an actor using symbols.

The analysis of "intelligent" or "conscious" behavior in terms of symbols has been especially emphasized by George Herbert Mead (*Mind, Self and Society*, University of Chicago

12. On the general concept, see C. W. Morris, *Signs, Language and Behavior*, Prentice-Hall, 1946. We use the word "symbol" rather than Morris' "sign" to accord with a more familiar usage in the social sciences. Symbols will be discussed in more detail in Chapter II, and political symbols in Chapter VIII.

13. On the general significance for the social sciences of the study of symbols, see H. D. Lasswell, 1948, 1949.

Press, 1934). The self is constituted in the process of using significant symbols to react to its own acts from the standpoint of those with whom it interacts—in the process, that is, of "taking the role of the generalized other." "Ego" is thus not to be understood in the psychonalytic sense as referring only to certain components of the personality (the reality-testing functions), but simply as a designation for any "minded" organism. An actor is an ego if he is a symbol user. (The word "self" will shortly be introduced for a more complex notion.)

The choice of the present definition emphasizes that political science need make no a priori assumptions as to what is essential in or most characteristic of human conduct other than the use of symbols. It is not presupposed either that man is essentially "rational" or that he is dominated by some particular drive or other (love of gain, glory, or power).[14] In what respects, to what degree, and under what conditions men do behave "rationally" or in accord with such drives is not to be prejudged in the conceptual framework, but must be determined by an investigation of men's acts under various conditions—and of the role of various kinds of symbols in those acts.

DF. *Identification* is the process by which a symbol user symbolizes his ego as a member of some aggregate or group of egos (X identifies with the Y's if X symbolizes X as a Y).

Symbolizing distinguishes the process but does not exhaustively characterize it: other acts, externalized as well as internalized, occur in conformity with the symbolic relationship. (Such acts may be taken as indices of identification in the absence of overt symbolic processes.) A process of identification may mark a profound change in the life of the individual. To become an active member of a revolutionary party, or to join the "resistance" against a foreign conqueror, is to put everything at stake.

Identification serves as the mechanism for the creation of the

14. Aristotle's observation that "political science does not make men, but takes them from nature and uses them" (*Politics*, I, 10) embodies a sound empiricism which renders questionable any serious attempts to implement the conception of man as essentially a "rational animal." Man is just as essentially irrational and nonrational. As Ernest Barker points out, "Man is a mixed being. Human nature in politics, like human nature in marriage and indeed in any other institution, is a mixed thing. Both reason and instinct are needed; and they may agree and serve one another, if they may also pull different ways" (1942, 77–8).

political "we." It is this "we" which lies at the center of political phenomena. Political demands are made in behalf of the egos with which a given ego identifies, and are justified by reference to the resulting "we." Politics begins when egos are emotionally bound together in relation to such demands in the name of the identified groups.[15]

DF. An *identification statement* is one specifying the ego with which a given ego identifies. A *symbol of identification* is one referring in identification statements to an ego or egos.

"I am an American," "He is a Communist" are identification statements, "American" and "Communist" symbols of identification. The study of such symbols is one of the important tasks of political science: with what frequencies are the various symbols invoked in different situations, and with what other acts, symbolic and externalized, are they correlated?

A satisfactory geography of politics would chart the symbols which men invoke to justify their pretensions, and disclose the nature of the acts with which each symbol is affiliated. Our usual maps show the world of "states," but the world of politics is richer, including acts justified in the name of churches, races, nationalities, tribes, classes, and dynasties (Lasswell, 1935, 30).

DF. The *self* is the ego and whatever it identifies with that ego.

The concept is closely related to what William James designated as the "social self": A man "has as many different social selves as there are distinct groups of persons about whose opinion he cares. He generally shows a different side of himself to each of these different groups." [16] The self as here defined is the set of these "different sides" in their inter-relatedness. It thus comprises all the roles which the ego adopts, and

15. For an elaboration of this point see H. D. Lasswell, 1930, especially 185–6. In general, variations in identification are correlated with variations in response: what we do depends, among other things, on the "we" that is active. Prediction depends on a knowledge of the roles in which action will occur. Identifications, in short, are an important component of predisposition.

16. William James, *Psychology,* Henry Holt, 1892, I, 294. Compare also F. H. Giddings, *Inductive Sociology,* Macmillan, 1901, 10: "The Unit of investigation in sociology is the socius—that is to say, the individual who is not only an animal and a conscious mind, but also a companion, a learner, a teacher, and co-worker."

is characterized by specifying the individuals and groups with which the ego identifies.

It is the self in this sense which was previously referred to as the political "we." The individual enters the political arena not as an ego but as a self. Political acts depend upon the symbolization of the individual in terms of a more inclusive self which champions a set of demands for social action. The invocation of this more inclusive self is not limited to discontent, but takes place in a wide variety of attitudes and acts manifested in interpersonal relations.

DF. A *personality trait* is a kind of act characteristic of a self. The *personality* is the totality of the personality traits pertaining to an actor. A *person* is an actor characterized as to personality.

A personality trait is an act typically performed by the actor in a certain kind of situation. Since acts may be internalized, personality traits include habits of thought and feeling as well as of overt action. The analysis of personality into component traits does not rob it of any empirical wholeness: relations among traits are themselves traits as here defined. A person with the traits of aggressiveness and generosity may also have the trait of following one with the other.

The personality structure of the person, it may be noted, does not include all the factors that predispose him toward meeting a given environment with a certain response. The predisposition in a given situation may include components not sufficiently typical to be regarded as personality traits.

We shall speak of an act or situation as "interpersonal" when more than one person is involved, regardless of the kind or degree of interaction taking place.

DF. Interpersonal relations are *personalized* or *impersonalized* according to the degree to which the whole personality is taken into account in the relation.

We personalize the administration of laws and regulations when we take into consideration the thoughts, feelings, and circumstances of the human beings affected, and seek to harmonize the working of the rule with special circumstances, without perverting the rule. Since many rules are made with thousands or millions of individuals in view, and with adminis trative convenience in mind, it is notorious that the rule as promulgated is bound to impose disproportionate hardship if "mechanically" applied; that is, applied with disregard of the circumstances of the specific case. Some officials accentuate the "mechanical" features by impersonalizing each client or case as much as possible. Others go a long way toward personalizing the relationship, without sacrificing the aims sought by the statute or ordinance. In many circumstances, of course, the personalizing goes so far that the common good is endangered ("What is the law among friends?").

In political science as in other social sciences specialists gravitate in two directions, toward emphasizing the personal or the impersonal. Political biography—which is cultivated chiefly by historians—has kept alive the more personal dimension of politics, while treatises on public law are usually at the opposite pole. With the rise of modern methods of personality and community study, the rank and file of the political process is brought more sharply into focus, and more data are at hand for understanding how political institutions are experienced by the people who work them, or are passively exposed to them.

To some extent the "humanizing" trend in political science has always been represented in the "classics," usually in the form of some theory of "human nature." Hobbes—to go no further back—devoted a considerable part of his *Leviathan* to matters of psychology. Frequently, however, this emphasis on psychology has remained in impersonal terms, and psychological theory has been drawn upon for general propositions about "aggressiveness" or "generosity" or some other trait of "human nature," and these borrowed generalizations have been used to support an abstract analysis or polemic. To humanize political relationships, it is necessary to have and to apply methods of establishing direct contact with persons (and of making reliable records for analytic purposes of what is said and done in specific situations).[17]

17. In recent years the humanizing and concretizing of political science has been stimulated by Graham Wallas (1908) and his students. As Walter Lippmann put it (*Preface to Politics*, M. Kennerley, 1913, 83–4 and 32): "When we recognize that the focus of politics is shifting from a mechanical to a human center, we shall have reached what is, I believe, the most essential idea in modern politics . . . The deepest error of our political thinking [is] to talk of politics without reference to human beings." Toynbee has aptly designated this error the *apathetic fallacy:* while the "pathetic fallacy" consists in imaginatively endowing inanimate objects with life, we now fall victims to the inverse fallacy of treating living creatures as though they were inanimate.

As an index of the degree to which any situation is personalized, we may take the substitutability of persons. The more difference a particular substitution makes, the more personal the relationship; and conversely, the less difference, the more the relation approaches the impersonal.

II

PERSPECTIVES

The persons active in politics make demands for values (on themselves and others) on the basis of various expectations. Patterns of attention, sentiment, interest, loyalty, and faith are among the perspectives of political action.

§2.1 *Values and Demands*

UNDEFINED. *Value, Valuation*

A VALUE is a desired event—a goal event. That X values Y means that X acts so as to bring about the consummation of Y. The act of valuing we call "valuation," and we speak of the object or situation desired as the "value." [1] The concept of value is thus to be understood in the sense of objective relativism (as elaborated, for example, by Ralph Barton Perry in his *General Theory of Value*, Longmans, Green, 1926). The proposition that Y is a value for X is as "objective" as any other proposition about a matter of fact: its truth depends upon the fact which it asserts to be the case, and is independent, in general, of the person asserting the proposition. Values are relative in the specific sense that Y is said to be a value only for some X or other (it is a value relative to X); wherever the X is not made explicit, it is said to be understood.

It is not necessary that Y be symbolized by X as a value—or even that it be symbolized by X at all—to be a value for X. In Dewey's terms, we are speaking of ends which are not necessarily (but which may be) ends-in-view. Further, both intrinsic and instrumental values are comprised in the concept

1. The characterization of a value as what is desired (aimed at, wished for, and so on) is not to be construed as restricting valuation to the phases of impulse and subjectivity. On the contrary, by valuation we mean the whole act. The phase of expression is of particular importance; intentions alone are significant only in terms of the patterns of completed action which they determine. The completed action need not, however, be successful; we may speak of "valuation" whether or not the value is attained, and gratification abolishes tension.

of value: Y may be valued on its own account, or for some Z to which it is believed to lead.

From the conception of value in terms of an *act* of valuing, it follows that values are conflicting, facilitative, or compatible according as the acts of valuation are such. Conflict and facilitation of values are not deducible from incompatibilities or consonance of symbolizations, but depend on the relations of the acts in which the valuations consist. Agreement or divergence in professed aims, for example, is not determinative (and often not even a reliable index) of facilitation or conflict of the relevant values. These relations depend on whether the professions are acted upon, and on the nature of the acts in which the aims find expression in the concrete situation.

The derivation of values from acts of valuation relates them directly to the concept of personality as the characteristic patterns of the person's action. To specify a person's values and to characterize his personality is to give equivalent descriptions of the same acts, the one locution directing attention to the environment, the other to the actor. And the same is true, of course, of groups of persons. Hence we will speak later of the *values* of a group, rather than of "group character" or similar notions.[2] One index of the values of a group is explicit statements made by its members.

DF. A *demand statement* is one expressing a valuation by the maker of the statement. A *symbol of demand* is one used in demand statements to refer to the value.

We speak of all expressions of valuation as "demands" regardless of the degree of intensity with which they are uttered. They are mild *preference* statements: "Full employment seems desirable"; and there are *volitional* statements: "There *must* be full employment!" These are commitments of the statement maker which, taken literally, enable the listener-observer to predict that the speaker is prepared to act in certain ways to bring about the positive values or to diminish the likelihood of occurrence of the negative ones. (The prediction may, of course, be in error if, for instance, the speaker is lying.)

In the statements quoted just above, some words refer to

2. Compare Rousseau, *Social Contract,* IV, 7: "It is useless to distinguish the character of a nation from the objects they esteem, for all these things depend on the same principle, and are necessarily intermixed."

the value or express the valuation. "Full employment" is a symbol naming what is valued, and "seems desirable" and "*must* be" signify the nature of the speaker's commitment. By taking note of the demand symbols that figure in the programs of political parties, the constitutions of states, or the speeches of leaders, we have a convenient method of describing the pattern of demands and noting trends. Between 1918 and 1944, for example, there was an unmistakable decline in the symbols of demand for *world revolution* in the slogans launched by the Communist party of the Soviet Union. Demands for *national* security, on the other hand, were more frequently made.[3]

When complete, demand statements explicitly refer to the ego or egos for whom what is demanded is a value: the statement includes symbols of identification. The slogan "Fifty Four Forty or Fight!" was, formally speaking, incomplete; though from the context no one doubts that "We Americans" made the demand. Valuation has a social character: not the bare ego, but the self in its various roles—identifications—has one set of values rather than another. The demands that a person makes are determined to a large extent by the groups, classes, and society to which he belongs. And these in turn determine the political effectiveness of the demand.

DF. A *demand aggregate* consists of persons making the same demand.

The members of a demand aggregate need be engaged in no interactions with one another, so far as the definition is concerned. Sameness of demand requires, however, that the persons in the aggregate not only demand the same value, but demand it for the same person or persons.[4]

PROP. The frequency of a demand statement in a situation varies with the intensity in that situation of the valuation signified.

An important characteristic of political situations is their intensity. The frequency with which demand statements are

3. See the charts in Lasswell, Leites, and Associates, 1949, chap. x (with Sergius Yakobson).

4. Throughout, the word "aggregate" will be used for the concept of mere uniformity ("parallelism") in acts. Other words, especially the term "group," will be introduced for the cases where certain patterns of inter-personal relations are superimposed on (or replace) such uniformities.

circulated is one index of intensity. It provides *some* basis for predictions of the extent of the sacrifice the participants in the situation are prepared to make to attain their demands. Of course, intensity might also be expressed by various stylistic characteristics rather than by frequent repetition of the demand; and conversely, frequency may be due not so much to intensity as to ritualistic and other functions performed by the demand statement. But frequency may serve as a first approximation to the measure of intensity, not only for demands but for other types of symbols (identifications, expectations) as well.[5]

PROP. The probability that an aggregate of persons will identify with one another varies with the number and intensity of shared demands.

The growth of a larger political unity is fostered by the identifications that occur, for instance, among those who make hostile demands on a common enemy. The members of the thirteen original colonies in this country became more closely identified with one another as "Americans" during the long struggle to modify British imperial policy, and later to throw off imperial rule. A national self arose to supplement and to include each colonial self in the personality of more and more persons. Hostile demands, of course, are by no means the only ones that foster identification; *any* shared demands (valuations) may have this effect.

§2.2 *Sentiments and Expectations*

UNDEFINED. *Sentiment*, *Sentiment Symbol*

The term "sentiment" is used rather than "emotion" or "feeling" to convey the idea of an attitude permeated by feeling rather than the undirected feeling itself. A "sentiment symbol" signifies not an emotion but *with* emotion whatever referent it has.

There are identifications without sentiment, as when one includes within the self the recognition that one resides in a community to which he is indifferent. And there are shared de-

5. Correlations between frequency of specified demand symbols and intensity of the political situation in which they are circulated are discussed in Lasswell and Blumenstock, 1939.

mands that result in neither identification nor sentimentalization (many "deals" made in politics). In the main, however, all political symbols are sentimentalized to some degree, especially the identifications with locality, church, party, nation.

A sentiment aggregate may be included within a demand aggregate, therefore, and consists of persons with a certain degree of emotional involvement in the demand. The abolitionist movement included persons of highly emotionalized responses as well as others more detached, for whom the movement provided an instrument of power striving.

DF. The degree of *concordance* of an aggregate is the extent to which there is a sharing of sentiment in the aggregate.

Complete concordance thus signifies homogeneity of sentiment throughout the aggregate. But even complete concordance leaves room for disagreement as to demands. Two groups may agree in a patriotic sentiment, but espouse different demands on its basis; and conversely, concordance alone is not sufficient to integrate conflicting demands. These relations are exhaustively exemplified in the history of political movements like nationalism.[6]

PROP. Concordance varies with the frequency of use of the corresponding sentiment symbol.

As Charles E. Merriam strongly emphasized in the concluding volume of the "Civic Training Series," the main control over the young comes from monopoly of what is brought to their attention. The effect of repeating whatever pattern of political symbols is current in the community is to perpetuate the pattern by limiting the alternatives for sentimentalization open to the rising generation (Merriam, 1931).

The correlation formulated in the hypothesis also has the consequence that direct and explicit refutation of certain types of propaganda often contributes to its effectiveness rather than the contrary. The repetition in the refutation of the negative sentiment symbols may spread and reinforce the sentiment by reaching a wider audience, and by restimulating a latent or dormant sentiment.

6. See Hans Kohn, *The Idea of Nationalism,* Macmillan, 1944, and Frederick Hertz, *Nationality in History and Politics,* K. Paul, Trench, Trubner, 1944.

DF. An *expectation statement* is one symbolizing the (past, present, or future) occurrence of a state of affairs without demands or identifications. A *symbol of expectation* is one used in expectation statements to characterize the state of affairs.[7]

The statement "There will never be a third World War" taken literally, is a reference to a future state of affairs. The person uttering the statement does not make explicit whether or not it is in accord with his preferences—he is making no demand. And the statement does not delimit the boundaries of the self; it contains no identification. The statement simply symbolizes the (non) occurrence of a certain state of affairs; it is "matter of fact," "descriptive."

One index of how persons or groups will act is the flow of different kinds of expectation statements, and the currency of symbols employed in them. We can classify expectations, for instance, as "optimistic" or "pessimistic" about each constituent of the self—with regard to imminence of recovery or death, of national victory or defeat, and the like (see §6.1). A fundamental fact about the political and social history of mankind is optimism or pessimism about the end of the world, and about the prospects of progress (of achieving a more abundant life) on earth. Expectation symbols like "progress" become sentimentalized and intertwined with demands for the attainment of a better world.[8]

7. The term "expectation" has the disadvantage of seeming to refer exclusively to events constituting the future, but it emphasizes that belief is here construed in terms of projected action, in conformity with our concern with the completed act rather than only the phase of subjectivity. A belief, even about the past, is not merely a "state of mind," but a state of the whole organism in relation to future acts. (It is such acts, and not merely the statement, which serve as indices of belief.) Usage among economists has recently tended to crystallize around the term "expectation," the terms "ex-ante" and "ex-post" being used for future and past references, respectively. See Bertil Ohlin, "Some Notes on the Stockholm Theory of Savings and Investment," reprinted in *Readings in Business Cycle Theory,* Selected by a Committee of the American Economic Association, Blakiston, 1944, 87 ff.

8. On the history of the expectation of progress, see J. B. Bury, *The Idea of Progress,* Macmillan, 1921. A. Lawrence Lowell (1926, chap. vii) used a "sanguine" or "not sanguine" disposition as one of the fundamental dimensions in classifying political attitudes. "Reactionaries," for instance, he characterizes as discontented with things as they are and pessimistic about improvement; the discontented and the sanguine are "radicals." (The contented and sanguine are "liberals," and contented and nonsanguine "conservatives.") On the significance of expectations about the past, see G. P. Gooch's study of the redefining of history and its interaction with nationalism, *Studies in Modern History,* Longmans, Green, 1931.

Aggregates with regard to given expectations and demands rarely coincide with one another. Not all the persons making a certain demand do so on the basis of the same expectations; and not all the persons sharing an expectation will make the same demands on its basis. In general, judgments of value cannot be deduced from propositions of fact, or conversely; and there is no invariant empirical connection between them. Expectations and demands are two distinct factors entering into interpersonal relations, neither of which can be regarded as reducible to the other and of no independent importance.

DF. A *normatively ambiguous* statement is one signifying both an expectation and a demand.

Consider, for a moment, the following statement uttered by a law teacher who is expounding a case, a legal adviser who is arguing with a client, or an advocate who is addressing the court: "This is the law (followed by a statement of a 'doctrine')." This statement may be treated as a summary of past statements made by sources who are treated as qualified spokesmen (authorities). It may also be taken to refer to future events, predicting what certain authorities will say (even though there is doubt about what they have said in the past); or it may be construed as a declaration of preference by the professor, adviser, advocate—a statement of what the speaker thinks the law should be even though the authorities (before or after) dissent. If this last construction is put upon the words, the speaker may affirm that he is misunderstood, since he did not use words that categorically convey preference; nevertheless, the listener may believe that the speaker lays himself open because so many talkers do in practice say "the law is so and so" when what they mean—in the sense of what they say if challenged—is a preference for the law to be so and so. Under some circumstances the statement goes beyond a simple preference and becomes a volition to do whatever is feasible to get the "should" accepted as an "is."

Hence if we take the statement of the "law" at face value we may find it ambiguous; and we can call it *normative-ambiguous*, because the word "law" is used, and "law" is a word that refers to norms, even though it is unclear whether the norm in question pertains exclusively to the speaker, whether it is shared by the speaker with others, or whether, though a norm of others, it is not the norm of the speaker at all. Common-sense experience emphasizes the enormous rôle of such normative-ambiguous statements in the discourse that purports to expound "law" or "ethics" or "Divine Will." "That is right (morally)" is a sentence open to all the doubts raised about the "this is the law" sentence; and "this is God's Will" is no whit less ambiguous. By evoking such word sequences a speaker may conceal his own preference or volition on contentious matters and increase the attention paid to what he says by enunciating norms whose sponsor appears to transcend the speaker.[9]

§2.3 *Interest and the Attention Frame*

DF. An *interest* is a pattern of demands and its supporting expectations.

Compare with this definition Perry's characterization of an interest as involving a "governing propensity" combined with expectations. The point that the definition aims to bring out is simply that an interest is neither a blind desire nor a knowing untinged by valuation. In every interest analysis discloses competent demands and expectations both.

In being reduced to demands and expectations, interests have been defined in terms of acts (including, as always, internalized acts). That a person professes an interest, however sincerely, does not entail, therefore, that he does in fact have it. Further, interests can be spoken of on this basis as facilitative, compatible, or conflicting with other interests (or other sorts of acts). Conflicts arising from incompatible expectations are those designated in §1.2 as "secondary"; conflicts between interests based on the same expectations are "primary." The former may be resolved when further inquiry decides between the alternative expectations; but the latter type of conflict is not removed merely by accumulation of evidence. (Compare differences in policy on public health with differences in policy on public morals.)

DF. *Valid interests* are those of which the component expectations are warranted by evidence available to inquiry; *assumed interests,* those in which the expectations are not warranted.

9. Lasswell and McDougal, "Legal Education and Public Policy," *Yale Law Journal,* Vol. 52, No. 2, March, 1943, 266–7 (reprinted in Lasswell, 1947, 87–8). A theoretical discussion of the normatively ambiguous character of value judgments, especially in moral discourse, is to be found in C. L. Stevenson, *Ethics and Language,* Yale University Press, 1944.

The difference between assumed and valid interests is that formulated in the statements that a person *has* an interest in X and that X is *to* his interest. The latter asserts that in fact X constitutes or will lead to the attainment of the person's values. A ruler may be interested in making war, although it would be *in fact* ruinous; a group may support a particular candidate on the false expectation that he will implement a specific policy when elected. Such interests are assumed but not valid.

The determination of whether an interest is valid in this sense is notoriously difficult, for the component expectations concern not merely the effectiveness of a particular course of action for the satisfaction of the demands in question, but also the relation of these demands to other demands of the person. An interest is appraised in terms of its relation to the entire system of interests (values) of the ego and those with whom it identifies. But like all questions of evidence, the validation of interests is a matter of degree, and the process of testing is continuous. As interested action proceeds, assumed interests tend more and more to be replaced by valid interests—except as inquiry or the dissemination of its results is interfered with.[10] (And the hypothesis might be put forward that this transformation is the more likely the more intense the demands in question. As Machiavelli observes, "Where men's lives and fortunes are at stake they are not all insane.")

DF. A *faith* is a sentimentalized expectation; a *loyalty* a sentimentalized identification or demand.

It is irrelevant to the definition whether the sentiment is evoked by the expectation, or whether on the contrary the expectation is elaborated as a justification ("rationalization") of the sentiment. The definition does not make all faiths irrational: the expectation may or may not be based on evidence. A faith is defined as an expectation in which there is some considerable emotional involvement; with the conditions under which such involvement takes place we are not here concerned. Sorel's discussion of the "myth of the general strike" provides an example of the political significance of such faiths.

10. Hence, availability of evidence and information, especially concerning interpersonal relations, is itself a value—important, if for no other reason, for the realization of all other values.

The alternatives in the definition of a loyalty correspond to loyalty to a person or to a cause. The two types are in constant interaction: identifications are both based upon and give rise to the sharing of demands; action in the service of a cause both results from and leads to identifications. Where necessary, the two can be distinguished as *personal* and *programmatic* loyalty. (Of course, personal loyalty in this sense includes what is called "group loyalty"; the identification can be with one person or many.)

DF. A *perspective* is a pattern of identifications, demands, and expectations.

Certain identifications, demands, and expectations tend to be clustered, as in the case of the person who is strongly identified with humanity as a whole; he is likely to support a world order, and to cherish some optimism about at least the long-range prospects of mankind. A perspective need not be a logically unified whole, and indeed seldom is. It may include "stray" identifications, demands, and expectations, so to speak, as well as integrated interests, faiths, and loyalties. It may even include in varying degrees, conflicting commitments of the ego and the self.

An *attitude* may be distinguished from a perspective as a tendency to complete acts by which a given perspective is externalized. Thus an apolitical person may be said to have no political attitudes, but may nevertheless entertain political perspectives; a ruling group may have war-like perspectives but not adopt a war-like attitude.

DF. A *practice* is an act characterized according to the kind of operation and the perspectives in which it is performed.

Acts consisting of the same operations may constitute different practices for different persons; and the same or very similar perspectives may be associated with different operations. Of two ballots cast for the same candidate, one may have been a "protest vote" and the other support in expectation of the candidate's election. Conversely, the different operations of not voting at all and of voting for a minority candidate may both have been expressions of "protest." Clearly, the phrase "protest vote" refers to a practice, not merely an operation.[11]

11. On the distinction between operations and perspectives in the analysis of political practices, see R. M. MacIver, 1947, 4.

DF. The *attention frame* of a person or group in a situation is composed of the symbols coming to their focus of attention in that situation. The *milieu* is the part of the environment symbolized by the attention frame (the remaining part is *surroundings*).

"One of the reasons that two honest men attach different weight to the various factors in a problem lies in the degree to which their attention is directed to them" (Lowell, 1926, 21). More than that: all response is a reaction, on the basis of predisposition, to those parts of the environment that impinge upon attention.

Often the environment is effective only through the mediation of symbols. Especially is this true in the case of political action, where the environment responded to is both spatially and logically "distant." The citizen angered at "the treachery of a foreign Power" or enthusiastic about "the regeneration of his Party" is responding not to something directly confronting him, but to something symbolically mediated.[12]

Often, of course, there may be nothing in the environment corresponding to the symbolization, or what there is may be seriously distorted by the symbols:

> People as ignorant as the modern citizen body is left by our social system make of it a picture for themselves which deludes them in their search for the causes of their misfortune. . . . Myth and legend surround them on every side (Laski, 1925, 101).

But the attention frame is not *necessarily* deluding; though it be a picture, it may be a true picture. That the environment is not taken account of directly but only through the mediation of symbols does not mean that it is actually not taken account of at all. Events may, and in the case of warranted knowledge *do*, correspond to our symbolization of them.[13] Ra-

12. An important part of the environment consists of perspectives of other persons, and these come to attention largely by exposure to symbols. See, for instance, Tawney, *Religion and the Rise of Capitalism,* J. Murray, 1926, 29: "There is a moral and religious, as well as a material, environment, which sets its stamp on the individual, even when he is least conscious of it. And the effect of changes in this environment is not less profound."

13. The fact that the symbols are in many respects "socially determined" does not at all exclude the possibility of such correspondence, but is among the conditions affecting its occurrence. That there is a sociology of knowledge does not entail that there is, after all, no knowledge, but only that there is no knowledge apart from a process of inquiry, which is conditioned by interpersonal factors among others. Mannheim (1936) is not sufficiently clear on this point.

tional public opinion—indeed, rational response of any kind—is therefore impossible without a properly organized frame of attention.

It is precisely this task of organizing attention that gives point to many of the rules and procedures (the practices) of courts, legislatures, and other agencies of government. The rules of evidence are aimed in part at the exclusion from the attention of judge and jury of matters that are deemed irrelevant. The rules of order in legislative assemblies and public meetings are effective in the degree that they provide for an orderly sequence of attention. The intelligence services of the army, navy, and foreign offices—to name only a few representative arms of government—are directly charged with heavy responsibility for what is worth bringing to the attention of generals, admirals, secretaries of state, and heads of states. If we broaden the concept of "intelligence" to mean the statements on the basis of which decisions are made, it is apparent that in a democratic society, where a share in decision making is widespread, the possibility of rational public opinion depends in no small measure on the manner in which the frame of public attention is organized by the media of mass communication.

The attention frame leaves its mark on the perspectives of the person and the group; and, in turn, what is perceived is modified by the perspectives in which the situation is approached. Deeply biased persons frequently do not allow themselves to realize facts and symbols disturbing to their perspectives. Walter Lippmann (1922, 20–1) has elaborated the political significance of this point:

> When full allowance has been made for deliberate fraud, political science has still to account for such facts as two nations attacking one another, each convinced that it is acting in self-defense, or two classes at war, each certain that it speaks for the common interest. They live, we are likely to say, in different worlds. More accurately, they live in the same world, but they think and feel in different ones. It is to these special worlds, it is to these private, or group, or class, or provincial, or occupation, or sectarian artifacts, that the political adjustment of mankind in the great society takes place.

The development of modern social and psychological sciences has provided new ways of collecting information about the attention frame and the milieu. Individuals can keep diaries of their daily round of activity, noting the people with whom they come in contact, and the media of communication to which they expose themselves. Other attention indices are book sales and library circulation, newspaper and magazine circulation, audiences in motion picture theaters, radio audiences, spectators and participants in demonstrations, lectures, forums. The contents of what is disseminated through these media can be described; and interviews of varying duration can be conducted with a view to unveiling the current attention frame and milieu perspectives.[14]

14. For a guide to current techniques of observation, see B. L. Smith, H. D. Lasswell, and R. D. Casey, *Propaganda, Communication and Public Opinion*, Princeton University Press, 1946.

III

GROUPS

Groups are formed by integrating diversified perspectives and operations. The effect of a group on values is determined in part by morale, which in turn is affected by permeability and circulation in the group. A group acts as a crowd or as a public in internal and external relations of accommodation and conflict. Culture (group) traits are patterned as institutions, which include mores and countermores (together constituting the social order), as well as expediencies.

§3.1 *Organization*

DF. *Coordination* is integration of diversified acts.

Degree of coordination is a measure both of how far acts are diversified and how far integrated. Soldiers on a drill ground exhibit little diversification; on the other hand, workers on an assembly line may perform many different operations. We speak of coordination in the second case, but not the first, though both sets of acts are integrated. Again, the diversified acts must support one another: conflicting or even compatible policies of distinct governmental agencies do not exemplify coordination.

Generally speaking, only some of the acts performed by a given aggregate are coordinated. The *extent* of coordination is the proportion of these acts to all the acts. An army exhibits a high extent as well as degree of coordination: almost all the acts of a soldier fall within a pattern of mutual support and diversification. Workers in a mass production industry may exhibit a high degree but low extent of coordination, if they have a considerable amount of uncontrolled leisure.

PROP. The noncoordinated acts of an aggregate tend to be compatible with those which are coordinated.

What is done outside the framework of the division of labor in a society is, on the hypothesis, shaped into compatability with the latter; the pattern would otherwise not be a stable one. Leisure-time activity must not conflict with the arrangement of work, and gives way to the coordinated acts, which are expressive of more intense demands—more intense because a pattern of coordination is maintained only at the expense of other values.

The hypothesis is illustrated by the development of sumptuary legislation (see Ernst Freund, *Standards of American Legislation*, University of Chicago Press, 1917). Apart from laws, there has been in modern society a spontaneous adaptation of noncoordinated activity to the skills and conditions of factory work. The division of labor in highly industrialized societies has been accompanied by coordinated housing, recreation, and so on. Alteration in religious practices (perspectives and operations) is discussed from a similar standpoint by Tawney, *Religion and the Rise of Capitalism*, J. Murray, 1926, and M. Weber, *The Protestant Ethic and the Spirit of Capitalism*, G. Allen & Unwin, 1930.

PROP. Identification varies with coordination.

The hypothesis is that persons tend to identify with those with whose acts their own are coordinated: a major basis of identification is sharing in a division of labor. The "we" is often a working team; the soldier often exhibits a more marked attachment to his "outfit" than to his officers, the party worker is often more closely identified with the boss of his own ward than with the "standard-bearer" of the party.

DF. *Cooperation* is the integration of diversified operations; *solidarity*, of diversified perspectives.

When only operations are involved, coordination is purely mechanical; coordination may have reference instead to integration of identifications, demands, and expectations. Cooperation, then, is "doing" together; solidarity is "thinking" and "feeling" together.

Solidarity does not consist in a simple parallelism of subjectivity. This would provide compatibility but not necessarily facilitation. For an aggregate to exhibit solidarity, the persons in the aggregate must take account of the perspectives of the others, identify with the others, be interested in their interests. There is not merely a number of egos making the same demand, for instance, but the demand is made in behalf of a self including the various egos.[1]

PROP. Solidarity and cooperation approach covariance in the degree that the perspectives and operations coordinated are intense.

Integration of intense perspectives evokes cooperation for the attainment of the values in those perspectives; cooperation in important activity evokes solidarity. On the other hand, breakdown in either tends, on the hypothesis, to breakdown in the other. Persons reciprocally sharing intense political demands may form a party or seek other patterns of cooperation for the attainment of the demands; joint participation in, say, a military operation enhances the solidarity of the participants. In situations of economic depression or military defeat, breakdown is reflected in divisive and conflicting perspectives, and such perspectives in turn interfere with the reestablishment of patterns of cooperation.[2]

DF. *Organization* is a pattern of solidarity and cooperation.

Action is organized when, though diversified, it is integrated, and the integration extends not only to the operations but to the perspectives in which the operations are performed as well.

DF. A *group* is an organized aggregate. An *association* is a highly organized group, a *demigroup* one with a lower degree of organization.

An aggregate of persons mechanically cooperating with one another does not constitute a group, nor is a group constituted merely by the sharing of reciprocal perspectives. Even mutual identification among the members of an aggregate does

1. The same point may be made by defining solidarity as the sharing of perspectives exhibiting reciprocity without conflict. Compare Timasheff, 1939, 74: "The existence of parallel convictions in a certain number of group-members does not form a group conviction. Society is a sum of interacting individuals; group-conviction is therefore the similar conviction of group-members insofar as this conformity is based upon social interaction." The concept of a group will shortly be introduced in terms of solidarity and cooperation.

2. Thus the distinction between solidarity and cooperation is important only for the political scientist, not from the standpoint of the actors themselves. In coordinated action no sharp discrimination is made between symbol and non-symbol events: solidarity and cooperation are both involved, and in mutual dependence.

not constitute a group as here defined if there are no diversified and integrated patterns of action. Skilled workers may identify themselves as such, but do not form a group unless their acts are integrated with one another on the basis of the identification.

Groups may, of course, exhibit varying amounts of solidarity and cooperation, provided both are present to some degree. There may be loose organization with respect to a wide range of shared interests, faiths, and loyalties; or the group may be highly organized for the satisfaction of a narrow demand. The terms "association" and "demigroup" are introduced to take account of the varying degrees in which the group characteristic may be present. Where the diversification, integration of operations, and solidarity are all considerable we speak of an association: the members of an association participate in a relatively complex and rigid division of labor in which both the operations and perspectives of each person are smoothly integrated with those of the others. In a demigroup, either cooperation or solidarity or both are relatively slight. Rather than an inclusive identification symbol for the whole group, there may be only over-lapping partial identification symbols—as in the case of a state where patriotic or nationalist perspectives are minimal. Or the division of labor may be of low degree or extent, the integrated operations perhaps consisting of little more than participation in an occasional ceremonial observance, exemplified by an aggregate of coreligionists without an organized church, or a very temporary pattern of loosely integrated action, as in the case of a lynch mob. In short, we do not distinguish absolutely between groups and nongroups, but focus attention on the extent and complexity of the interpersonal relations among the members of specified aggregates.[3]

The importance of the group concept for political science need not be enlarged upon. Beard's emphatic statement (1934, 67) is scarcely an exaggeration: "This great fact stands out clearly, that through the centuries—down until our own day—group interests were recognized as forming the very essence of politics both in theory and practice." Yet, regardless of the

3. The internal structure of groups will be discussed in Chapter 7. Classes will be defined as particular kinds of aggregates which may or may not be organized as groups.

importance which groups empirically do have, the concept is not to be taken as logically fundamental, in the sense that political phenomena are to be defined exclusively in terms of groups. We are interested in neither groups nor individuals as "social atoms," but in interpersonal relations, which under specified conditions exhibit organization of varying kinds and degrees.[4]

PROP. The tendency for a specified group to emerge varies with (1) the intensity of perspectives for solidarity and their integration with predispositions, and (2) expectation of difficulty in attaining values by private operations.

The more intense reciprocally shared faiths, loyalties, and interests, the greater the likelihood of organizing to satisfy them. But intensity is not enough; group formation is obstructed if equally intense predispositions of the person are in conflict with the proposed group perspectives. Particularly effective elements of predisposition are loyalties to and identifications with preexistent groupings. Some conflict of operations is bound to occur between the new group and the old: time, energy, and resources are limited. More important is the fact that an established group membership entails more or less rigidity of perspective. Class loyalties and national loyalties may clash.[5]

Reference to the second factor puts emphasis on environmental conditions of group formation, effective through expectations. A group is the more likely to arise the more difficult it is expected to be, by acting alone or in an unorganized way with others, to attain a demand, satisfy an interest, or maintain and propagate a faith.

4. The present approach thus differs from doctrines like that of Gierke and Maitland that "the state is not a collection of individuals but an aggregation of groups." It is a question of how the term "state" is to be defined and used in political theory, not of whether the state "really" consists of groups or individuals. Definition in terms of persons and their interactions seems to us more fruitful, since it provides directly for both organized and unorganized ("individual") patterns of action.

5. To be sure, there does seem to be a tendency for the ego to form a more and more inclusive self. This is the predispositional basis for group formation—man is a gregarious animal in the phase of subjectivity as well as expression. But limits to this tendency are imposed by the self in the same process: the identifications already established narrow the range of possibilities of further identification. Sebastian de Grazia stresses the latter in *The Political Community, a Study of Anomie,* University of Chicago Press, 1948.

The tendency to form groups for the attainment of ends has been called by Gumplowicz, Ward, and others the *principle of synergism:*

> the phenomenon which consists in the fact that invariably in associated forms of life, definite groups of men, feeling themselves closely bound together by common interests, endeavour to function as a single element in the struggle for domination.[6]

The present hypothesis is that they are most likely to do so where the interests in question exceed a certain intensity, where they are integrated with wider perspectives already adopted, and where the expectation is that "domination" is impossible without "functioning as a single element."

DF. The degree of a person's *participation* in a group is the extent and intensity of his solidarity and cooperation with the group. The *morale* of a group is the degree of participation of its members.

Such designations as "sympathizer," "supporter," "dues paying member," "member in good standing," "active member" are common ways of taking account of varying degrees of participation. Since intensity, by which participation has been defined, is persistence in a course of action regardless of interference, the morale of a group as here defined is the degree to which the group maintains its identity and activity as a group in the face of adversity: it is the ability to withstand deprivations. And since participation involves both operations and perspectives, both are comprised in morale as well. Cooperation may continue at a high level even though solidarity has been undermined (though rarely the converse); and in such a case we may still speak of relatively high morale, though it may be unstable. An army may continue to fight even after it has lost faith in its commanders, interest in victory, or loyalty to the cause. Morale has completely collapsed only when it throws down its arms. In short, though solidarity implies a high morale, the converse is not necessarily true. It is on this fact that the possibility of external destruction of morale depends: weakness in solidarity provides the predispositional basis on which environmental stimuli can be effective.

6. Consult Barnes, 1924, 53, and MacLeod, 1931, 49.

DF. A *territorial group* is one for which activity in a specified geographical area is a necessary condition of participation; a *functional group*, engaging in specified practices.

The classification is neither exclusive nor exhaustive. Both conditions might be required, or neither. Other common conditions of participation are ethnic or religious origin or affiliation. Where the conditions in question are sufficient as well as necessary, we may speak of *purely* territorial or functional groups.

DF. The *permeability* of a group is the ease with which a person can become a participant.

Permeability can be measured in various ways. If economic status is a condition of group membership, the higher the status required, the less permeable the group. The permeability of a territorial group depends on immigration or rental restrictions. A group requiring acceptance of a large number of specific dogmas is less permeable than one requiring only agreement in "general aims." And so on. Permeability may be indirectly measured by the frequency of new accessions to the group in relation to eligibility.

DF. The *circulation* of a group is the degree of change in group membership, independently of change in size of the group.

The definition excludes changes consisting in gain only or loss only of membership: the circulation is the rate at which replacements occur, the "turnover." In a given time interval a group may rapidly increase or decrease in size with little or no circulation, or have high circulation and remain constant in size.

PROP. The morale of a group varies inversely with its circulation.

A "tightly knit group" significantly means both a group difficult to enter and one whose members closely identify with one another. The less permeable the group, the more value attaches to membership and, in turn, the more intense the adherence to group perspectives.

Of course, slight circulation—in particular, replacement of the disaffected by persons with intense group perspectives—

may raise morale considerably. But the effect is reversed, on the hypothesis, if the replacements are extensive and continuous. The result may be a sharp cleavage between the old members and the new which seriously interferes with both solidarity and cooperation. Roberto Michels (*Italien von Heute*) has described the "accordion rhythm" of revolutionary parties, which is generated by the interplay of permeability and solidarity. After the seizure of power, the party takes in members who are less thoroughly indoctrinated than the seasoned veterans. Presently these "opportunistic" elements arouse alarm among the older leaders and theorists, generating a "purge" that contracts the size of the party (see below, pp. 368–9).

PROP. Conflict among given groups varies inversely with (1) the circulation in the groups, and (2) their mutual permeability.

Both factors lower the intensity of group participation, and hence the likelihood that such participation will continue in the face of conflict with other groups. The second factor is particularly important: conflict will be minimized by expectations of possible membership in the other group. The point has frequently been commented on in the special case of economic groupings, especially in terms of class alignments:

> In a society where movement from a lower to a higher class occurs to a great extent and where the workers are not politically subordinated, class conflicts are attenuated and the ideology of the class struggle finds it difficult to gain a foothold (P. Mombert, "Class," in *ESS*).

DF. The *social mobility* of a person is the degree to which he participates in new groups.

It is a measure of the frequency with which the person ceases to participate in some groups and enters into others (see P. Sorokin, *Social Mobility*, Harper, 1927). The proposition on the inverse relation of circulation and morale may be restated in terms of social mobility. The higher the mobility of an aggregate of persons, the less likely are they to attain solidarity, and hence high morale, in whatever groupings they are participants.

DF. The degree of *accommodation* by a group is the inverse of the intensity of group acts in conflicts with other groups.

Low accommodations by a group is not to be confused with fanaticism of its participants. Fanaticism may be defined as the intense maintenance of a perspective by a person; accommodation is defined with respect to a group, and moreover refers to practices rather than perspectives only. A group might have low accommodation even though its members are not fanatic: the course of action involving conflict might be persisted in in spite of reluctance on the part of the participants —as is the case where morale is low but discipline severe.

Of course, a given group may be highly accommodating to some groups and not others, or accommodating with regard to certain of its acts and not others. A particular problem requires specification of the "area" and "objects" of accommodation.

PROP. The circulation of a group varies with its accommodation.

The hypothesis is that the more intense the group in its conflicts with others, the more difficulties in the way of new accessions to membership—greater sacrifices are required—and the more obstacles the group will put in the way of dropping membership. Conversely, the greater the accommodation, the more permeable the group, and the weaker the demands on participants to continue participation. It may be expected, therefore, that the low accommodation (militant) groups will be most stable in membership.

PROP. Large changes in the degree of accommodation are accompanied by a high degree of circulation.

As the group increases in accommodation, the more fanatic will be alienated by the adulteration of the program, and others will be drawn into the group; in the converse direction, moderates are repelled and extremists drawn in.[7] Of course, large changes in any characteristic of the group may result in high circulation, but changes in this character of the group are especially important, since they are likely to concern personality traits of the participants (Lasswell and Blumenstock, 1939,

7. This proposition is not incompatible with the preceding one: in the interval from high to low accommodation there may be high circulation, but the circulation at the end of the interval will be less, on the preceding hypothesis, than at the beginning. The two propositions together imply that the lowest circulation will characterize a group that is and remains militant.

chap. xv). By contrast, new demands and expectations may replace the old with comparatively little shift in membership if the leadership is unchanged and *symbols* of identification, demand, and expectation remain constant.

§3.2 *Publics, Public Opinion, and General Interests*

DF. An *opinion* in a group is a demand or expectation controvertible in the group; a *consensus*, noncontrovertible.

That a demand or expectation is controvertible in a group means that disagreement with it does not forfeit group membership or evoke other equally severe sanctions. A perspective is a matter of consensus rather than opinion when disagreement with it is not countenanced. Usually disagreement is visited by severe sanctions; and at any rate, it does violence to the sentiments and expectations of the group—it is shocking and astonishing.

Opinion is not passive or quiescent but involves, in general, a phase of expression in which it is made effective to some degree or other. Stress toward completion of the act of "holding" an opinion characterizes the *intensity* of the opinion. Explicit and detailed symbolization of the perspectives and operations respectively determining and determined by the opinion may be called the *symbolic* and *operational elaboration* of the opinion. The former is a presentation of the purported ground for the opinion, the latter a specification of the action called for by the opinion.[8] In terms of its symbolic elaboration, opinion may be characterized as "informed" or not, sentimentalized to various degrees, and so on.[9]

PROP. An opinion aggregate is the more likely to attain solidarity the more highly controversial the opinion, and the more the aggregate is in a minority.

8. See George C. Thompson, *Public Opinion and Lord Beaconsfield,* Macmillan, 1886, and the discussion in Lasswell, 1935, 195. "The term 'elaboration,'" Thompson writes, "may be used to denote either on the one hand definiteness with regard to practical action, or on the other the degree to which the opinion in question results from a thought-out political theory; let us say, its theoretical completeness." On the basis of the operational elaboration of opinion, Thompson introduces an interesting set of distinctions. An opinion consisting only in a general preference he calls a *bias;* a wish for a particular end or course of action, a *notion;* and beliefs as to the best practical means for achieving the ends desired, *policies;* patterns of closely related notions he calls *views.*

9. On the significance for politics of various types of symbolic elaboration, see, for instance, Lippmann, 1922, and Lowell, 1913.

Intense conflict with other opinions enhances mutual identification of those sharing the given opinion. The perspective of each person gives support to its maintenance by the others: demands can be made in the name of a self transcending the individual ego, expectations can claim warrant by being shared.

The smaller the minority, the more important is solidarity to make its opinion effective. And a minority is more favorably predisposed to solidarity because the need for justification of the perspective by other egos is more intensely felt. (There is, of course, a lower limit to the minority status beyond which solidarity is no longer likely; it is perhaps that below which the minority is too small to be either effective or subjected to attack.) The formation of blocs in legislative bodies and factions in political parties exemplifies the hypothesis.

DF. A *public* consists of the persons in the group who have or expect to have an opinion. *Public opinion* is the distribution of opinion in a public.

A public is defined in relation to a group so as to provide that divergencies of opinion within a public be superimposed on a basic consensus. Where such consensus is lacking, we have not one but several publics.[10]

Note that the public is narrower in scope than the attention aggregate. To be a member of the public it is necessary to expect that one can have some effect on the formation of policy. On some questions a person may be undecided; he does not drop out of the public until he ceases to expect to participate at some time or on some questions. The degree of participation may change from issue to issue even though the public does not. Indices of the public include such acts as speaking, writing, canvassing, contributing to parties and causes. (The expectations of the inactive can only be determined by intensive methods of observation.)

Public opinion comprises all of the opinions maintained by various parts of the public in question, as well as a specification of the parts having no opinion. When "public opinion" is spoken of in the singular, some one dominant opinion is referred to. The indices by which dominance has been determined

10. The point is emphasized by Lowell, 1913, 9: "A body of men are politically capable of a public opinion only so far as they are agreed upon the ends and aims of government and upon the principles by which these ends shall be attained." This is a matter of definition, of course; but the definition is a useful one.

must then be specified. The *dominant opinion* is not necessarily the *majority opinion;* the opinion of an influential minority may be that which is actually effective.[11]

DF. A *crowd* consists of the persons in a group who are expressing a consensus.

As a reaction against Le Bon's overgeneralization of the crowd concept, both "crowd" and "public" received sharper definition (consult Robert E. Park, *Masse und Publikum,* Buchdruckerei Lack & Granau, 1904). When a group is making nondebatable demands, it is acting as a crowd. (A crowd in action is a *mob.*) When the bounds of identification disappear and the person is concerned for his own ego, we have *panic.* In a crowd there is *psychic contagion,* a maximum of sincere, unreflective, excited dissemination of symbols.

DF. An *interest group* is an interest aggregate organized for the satisfaction of the interest.

All groups might be regarded as interest groups, since they all involve demands (preferences if not determinations) and expectations. But we may distinguish among various patterns of group activity those concerned with the satisfaction of interests—rather than, say, propagation of faiths or evocation of loyalties—and characterize the group as an interest group with regard to these patterns.[12]

DF. A *special interest group* is one such that in fact or on its own expectation the satisfaction of its interest significantly exceeds that of the interests of those outside the group. A *general interest group* is one having, to a significant degree, other than special interests.

If a trade association or pressure group is "out to smash" another organization, it is—in terms of its own expectations

11. This distinction is emphasized and developed in the Thompson work cited on p. 38, n. 8.

12. Coordinate concepts of "faith" and "loyalty groups" might be introduced analogously. Agencies for the maintenance of morale might be described as loyalty groups, organizations devoted to proselytizing as faith groups. But the concept of an interest group is far more useful: various sociological theorists construe society as a complex of conflicting interest groups, and view this conflict as "the vital and dynamic factor" in the social process. See, for instance, Albion W. Small, *General Sociology,* University of Chicago Press, 1914, and consult Barnes, 1924.

—a special interest group. However, the nongratification of other groups is not always involved; indeed, advantages may accrue to outsiders, as when insurance companies combine to reduce accident rates by public education. What is in question are the comparative advantages to the group and to outsiders.

By the characterization "in fact" we refer to scientific and impartial estimates. We recognize that the self-estimates by group leaders (and members) *may* coincide with that of qualified scientists. Often, however, self-appraisals are false (even without hypocrisy); and those who think they serve the general interest are blinded to important advantages to themselves.

Every group has *some* special interests—for instance, those in its own existence and activity *as* a group. But not all special interests are necessarily in conflict; they may be compatible or even in some cases facilitative of one another. And in changing circumstances, special interests may come to be in the general interest: the special interests of the military become general interests in time of war.[13] Of course, changes may equally take place in the opposite direction: an army brought into being for national defense may become the organ of national tyranny.

A difficulty in the classification of a particular aggregate as a general or special interest group is the number of interests that may be deliberately pursued, or actively affected, by a group. Consequences, furthermore, are often not visible over short periods of time. Professional associations are frequently given the benefit of the assumption that they serve the general interest; yet, as Graham Wallas (*Our Social Heritage*, Yale University Press, 1921) showed so well, the adjustment of professions to the common good is no simple matter. A difficulty in the classification of a particular aggregate as a general or special interest group is the number of interests that may be deliberately pursued, or actively affected, by a group. Consequences, furthermore, are often not visible over short periods of time.

13. The position taken by Michels (1915, 389) stands in need, therefore, of considerable qualification: "By a universally applicable social law [*sic*], every organ of the collectivity brought into existence through the need for the division of labor, creates for itself, as soon as it becomes consolidated, interests peculiar to itself. The existence of these special interests involves a necessary conflict with the interests of the collectivity."

PROP. The accommodation by and circulation of an interest group vary with the degree to which it is concerned with general rather than special interests.

The hypothesis is simply that the more general the interest, in the present sense of wide dispersion of the benefits of the satisfaction of the interest, the less intense the interested activity. On the whole, greater perseverance characterizes the pursuit of special advantages than of general improvement.[14] Moreover, a general interest group is more permeable, requiring only a perspective of "public spiritedness" rather than adherence to some special interest. And with the lesser intensity of such perspectives, frequent shifts in membership are to be expected as obstacles are encountered.

DF. The *expediency interests* of a group are those instrumental to the group process (structure and function) of the group. Its *principled interests* are those for the satisfaction of which the group attained solidarity.

A single interest—for example, an interest in peace—might in different respects involve both expediency and principle. There is intended no absolutistic differentiation between ends and means.

The distinction between expediency and principled interests has been elaborated by C. J. Friedrich (1937, 292–5), especially in application to political parties; he calls them "material and ideal objectives." Both sorts of interests, Friedrich points out, are present in all parties (groups): "The distinction between patronage parties and parties of principle is untenable. There is no such thing as a party which lacks either of these elements completely." This is not to say, however, that both kinds of interests are always present and equally effective.

PROP. As principled interests are satisfied in action, or the expectation of satisfaction is postponed, expediency interests become more pronounced.

Both these conditions are likely to occur as the group increases in size and age. Of course, it is not size itself which is

14. There is involved here no assumption of a universal egoism: the special advantage in question is that of the group, and may not apply to its members distributively. And if the term "egoism" is widened to include action on behalf of those with whom the ego identifies, it loses empirical content; such action is itself an index of the existence of an identification (self).

important, but the heterogeneity of perspective which is likely to accompany increase in size. As Friedrich observes,

It is evident that a party in order to hold together a rather heterogeneous following will shun a decided stand on questions of principles, while at the same time making concessions to a variety of theoretically perhaps incompatible interests.

Size in itself makes more difficult the integration of operations. Such integration becomes an increasing object of concern as the group grows older and the conditions taken into account in the original pattern of cooperation change with time. Michels (1915, 366) concludes that "as the organization increases in size, the struggle for great principles becomes impossible." [15] But the connection with size and age is not unvarying, since groups can revitalize old principles or add new ones.

In a sense "age" is a misleading term that avoids specifying the variables that are actually interacting with one another. Usually the word is one of ambiguous reference, and can be given significance only as a concealed hypothesis to the effect that the interaction of all relevant variables will result in bringing about a certain pattern of equilibrium. Such hypotheses take on some dignity when they are made in forthright terms, and subjected to the test of verification, as in Arnold J. Toynbee's *Study of History*. But the conception of definitely timed (or even of shifting) "stages" in social or political processes is far from established. The history of the Roman Catholic Church, and of certain other long-lived groups, cast serious doubt on "stages." Rather, the changing equilibrium among the significantly interacting variables has resulted in periods of "revitalization" and "decay" (to use biological metaphors); or, to speak more precisely, periods of relative stress on principled interests have reappeared more than once.

PROP. Groups are more accommodating with regard to principled than expediency interests.

15. Compare also M. Ostrogorski, 1926, 103: "For thirty years there has lasted under slightly varying aspects a situation always fundamentally the same: parties scattered, decomposed, and unable to hold together by any natural affinities, while the old organizations still subsist, reduced to the state of electoral machines for manipulating the elections, dividing the electors into two rival camps and setting them at one another like marionettes."

Concession and compromise will be more frequent and extensive when they concern demands not directly related to the survival and functioning of the group as such. Two important corollaries follow from the hypothesis. One is that expediency interests are relatively more constant than principled interests. This may be seen in the transformation of revolutionary parties with the attainment of power (see §10.4).

A second corollary is that principled interests are modified as they come into conflict with expediency interests. Demands involving action which threatens the pattern of organization are altered or abandoned altogether in the interests of organization (though the *symbols* of demand are frequently retained). As Michels puts it (1915, 373):

> From a means, organization becomes an end. To the institutions and qualities which at the outset were destined simply to ensure the good working of the party machine (subordination, the harmonious co-operation of individual members, hierarchical relationships, discretion, propriety of conduct), a greater importance comes ultimately to be attached than to the productivity of the machine. Henceforward the sole preoccupation is to avoid anything which may clog the machinery.

Again, this is too unqualified a formulation: we do not say that expediency becomes the *sole* preoccupation, but only that it tends to take precedence over principles when conflict arises. Moreover, there is no need to adopt here Michels' standpoint, according to which a principled stage is followed by "degeneration" to expediency.[16]

PROP. Principled interests are subordinated to expediency interests in the degree that the group expects general support without emphasis on principles, or expects attainment of its demands without general support.

With regard to its expediency interests, every group is a special interest group. Where general support is valued, it must be sought, therefore, on the basis of principled interests.

16. Another not untypical "stage" hypothesis—subject to the reservations noted above—asserts that the "agitational" phase of social action moves into the "organizational." Religion allegedly becomes magic, and "ideology" becomes "phraseology"; the tactician substitutes for the prophet, and the bureaucrat for the enthusiast. All this signifies, in our terms, the relative eclipse of principled interests. (R. Mayreder, *Der typische Verlauf Sozialer Bewegungen,* 2d ed. Vienna, 1926.)

(Any direct interest in other groups is, from the standpoint of the given group, a principled interest.)

The hypothesis is clearly exemplified by political parties, though it applies to other types of groups as well. Friedrich (1937, 293) maintains:

> The ideal objectives are forced upon parties by their struggle for gaining control of the government. It is a platitude of practical politics that the outs are invariably more emphatic in their advocacy of principles than the ins.

It follows from the proposition that the demand statements most prominently brought to the focus of attention of non-group members will symbolize principled rather than expediency interests. The demands of the group are presented to outsiders so as to maximize support of the group. In internal bulletins, on the other hand, expediency interests can be given fuller symbolization; support is not in question, or not to the same degree.

If the members of the group are stratified by degree of participation, similar considerations can be applied to the group itself. The less the degree of participation, the greater the prominence of symbols of principled interests which will be brought to the focus of attention. Memoranda circulating within the executive committee, say, would, on the hypothesis, deal more with expediency interests than would those disseminated among the entire membership.

DF. *Group consciousness* is the degree to which there is identification with the group based on solidarity in relation to valid interests; *false group consciousness*, in relation to assumed interests only.

Group consciousness, on this definition, is more than simply identification with the group. We do not speak of group consciousness if there is identification without reciprocal sharing of perspectives. The identification "I am an American" is not always accompanied by an explicit set of demands and expectations specifying what it is to be an American. A high frequency and intensity of such identifications do not in themselves constitute national consciousness. The latter involves not only identification, but solidarity as to interests, faiths, and loyalties.

Further, group consciousness requires that the interests

shared be empirically warranted as being *to* the interest of the members of the group. If participation in the group is in fact inimical to the interests of the participants, we can speak only of false consciousness. Nationalism, to pursue the example, involves a conception of "national interest," but this phrase does not always signify what is to the interest of the nation. Nationalism coincides with national consciousness only where there is awareness of what is in fact to the nation's interest, and where solidarity is attained on *this* basis and not in terms of interests falsely accepted as such.[17]

PROP. Group consciousness initially increases with conflict with other groups with equal or higher degrees of consciousness.

Such conflict strengthens, at least at the outset, existing patterns of solidarity: the "we" becomes crystallized and important as over against a blatant "they." The most familiar example is the increase of patriotism in wartime, involving not merely a strengthening of identifications, but of interests, faiths, and loyalties as well. The exigencies of conflict, moreover, heighten awareness of the valid interests of the group as a whole: defense against the common enemy is an interest in common, facilitating the recognition of other shared interests.[18]

The hypothesis is only of an initial increase, however. Two factors are important for the persistence of the heightened consciousness: the balance of expected success over sacrifices demanded, and the initial intensity of group participation. In the face of the necessity of continued sacrifice without expectations of ultimate success, solidarity may progressively weaken and ultimately break down completely as conflict continues. A differentiation between "we" and "they" emerges *within* the group (between the rank and file and the leaders, for example, or between the people and the government); "their" interests

17. "Group consciousness" is a generalization of the Marxist concept applied to the special groupings called classes. The Marxists have especially emphasized as a component of class consciousness awareness of valid interests: identification with a class other than that to which a person belongs by virtue of his economic status and function, far from constituting class consciousness on that usage, represents quite a contrary state of affairs.

18. Compare M. Ginsberg, "Class Consciousness" in *ESS:* "The possession of common interests by members of a group is often brought into consciousness by the need of defense against a common enemy, imaginary or real, and especially of being pitted against another group already conscious of itself."

do not coincide with ours, "they" are responsible for the conflict or at any rate for the defeat, and so on.

If, however, intensity of group participation is initially high, even bitter and costly defeat may serve only to heighten group solidarity and consciousness. The defeat may itself provide common interests—in rehabilitation and revenge, for example—and increase awareness of what is *to* the group interest.[19]

§3.3 *Society and Institutions*

DF. A *cultural trait* is an act characteristic of a group.

An act is characteristic when it recurs under comparable circumstances. It is no simple matter, however, to decide in all cases whether the circumstances *are* comparable and the act has in fact recurred. Among social scientists it is the social anthropologists who have had to deal most intimately with the descriptive problems involved, since they have done field work among groups whose culture contrasts most sharply with our own.[20]

Note that traits of culture may be *personality types*, if the recurrence of a given form can be demonstrated—if, for example, superaggressive and destructive types appear among the political leaders of the group. Certain *personality traits* may occur widely, although combined in various patterns of personality. *Group acts favorable to certain personality types and personality traits* may also be distinguishable; such as the maintenance of large armies. *Other interpersonal practices* complete the inventory of culture traits.

DF. An *institution* is a pattern composed of culture traits specialized to the shaping and distribution of a particular value (or set of values). The *culture* of a group is the totality of its culture traits. A *society* is a group with its culture.

19. See N. C. Leites and I. de Sola Poole, "Communist Propaganda in Reaction to Frustration," Library of Congress, *Experimental Division for the Study of War Time Communications*, Document No. 27, 1942 (reprinted in Lasswell, Leites, and Associates, 1949, chap. xii).

20. Lasswell, 1939, 535–6. Some of the most suggestive writing on methods of field observation has been done by Bronislav Malinowski. A pioneer example of photographic recording is Gregory Bateson and Margaret Mead, *Balinese Character; A Photographic Analysis*, Special Publications of the New York Academy of Sciences, Vol. II, 1942.

When we speak of the institutions of government that prevail in a given group, we are describing some of the culture traits that are present; we are selecting practices that, from a specified (value) standpoint, are closely interrelated.

Although an attempt has been made to reserve the term "culture" for trait-patterns of groups that are distinctive in the list of all known contemporary and historic times, usage has robbed the term of this meaning. Nonetheless, it is still convenient to use the word "group" in referring to some interpersonal relations which do not reach the degree of elaborateness that justifies the use of the term "culture." A transitory party faction is a group, though not a culture. The term "society" includes reference to people and basic traits of action in the same way that "personality" includes reference to the person and his basic action traits.

For many purposes it is convenient to have a synoptic term for all the perspectives of a culture (*symbol culture;* often called "ideal culture"). It is also useful to have a word for the operations performed on the physical environment, and the materials on which they have been performed. The ensemble is often called *material cultures;* if it is desired to distinguish the materials, they can be designated *culture materials.*[21]

As a means of classifying acts that conform to the traits of a culture, we may speak of *conduct.* When acts are spoken of with no implications for their relation to culture, the word *behavior* is convenient. Obviously, the members of a group always engage in much behavior that is not conduct.

DF. A *sanction* is conduct in response to an act (in terms of its conformity or nonconformity to culture traits) that is expected to modify future acts in the direction of conformity, or to nullify any damage to society resulting from the act.

The sanction might consist in the manipulation of symbols (praise or censure), or in a redistribution of goods and services, or in the use of violence, or, speaking generally, in reward or punishment by way of any value whatever. The sanction is *positive* when it enhances values for the actor to whom it is

21. See, on the concepts of this section, the essays in *The Science of Man in the World Crisis,* Ralph Linton, ed., Columbia University Press, 1945, especially "The Concept of Culture" by Clyde Kluckhohn and William H. Kelly, and "The Concept of Basic Personality Structure as an Operational Tool in the Social Sciences" by Abram Kardiner.

applied, *negative* when it deprives him of values. It is to be noted that a sanction is itself conduct, that is, action in accord with the culture traits; the sanctions in force in a given group conform to the group perspectives.

DF. A *commitment* is a projected act with the expectation that negative sanctions will be applied if the act is not completed.

In most cultures, commitment involves, at bottom, expectations of violence—"Covenants without swords are but words," in Hobbes's phrase. But sanctions may concern other values than personal safety.

Consent might be defined as commitment to the satisfaction of a demand. This definition emphasizes the active character of consent; but of course the act may be internalized. The point is that in giving consent, values are put at stake: consent is incompatible with indifference. Often this order of definition is reversed, commitment being defined in terms of consent to specified action. But it then becomes necessary to distinguish between genuine and merely verbal consent; and this is done ultimately, by reference to expectations of sanctions, as in the present procedure.

In particular, "silence is consent" only if it is an index of expectations, not simply of consequent deprivation, but of acts of deprivation which are in accord with culture traits—in short, expectations of sanctions as here defined. The victim of robbery is not genuinely consenting to being robbed; he genuinely prefers being robbed to the threatened violence, but such violence is not the application of a sanction. It does not accord with the culture traits, and is itself subject to sanctions.

DF. The *mores* are culture traits, deviations from which are expected to be met (and actually are met) by relatively severe sanctions. *Countermores* are culture traits symbolized by the group as deviations from the mores, and yet are expected to occur. *Expediencies* are culture traits which are neither mores nor countermores.

That culture traits tend to be sentimentalized, and defended when deviated from, is a general observation often confirmed.[22]

22. For an elaboration of this point see, for instance, W. G. Sumner's *Folkways*, Ginn, 1940 and Westermarck's *Origin and Development of the Moral Ideas*, Macmillan, 1906.

It is significant, however, that many activities which are disapproved of by those who bear a given culture are, nevertheless, expected to take place. Bribery may be almost universally reprobated, yet it is taken for granted that some officials will succumb to temptation. A certain volume of countermores activities are thus "normal" (in both a statistical and normative sense), and must be included by the candid observer as part of the culture.

There are, however, violations of the mores so shocking that they are not expected to happen, and when isolated instances do occur, they are dismissed as "inhuman" (as something wholly apart from culture). (Consider the inviolability of the chief priest in some cultures.) Deviations from many patterns of a culture are ignored altogether or meet with mild disapproval. Continual innovation may be expected and accepted in many spheres, not only of material culture.

Resembling the separation of cultural patterns into mores, countermores, and expediencies is the classification of traits of personality into three categories: those sustained by the conscience, those appealing to impulses and modes of expression in conflict with conscience, and others. For convenience, we may refer to patterns of *conscience*, *impulse*, and *reason* (in a sense roughly corresponding to the psychoanalytic categories of superego, id, and ego). On reflection it is plain that the mores of a group must be sustained by the conscience of most group members. But it is possible in large, complex societies for some child to grow to maturity in subenvironments that attach the conscience to conduct that is countermores from the perspective of the society as a whole. Religious dissenters may refuse to bear arms in defense of the state; or back-country distillers may hate revenue officers.

DF. The *social order* is the pattern of mores and countermores institutions.

The social order comprises the practices of custom, morality, religion, and so on, and the expected deviations from them. It is the pattern of acts subject—in fact or only in the group perspectives—to the application of sanctions. When a practice ceases to be treated or symbolized as subject to sanctions, we say it has been made "technical." It has become a matter of expediency, not morality.

DF. *Technology* consists in the operations by which the group manipulates its culture materials.

Part of the technology is hedged about by sanctions, and is therefore included in the social order (animals for food, for instance, may be killed only in a ritually prescribed manner). Other parts of a given technology may be almost wholly free of entangling sanctions. The former are group *techniques;* the latter are group *technics. Technicalization* is a transformation from technique to technic, from involvement with mores and countermores to expediency alone.[23]

It is often affirmed that one pervasive factor in the insecurities of the modern world is the encroachment of the scientific-explanatory and the engineering-manipulative perspective into every realm of culture, resulting in the "atomizing" of society and the disappearance of social order.[24]

23. This difference between technique and technic has much in common with Durkheim's distinction between the "sacred" and "profane." Secularization is an approach to technicalization: practices have been freed of, at any rate, divine sanctions. See Emile Durkheim's *Elementary Forms of the Religious Life* (Macmillan, 1915) and *The Division of Labor in Society* (Macmillan, 1933).

24. Assertions of this type have been prevalent among the "materialistic" Marxists and the apologists of many religious groups. Examples of the latter: Karl Polanyi, *The Great Transformation,* Farrar & Rinehart, 1944; N. Berdyaev, *The Destiny of Man,* Scribner's, 1937.

PART TWO

The political interactions of various persons and groups are constituted by patterns of *influence* and *power*, manifested in and affected by *symbols*, and stabilized in characteristic political *practices*.

IV

INFLUENCE

By influence is meant the value position and potential of a person or group. Values may be grouped under "welfare" and "deference," and positions described in regard to each value (or set of values). Positions in descending order of influence are occupied by the elect, mid-elect, and reject. Classes and social structures are defined in relation to the shaping and distribution of values.

§4.1 *Values and Value Position*

UNDEFINED. *Welfare values, deference values*

VALUES ARE the goal-events of acts of valuation (see §2.1). We are concerned for the most part with two important groups of values; but it is not assumed that these are the only values which may be objects of scientific inquiry or practical action. By "welfare values" we mean those whose possession to a certain degree is a necessary condition for the maintenance of the physical activity of the person. Among welfare values we are especially concerned with well-being, wealth, skill, and enlightenment. By *well-being* is meant the health and safety of the organism. *Wealth* is income: services of goods and persons accruing to the individual in any way whatever.[1] *Skill* is proficiency in any practice whatever, whether in arts or crafts, trade or profession. By *enlightenment* we mean knowledge, insight, and information concerning personal and cultural relations.

Deference values are those that consist in being taken into

1. It is not in accord with present-day usage to adopt Adam Smith's "wealth" as the most suitable single term for the subject matter of economics. "Income" is distinguished for many purposes from "wealth," and the phrase "goods and services" is often employed to define the field of economics. The point is also often made that "goods" can be reduced to "services," since it is the services of the goods, not their physical attributes, that have economic relevance. Seeking a single-term designation, we have preferred the venerable "wealth" to the less familiar "services."

consideration (in the acts of others and of the self). Most important of the deference values, for political science, is *power*. Other important deference values are respect, rectitude, and affection. *Respect* is the value of status, of honor, recognition, prestige, the "glory" or "reputation" which Hobbes classes with gain and safety as one of the three fundamental human motivations. *Rectitude* comprises the moral values—virtue, goodness, righteousness, and so on. *Affection*, finally, includes the values of love and friendship.

No assumptions will be made here as to the comparative intensity with which these values are held, or the importance assigned to them by various persons and groups. In some form and to some degree these values no doubt always play a role, and political scientists, ancient and modern, have seen in them the element of invariance which makes a political science possible. Machiavelli justifies the study of history with the observation that

> Whoever considers the past and the present will readily observe that all cities and all peoples are and ever have been animated by the same desires and the same passions; so that it is easy, by diligent study of the past, to foresee what is likely to happen in the future.

Bryce takes a similar position:

> There is in the phenomena of human society one "constant," one element or factor which is practically always the same, and therefore the basis of all the so-called "social sciences." This is human nature itself. All fairly normal men have like passions and desires. They are stirred by like motives, they think upon similar lines . . .[2]

But while there may be similarities of "motive, passion and desire" among various persons and cultures, there are differences as well, differences especially in the comparative importance attached to the various values. No generalizations can be made a priori concerning the scale of values of all groups and individuals. What the values are in a given situation must in principle be separately determined for each case.[3]

2. Machiavelli, *Discourses*, Bk. I, chap. 39; Bryce, 1924, I, 14.

3. On variation in basic values see, for instance, Ruth Benedict, *Patterns of Culture*, Houghton Mifflin, 1934. Repositories of data about variations from culture to culture and within a culture from time to time are W. G. Sumner and A. G. Keller, *The Science of Society*, Yale University Press, 1927; L. T. Hobhouse, *Morals in Evolution*, Henry Holt, 1915; E. Westermarck, *Origin and Development of the Moral Ideas*, Macmillan, 1906–08.

In particular, it is impossible to assign a universally dominant role to some one value or other. No single principle of motivation can be elaborated into a tenable "philosophy of history"—as though always and everywhere human conduct can be interpreted as a striving only for economic gain, or for political power, or for prestige and glory, or for love and affection. In a specific situation, any or all of these—and others as well—might be involved in different degrees. What values are operative to what extent can be determined only by specific empirical inquiry.

DF. The *value pattern* is the pattern of distribution of the values of a group among its members.

We shall use the term *distribution index* of a value to refer to some measure of the dispersion of the value pattern. The index will be spoken of in a positive sense: the greater the equality of the pattern, the higher the index. Hence a society in which power is concentrated in a few hands has a lower distribution index (for power) than one in which power is more widely shared. Similarly for other values: where the highest incomes are many times the lowest, the distribution index of wealth is lower than where the highest incomes are not so much in excess of the lowest; a society divided into castes has a lower distribution index for respect than one not so divided. And so on.

DF. *Value position* is the place occupied in the value pattern.

A person or group receiving a comparatively large share of the value will be said to occupy a *high* or *favorable* value position; the other extreme will be spoken of as a *low* or *unfavorable* value position.

PROP. The positions of a person or group in different value patterns tend to approximate one another.

This is not to say that any given value pattern tends to a more and more unequal distribution, but only that the patterns of different values tend to coincide. The hypothesis is not, for example, that the rich become richer and the poor poorer, but rather that the rich tend also to be the healthy, respected, informed, and so on, and the poor to be the sickly, despised, ignorant. Those with a high position in one value tend to attain high ones in others as well, and similarly with low position. The phenomenon described in the hypothesis can be termed *value agglutination*, and is to be distinguished from *value concentration*—a change in the shape of a single value pattern in the direction of less and less equality (a lowering of its distribution index). It is an example of value agglutination if, say, life expectancy and years of schooling completed both correlate positively with income; value concentration is exemplified in societies where respect, say, focuses on a small elect.

DF. A *competitive value* is one such that those who occupy different positions in the pattern symbolize themselves as conflicting; where the different positions are symbolized as compatible the value is *pluralistic;* and where facilitative, the value is *stratified.*

Differences in the sharing of a competitive value are not acquiesced in, but form the basis of conflict (competition). A stratified value, on the other hand, is expected to be unequally distributed, and the inequalities support one another. Different shares of pluralistic values are regarded as neither necessary nor intolerable.

Every value may have all three characteristics in some degree. Skill is a competitive value when the skilled try to interfere with the acquisition of skill by the less skilled—by maintaining impermeable guilds at a time of rising pressure for economic opportunity. Skill is a stratified value insofar as "masters" instruct "apprentices" while the latter endorse the special interests of the "masters." And it is pluralistic insofar as there is minimal interaction, whether of support or interference, between certain skill groups.

Even though a value exhibits all three characteristics in some situations, emphasis may rest on one. Wealth, for instance, is a competitive value in our society; well-being is pluralistic; and respect is stratified wherever castes survive. That a value which is competitive in one society may play a different role in another society is well-established. Respect is stratified in an "aristocracy," but is pluralistic or competitive in a "republic."

§4.2 *Influence*

DF. The *value potential* is the value position likely to be occupied as the outcome of conflict.

One index of the influence of a political party is the number of party members in office. The value potential (in terms of this index) is the number of party members likely to be in office after the next election, or the next uprising, or some other probable conflict. Obviously the value potential of any person or group in regard to any value is a matter of estimate.

DF. The *value expectancy* is the position expected by the self. The *value demanded* is the position sought by the self.

Note that the expectancy is the position which the actor thinks is probable, not that which is in fact probable, in the judgment of a qualified observer. The latter is the value potential.

The importance of the value demanded as a determiner of conduct has been explored by Kurt Lewin and other psychologists under the designation "aspiration level." It is clear that there is a positive relation between the intensity of action toward the attainment of a value and an optimistic expectancy regarding that value.[4]

DF. The *realism index* is the degree to which the value expectancy approaches the value potential.

It is not necessary that the expectations be realized and the demands gratified for the perspective to have been realistic; it is sufficient if such an outcome was probable. (The expectation of three "heads" in six tosses of a coin is realistic even if all six tosses result in "tails"; the expectation of six "tails" would have been unrealistic even though it was actually fulfilled.) Excessive optimism or pessimism are both unrealistic (a low realism index).

DF. The *actualization index* of a value pattern is the degree to which the pattern approximates the potential.

Only a small fraction of the members of a party may vote at an election; its influence has not been fully actualized. Similarly, there is a low actualization of influence for a state confined to a small territory and sphere of influence but with a large and efficient military machine. Different indices can be specified of the actualization of other values.

4. A succinct summary is in J. McV. Hunt, *Personality and Behavior Disorders; A Handbook Based on Experimental and Clinical Research,* Ronald Press, 1944, I, chap. x.

DF. The *demand ratio* is the ratio of demand to the initial position of the demand maker. The *realization ratio* is the ratio of the resulting position to expectancy.

Hence the demand ratio may be said to measure the degree of dissatisfaction with the existent distribution. The higher the ratio, the less satisfactory the distribution to those making the demands. It is the demand ratio, and not merely an unfavorable value position, which occasions stress toward changes in the practices of value distribution. As Michels puts it (1915, 236),

It is not the simple *existence* of oppressive conditions but it is the *recognition of these conditions by the oppressed,* which in the course of history has constituted the prime factor of class struggles.

Realization is not to be confused with actualization; the former compares results with expectancies, the latter with potentials. Demands may be realized without a high degree of actualization if they are unrealistically moderate (pessimistic).

DF. *Influence* is value position and potential.

It is important to take both potential and position into account. A group may be more and more influential even though its value position remains constant, if its potential is increasing (for instance, an increasingly popular and well-organized revolutionary party); and conversely a group may have little influence regardless of its value position, because of its low potential (as in the case of a ruling clique just before its overthrow).

The word "influence" is a verb as well as a noun: the possessing of a value is in general an interpersonal relation. This is true not merely because some values, such as the deference values, consist in such relations, but because the conduct of persons active in the shaping and distribution of the value is essential to its possession (enjoyment). The effective claim of an individual to a piece of real estate means that his acts in relation to the land are not interfered with by others.

When the study of politics is defined as the study of "influence and the influential" (Lasswell, 1936), its subject matter comprises more values than power, though it does not include all values. A limited list of values may be chosen for investigation in order to discover how they are interrelated in a given society, and from one society to another. Such choices are made from the standpoint of furthering the ongoing of inquiry.[5]

PROP. The permeability of a group varies inversely with its influence.

The relative permeability of a group with respect to another (that is, the degree to which candidates for membership in the first group belong to the second) varies inversely with the difference in influence of the two groups. A large stock-holder may more easily become a member of the board of directors than a small one.

Since potential as well as position determines permeability, admission of new members varies with the group's expectations of the resulting increase or decrease of its influence.

DF. *Security* is high value expectancy, position, and potential: realistic expectancy of maintaining influence.

Security involves, first, certain perspectives (the "sense of security"): demands and expectations as to the future value position of the self. The perspectives must be realistic—the expectations be in fact likely to be fulfilled—or there is only a "false" sense of security. And the actual value position must be comparatively high: the locus of security is in the present as well as the future.

DF. *Indulgence* is increase in influence; *deprivation* is decrease. The *I:D ratio* is the ratio of indulgence to deprivation in a specified situation.

Indulgence and deprivation are general terms for any improvement or deterioration in value position or potential. The concepts have nothing to do with the pleasure-pain ratio of the utilitarians; no useful purpose is served by describing all the various values in hedonic terms.[6]

5. During the nineteenth century the expansion of modern society gave prominence to specialized activity, and led to a corresponding specialization of scientific investigation. The science of economics became more distinct from the science of politics, and "political economy" went into the shadow. Recent crises have brought about a new rapprochement, reflected in the writings of Jacob Viner, for instance, and in such titles as Robert A. Brady, *Business as a System of Power,* Columbia University Press, 1943.

6. But so masterly was Jeremy Bentham as a user of language that it may be possible to interpret his treatment of the utilitarian categories in strict equivalence to our present usage (*The Theory of Legislation,* Harcourt, Brace, 1931 and *The Theory of Fictions,* Harcourt, Brace, 1932).

It follows from the definitions that all demands are to maximize indulgence over deprivation for the identified self, and that behavior is based on expectations as to the I:D ratio. Again, there is no utilitarian assumption here of "man the calculator," in the sense that *all* conduct is directed by *conscious* projection of alternative courses of action. Nothing more is involved than that values are valued, that conduct is goal-directed. Given certain goals, action is based on expectations of indulgence and deprivation with regard to those goals.

DF. The *elect* consists of those with the most influence; the *reject*, the least influence; the *mid-elect*, those belonging neither to the elect nor the reject.

Where it is convenient to make further differentiations, we speak of the *upper*, *mid-*, and *lower elect*. All the terms may be used with reference to position and potential in any single value pattern as well as to influence in general. For some values, however, special terms will be introduced—for example, we will speak of the elect and reject in relation to power as the "elite" and the "mass" respectively.

§4.3 *Social Structure*

DF. A *class* is a major aggregate of persons engaging in practices giving them a similar relation to the shaping and distribution (and enjoyment) of one or more specified values.

The concept of class is among the most confused and controversial in political theory. An important source of this confusion is the fact that the word "class" is normatively ambiguous to a very high degree. It is used with equal frequency, and intensity, as a descriptive category, and as a symbol of demand and identification; and seldom does the user make explicit which function the term is intended to serve. Like other terms here introduced, we shall use it solely in a descriptive sense; and though the frequency of its normative use entails a risk of misunderstanding, what the term symbolizes is important enough both in political practice and political science to justify retention of the familiar word.[7]

7. Compare Tawney, 1931, 65–6: "If the word 'class' is one which everyone dislikes, it is also one which no one in practice can escape from using. The sensible attitude is neither to ignore the influence obviously exercised by the

We define class in relation to some value or values; where these are not specified, they are to be understood as the set of all values important in the society. The *class structure* of society is the pattern of these classes. Although the classes most frequently discussed are economic, that is, defined with regard to wealth, one may also speak of classes with respect to other values. We refer to class as a "major" aggregate in order to emphasize the use of the term to describe the most prominent characteristic ways in which persons are related to values. Both the polemical and scientific usefulness of the word "class" comes in part from the tendency to employ but a small number of terms to specify classes. In some vocabularies we have the "bourgeoisie" over against the "proletariat," or the "ruling class" against the "ruled." Even where the differentiation is carried farther, and three-term, five-term, or even a more-term system is used, there is some inhibition upon the multiplying of distinctions. By contrast, terms that designate the distribution of occupations and skills in society must be numerous, or they are unusable.

A class is defined as an aggregate, not a group, in the sense of our previous definition: it may or may not be organized. We may speak of class solidarity and class consciousness under the same conditions as previously specified. In particular, it is to be noted that class consciousness is not logically necessary to the existence of a class. As R. H. Tawney puts it (1931, 66), the fact of class and the consciousness of class are different phenomena.

> The fact creates the consciousness, not the consciousness the fact. The former may exist without the latter, and a group may be marked by common characteristics, and occupy a distinctive position vis-à-vis other groups, without, except at moments of exceptional tension, being aware that it does so.

It must be emphasized that to speak of classes does not of itself imply the existence of a "class struggle." *Whether, to what degree, and under what conditions conflict occurs among specified classes is an empirical question which is in no way settled merely by invoking the concept of class.* Nor does the concept

---

phenomenon which it describes, as though it were indecent to mention it in polite society, nor to erect that phenomenon . . . into the unique reality to which all other aspects of social life are to be referred as their original source and all-sufficient explanation."

imply the existence of rigidly demarcated groupings sharply differentiated from one another; the permeability of a specified class is again a variable whose magnitude under given conditions must be empirically determined. What is required for the applicability of the term (and thus presupposed by its use) is only that there be available indices by which we can distinguish different relations to the shaping, distribution, and enjoyment of a specified value or set of values.[8]

DF. A *welfare class* is one defined with respect to welfare values; a *deference class*, with respect to deference values; a *social class*, one defined with respect to all the values important in the society.

There are as many kinds of classes as there are values, and within each kind as many classes as characteristic functions in the shaping and sharing of the value. Much of the controversy and confusion concerning the nature of classes stems from a failure to recognize this wide range of possibilities. More confusing, however, is the use of the term class, not as a classificatory term alone, nor even as a normatively ambiguous expression, but as an overcondensed way of stating hypotheses about the social process. Often the condensation of meaning occurs in a context that fails to make explicit what is being said.

To speak of class in the Marxist sense in reference to capitalist society is not only to categorize people according to their ownership relation to the tools of production. It is to put forward the hypothesis that persons so classified constitute social classes as well; and that social class position and potential are determined—allowing for some lag—by the economic class (by their share of wealth, measured by ownership of the instruments of production).

The term class can be disentangled from all forms of ambiguity by careful stipulating which value (or values) are

8. The suggestion has often been made that we "reject the very idea of classes, for the simple reason that we cannot discover any community which is really arranged in a number of distinct and distinguishable classes" (Barker, 1942, 117). This is to say that only terms of absolute precision are admissable in science. But clearly, a concept may be serviceable even though borderline cases arise in its application, and a system of classification may be important even though there is some degree of overlapping among its categories. We do not presuppose that all classes are absolutely distinct from one another, but only that some classes, under suitable conditions, can be distinguished from others with sufficient clarity to subserve the ongoing of inquiry.

meant, by openly declaring any normative judgments, and by making explicit whatever hypotheses are held about the determinative effect of any value position or potential upon any other position or potential. The hypothesis of value agglutination (p. 58) is that all values tend to be held in the same degree by a given group or aggregate in society. But it does not undertake to specify which values are more determinative than others. However, the statement of this hypothesis does invite inquiry directed toward the study of these relations in every concrete situation. Enough is already known about cultures to say that values are differently ranked in different societies; and to sustain the proposition that *control of the key values exercises a stronger determinative effect upon the control of all values than is exerted by the control of nonkey values.* (In assembling data bearing upon this hypothesis, circularity is avoided by choosing different indices for the "keyness" of a value than for "effect," [9])

DF. A *skill group* (or *aggregate*) consists of persons performing the same technological operation; the *skill structure* of society is the pattern of such groups and operations. An *occupation* is a practice pursued as a major activity by a person.

We do not limit the term occupation to the activity from which the person draws his chief income. It is consistent with the definition to recognize that goal values sought by particular persons may deviate from the goals usually dominant among those pursuing an occupation. A "gentleman farmer" does not work primarily with wealth in view, but is interested in respect, skill, well-being, or some other value. A person's *vocation* is what he is considered fit to exercise, and regards as the maximum realization of the demands of the self, even though there may be no opportunity to follow his bent.

Almost invariably an occupation involves one or more skills; hence the member of a particular occupational category can usually be included in several categories of skill. (Also, a person is usually in command of skills in addition to his occupational equipment; we may speak here of avocational skills.)

9. A striking instance of a key value that contrasts with our own society is the importance given by the Zuni Indians of the southwestern United States to a prominent position in ceremonial dances. In terms of our classification, the value involved is not primarily a welfare value (like wealth or even skill); what is desired is deference—and deference not in the form of power but respect (Benedict, *Patterns of Culture,* 1934).

Classes have often been defined in relation to skill, particularly in terms of occupation; occupation is said to be the essential determinant of class. Bryce, for example, analyzes the American class structure in these terms (1893, II, 297):

> Classes are in America by no means the same thing as in the greater nations of Europe. One must not, for political purposes, divide them as upper and lower, richer and poorer, but rather according to the occupations they respectively follow.

In other conceptions, what is held to be essential to class is not occupation but status. Tawney, for example, elaborates this interpretation (1931, 71):

> Class systems . . . have usually been associated—hence, indeed, the invidious suggestion which the word sometimes conveys—with differences, not merely of economic metier, but of social position, so that different groups have been distinguished from each other, not only, like different professions, by the nature of the service they render, but in status, in influence, and sometimes in consideration and respect. Even today, indeed, though less regularly than in the past, class tends to determine occupation rather than occupation class.

Where these are matters of definition, the distinction being made is between welfare and deference classes.[10] Often, however, they are construed (and intended) as hypotheses of empirical relationships among class, occupation, status, and other political variables. Bryce, for instance, is saying that political power in America is more affected by occupation than by the wealth or respect structure of society. Such empirical relationships cannot be stated in a general form for all societies, and often not even for all the various situations within a given society.

DF. *Status* is membership in a specified deference class. Social mobility is *vertical* or *horizontal* according to whether or not it includes change in status.

Rather than defining class in terms of status, we define status in relation to deference classes. To "have status" is to

10. Tawney also formulates in this passage a conception of class that coincides with our definition of "social class": "The conception of class . . . is comprehensive. It relates, not to this or that specific characteristic of a group, but to a totality of conditions by which several sides of life are affected."

occupy a favorable position in the pattern of such values as power and respect; and in general the status of a person is specifiable in terms of his relation to deference values. On the basis of status we differentiate between vertical and horizontal mobility. Change in occupation involving an increase in income, for example, represents vertical mobility only insofar as the improvement in wealth position is accompanied by indulgence as to respect, power, affection, and so on. In some societies everyone is assigned a definite "rank." The significance of such distinctions must be ascertained by empirical inquiry, since in some circumstances rank actually refers to respect as a value alone, while in other circumstances it has reference to all the deference values, in which case the value order accurately defines status. If welfare values are also accorded by rank, the latter demarcates social classes.

DF. A *caste* is a highly impermeable deference class with a high degree of solidarity.

We distinguish caste from class, first, by its lesser generality —it is defined in relation to deference values only—and second, by its properties of impermeability and solidarity, which by no means characterize all classes. Thus a hereditary aristocracy, for example, constitutes a caste as here defined. Like other classes, castes are not necessarily, though they may be, organized as groups. Though the element of solidarity is always present, cooperation may be minimal, and is often limited to the performance of purely ceremonial acts.

The most elaborate field studies in America of status have reported on the existence of caste, notably in Negro-White communities. Lloyd Warner and his associates are free from the temptation which Frederick Pollock complained was common in anthropology, "to go digging in savage muck-heaps and not look at what is happening under one's nose." [11]

The social structure is the pattern of shaping, distribution (and enjoyment) of all the various values that are comprised in influence. It is a description of the social structure which

11. Among the workable indices of caste difference—impermeable differences in respect position—are intermarriage, reciprocal dining invitations, exclusive clubs, exclusive pews, exclusive burial grounds (to specify but a few that were especially appropriate to New England). See W. L. Warner and P. S. Lunt, *The Status System of a Modern Community,* Yale University Press, 1942, and J. Dollard, *Caste and Class in a Southern Town,* Yale University Press, 1937.

answers the question "who gets what, when and how." (The concept of social structure is not to be confused with "social order," previously defined as the mores and countermores institutions—custom, religion, morality.)

It follows from the definition that the social structure is analyzable into relationships among classes (specified in relation to the values comprised in influence). Whatever groupings are relevant to the influence practices are by definition classes: they consist of persons with characteristic relations to specified values. But while it is a tautology that the social structure is a class structure, it is altogether an empirical question what the classes are, how they are related, how influence is distributed among them.

In particular, the conceptual framework cannot prejudge the importance of economic classes. In some societies deference values of one sort or another (and hence deference classes) might be more important than welfare values and classes, though of course both will always be involved to some degree. Tawney's insistence (1931, 67) on the recognition of the importance of various types of social groupings seems inescapable:

> Clearly, there are societies in which the position and relations of the groups composing them have been determined ultimately by the effect of conquest. Clearly, the rules under which property is held and transmitted have played a part in fixing the conditions by which different groups are distinguished from each other. Clearly, there are circumstances in which the biological characteristics of different groups are a relevant consideration. Clearly, the emergence of new social groups is a natural accompaniment of the differentiation of economic functions. . . . These different factors, however, have varying degrees of importance in different ages, different communities, and different connections.

Though it be true that economic classes are of predominant importance in our society, a general science of interpersonal relations cannot safely project the social structure of our own culture on all cultures. Further, while it may follow from the definitions that the history of all hitherto existing society is the history of classes, it is by no means necessarily true that the history is one of class struggle. Class collaboration is, under some circumstances, just as striking a feature of the social structure—as the Marxists recognize in inveighing against it. When the term "class struggle" is used in a descriptive sense rather than as a symbol of demand, it must be limited in its application: there are to be formulated conditions under which the relation between classes is one of conflict rather than integration.

PROP. Changes in the social structure are functions of large changes in coordination.

That is, the social structure alters with basic modifications in the productive processes, whether operations or perspectives. The further hypothesis may be put forward that changes in techniques have a greater effect on the social structure than do changes in the social order. Alterations in the expediencies of a society are more likely to modify (and to modify to a greater extent) the social structure than alterations in the mores.

§4.4 *Social Process*

DF. *Economy* is maximization of value: an act directed toward the attainment of a value V is economical with respect to a set of values L in the degree that it attains V with an optimal attainment of the L's.

The concept is defined relatively to some set of values, for an act may be economical with respect to one set and not another.[12] Where the set is not specified it is to be understood as all the values of the actor involved in the situation. What is chiefly important is that various values may be simultaneously relevant to the determination of economy: means cannot be appraised with respect to isolated ends, but rather in relation to complex goal patterns.

It follows from the definitions that *behavior tends to be what is expected to be most economical*—or, in the equivalent formulation of §4.2, that expected to maximize the I:D ratio.[13] The

12. The maximizing of values is concerned with net results, hence implies the minimizing of "cost" (negative values) in the sense of incurred losses or gains no longer possible. Such gains and losses, of course, are different, in general, for different values involved.

13. This is logically true because we determine what an individual's values are by his conduct. When he acts in what we believe to be a noneconomical manner, we infer either that his expectations are mistaken, or that his values are not what we supposed them to be.

qualification "expected to be most economical" is essential, for otherwise the proposition would be plainly false: people often act in ways which as a matter of fact are not economical with respect to their own values. It is entirely possible for a person to be mistaken not only as to means for attaining his values, but even as to what his values are.[14] The importance of the proposition is not nullified by its purely logical character; and, indeed, it is often regarded as a "basic postulate" of political theory.[15] Whenever a person chooses a course of action, we are to look for the specific values and expectations that make it appear to the actor most economical for him.

DF. The *pragmatization* of practices is the maximizing of their economy with respect to all the values of the actors. *Rationalization* of practices is their technicalization and pragmatization.

We speak of practices and institutions as pragmatized in the degree that means and ends are reciprocally determined so as to maximize the total values in the situation.[16] Rationalization (Zweckrationalizierung) involves not only a maximal realization of values, but also that the adaptation of means and ends to one another be achieved through expediences. For example, if religious doctrines impose sanctions for the utilization of certain materials, practices in accord with these doctrines are not rationalized, though they may be pragmatized in relation to the religious values. Rationalization, in short, requires that the only restrictions imposed on practice be those set ultimately by noncultural conditions (biological and environmental) for the attainment of goals.[17]

14. We say behavior "tends" to be that accepted as most economical because not all acts are taken to be equally expressive of valuations. An act may be performed, not from deliberate choice, but in accord with a routine so firmly established as to reduce deliberation to a minimum. In that case the act may very well differ from what the actor would have judged to be economical had he engaged in deliberation.

15. See, for example, Catlin, 1930, 108. A similar formulation is also given by Herbert Spencer in his *Principles of Sociology,* D. Appleton.

16. The term was chosen because of the special emphasis of pragmatism on this analysis and appraisal of conduct. See, for example, John Dewey's "Theory of Valuation," *International Encyclopedia of Unified Science,* Vol. II, No. 4, 1939, and his *Human Nature and Conduct,* Henry Holt, 1922.

17. These conditions must be taken comprehensively enough, however, to include whatever is relevant to *all* the values operative in the situation. Rationalization in the present sense is not to be confused with Comtean positivism. Hux-

DF. The *social process* is the totality of value processes for all the values important in the society.

In the following table we introduce terms for the phases of the social process with respect to the welfare and deference values introduced in §4.1. (The concepts will be discussed in connection with the analysis of power.) It may be repeated that the list of values is not exhaustive, even of the most important values. Some others, however, can be regarded as compounds of those given. Authority, for example, will later be dealt with as involving elements of power, respect, and rectitude.

DF. *Policy* is a projected program of goal values and practices: the *policy process* is the formulation, promulgation, and application of identifications, demands, and expectations concerning the future interpersonal relations of the self.

Projected action may be either private or social: it may concern either the actor alone or his relations with other persons. A course of action in relation to others we call a "policy" of the actor. The field of policy is constituted by interpersonal relations.[18]

DF. The *exercise of influence* (influence process) consists in affecting policies of others than the self.

To *have* influence is to occupy a high position (and potential) with respect to all the values important in the society. Influence is *exercised* when its possession affects the interpersonal relations of those (other than the self) active in the shaping and enjoyment of the values. This occurs in accord with what Friedrich (1937, 16–17) has called "the rule of anticipated reaction": policies are determined by expectations of the resulting conduct of those having the influence. The exercise of influence consists in this effect on the policy of others.[19]

---

ley's "brave new world" is not one in which institutions are rationalized, but only technicalized. Important values (for instance, the moral) were not taken into account; practices were ultimately not economical in relation to those values.

18. Thus the term "policy," as here defined, is not to be interpreted as restricted to expediency rather than principle; policy is involved in the adoption of any perspective—identification, demand, expectation—of the interpersonal relations of the self. A projected course of action is a policy whenever persons other than the actor are implicated in the acts in question.

19. Of course, the exercise of influence in particular ways is itself a policy

TABLE 1

Social Process

	Deference Values				Welfare Values			
Value	Power	Respect	Rectitude	Affection	Well-Being	Wealth	Skill	Enlightenment
Measure	Power	Status	Righteousness	Popularity	Well-Being	Wealth	Ability	Enlightenment
Elect	Elite	Select	Righteous	Popular	Fit	Wealthy	Able	Informed
Situation	Arena	Stage	Court	Circle	Habitat	Market	Shop	Forum
Interaction	Encounter	Confrontation	Appraisal	Sociality	Living	Exchange	Occupation	Disclosure
Shaping	Determination	Recognition	Moralization	Bestowal	Adaptation	Production	Praxis	Inquiry
Outcome	Decision	Prestige	Rightness	Cordiality	Vitality	Transaction	Performance	Knowledge
Ratio	Alignment	Distinction	Morality	Friendliness	Salubrity	Price	Craftsmanship	Informativeness
Enjoyment	Ascendency	Repute	Virtue	Friendship	Consummation	Consumption	Expression	Insight
Doctrine	Political Doctrine	Code of Honor	Moral Code	Code of Friendship	Hygiene	Economic Doctrine	Professional Standards	Standards of Disclosure
Science	Political Science	Science of Status	Social Ethics	Amicology	Social Biology	Economics	Science of Skill	Sociology of Knowledge

DF. The *weight* of influence is the degree to which policies are affected; the *domain* of influence, the persons whose policies are affected; the *scope* of influence, the values implicated in the policies.

The effect on policy brought about by influence varies, of course, in degree; we speak in this connection of the "weight" of influence being exercised. We may speak of the weight of influence as varying, for example, with changes in the prestige of the influential—the more a person is respected, the more effect his policies will have on those who accord him respect. And so on.

Amount of influence has a second dimension: the number of persons being influenced. This we call the "domain" of influence. Thus improvements in the technology of communication have enlarged the domains of influence; but by rendering the same domain subject to several centers of influence, in many cases they have lowered the weight of influence exercised by each of these centers.

Conduct is goal-directed and thus implicates values; the demands and expectations of which policy consists have reference to values. By the "scope" of influence we mean the values involved in the policies affected. In a given case influence may be exercised with regard to some values and not others: its scope is limited in various ways. Thus a friend may have influence with regard to the values of affection and respect—he may affect policies concerning those values—but not, say, the values of wealth or power. Amount of influence thus has reference to scope as well as to weight and domain.

---

of the person having the influence: it is a pattern of *his* interpersonal relations. Influence is being exercised when changes in the influence-policy are correlated with changes in the policies of those *over* whom it is being exercised.

V

POWER

Power is the deference value with which political science is especially concerned; it can be described in terms of its domain, scope, weight, and coerciveness. Forms of power can be distinguished according to the value upon which power is based. Influence relations for which power is a base are also classified.

§5.1 *Decisions and Power*

DF. A *decision* is a policy involving severe sanctions (deprivations).

SEVERE SANCTIONS are "involved" when they are expected to be used or are in fact applied to sustain a policy against opposition. Sanctions are "severe" in terms of the values prevailing in the culture concerned. There is no doubt about the extremity of violence; yet disgrace—the drastic withdrawal of respect—may play a more important role in many situations.

From the standpoint of society as a whole, it is often impossible to determine, without further information, whether a given legislative act, executive decree, administrative rule, or court judgment is a decision. Even measures that are not meant very seriously may be transformed into decisions at a later time, as when gambling laws—passed to quiet public clamor, though not expected by the best informed politicians to be enforced—are subsequently seized upon by a vigorous prosecutor and an inflamed public sentiment.

Since a decision is an *effective* determination of policy, it involves the total process of bringing about a specified course of action. In decision making only those participate whose acts do in fact matter. We do not speak of a vote being cast—save as an operation—if the ballot is not counted. And since the decision-making process includes application as well as formulation and promulgation of policy, those whose acts are affected also participate in decision making: by conformity to or disregard of the policy they help determine whether it is or is not in fact a decision. Laws are not made by legislatures alone, but by the law-abiding as well: a statute ceases to embody a law (except in a formal sense later discussed) in the degree that it is widely disregarded.

DF. *Power* is participation in the making of decisions: G has power over H with respect to the values K if G participates in the making of decisions affecting the K-policies of H.

The concept of power is perhaps the most fundamental in the whole of political science: the political process is the shaping, distribution, and exercise of power (in a wider sense, of all the deference values, or of influence in general).

> Politics, as a theoretical study, is concerned with the relations of men, in association and competition, submission and control, in so far as they seek, not the production and consumption of some article, but to have their way with their fellows. . . . What men seek in their political negotiations is power. . . .[1]

We have previously made it clear that political science can be usefully conceived, for many purposes, as concerned with more values than power alone. However broadly the scope of the subject may be defined, power is always included in the sense here used.

Power is here defined relationally, not as a simple property. Bertrand Russell (1938, 35) concisely defines power as "the production of intended effects," thus making it a property which can belong to a person or group considered in itself. But power in the political sense cannot be conceived as the ability to produce intended effects in general, but only such effects as directly involve other persons: political power is distinguished from power over nature as power over other men. Friedrich (1937, 12–14) emphasizes this point by formulating as an "axiom" concerning power that "it is a certain kind of human relationship." Tawney's definition (1931, 230) similarly restricts intended effects to those on the conduct of other persons: "Power may be defined as the capacity of an individual, or group of individuals, to modify the conduct of other individuals or groups in the manner which he desires. . . ." The making of decisions is an interpersonal process: the policies

1. Catlin, 1927, 210–11, 262; compare also Friedrich, 1937, 11.

which other persons are to pursue are what is decided upon. Power as participation in the making of decisions is an interpersonal relation.

It is, moreover, a triadic relation as here defined. "Power over whom" is not yet a complete specification: there must be added, "in such and such particulars" (the scope of power). A and B may each have power over C, but with regard to different areas of C's behavior, determining policies which C is to pursue in different fields; more simply, A and B may have power with respect to different values of C's. A's decisions may affect, say, C's shaping and enjoyment of economic values, and B's his share of respect.

The definition of power in terms of decision making adds an important element to "the production of intended effects on other persons"—namely, the availability of sanctions when the intended effects are not forthcoming. It is the threat of sanctions which differentiates power from influence in general. Power is a special case of the exercise of influence: it is the process of affecting policies of others with the help of (actual or threatened) severe deprivations for nonconformity with the policies intended.[2]

But—to repeat an earlier caution—this is not to say that the exercise of power rests always, or even generally, on violence. As Merriam warns (1934, 20):

> It cannot be concluded, as many have, that the essence of the power situation is force, in the sense of violence and physical brutality. Altruism as well as egoism has a place in human relations and organization, and cooperation has as genuine a position as coercion.

Power may rest on faiths and loyalties as well as interests, to say nothing of habit and apathy. And even when the element of constraint is prominent, it need not take the form of violence. Sanctions may be applied with regard to other values than physical safety and well-being. In short, power entails only effective control over policy; the means by which the control is made effective are many and varied.

The power relation presupposes specified valuations: we speak of power as a control over value practices and patterns.

2. Compare Locke's definition in his *Two Treatises of Government,* Bk. II, chap. i: "Political power, then, I take to be a right of making laws, with penalties of death, and consequently all less penalties . . ."

Values are presupposed, moreover, by sanctions, which are without effectiveness unless their application does in fact constitute a deprivation. As Friedrich points out (1937, 12), neither things nor ideas are

> power taken by themselves; they can become instruments in the hands of one seeking power. To convert them into power, the power-seeker must find human beings who value the things sufficiently to obey his orders in return. . . . It is, therefore, impossible to study politics as the process of acquiring, distributing, and losing power without taking into consideration the major objectives of the human beings involved in the situations studied.

Power is itself, of course, a value, and an extremely important one; but no assumption is made here as to its being always and everywhere more important than other values. Power, is, specifically, a deference value: to have power is to be taken into account in others' acts (policies).[3] It is important to distinguish clearly in concrete situations between power as a value and the values over which power is being exercised. One may have power over wealth ("economic power"), for example, without occupying a correspondingly favorable position with regard to wealth itself—as in the case, say, of powerful labor leaders. One may control the distribution of respect without being respected, as may be true of a publisher or propagandist. And so on.

Since power is comprised under influence, we may speak of the weight, scope, and domain of power in the senses defined for the exercise of influence. The weight of power is the degree of participation in the making of decisions; its scope consists of the values whose shaping and enjoyment are controlled; the domain of power consists of the persons over whom power is exercised. All three enter into the notion of "amount" of power. Increase or decrease in power may involve a change in its weight (as when limitations on suffrage are imposed or lifted), in its scope (as when economic practices are brought under or freed from control), or in its domain (as when a state brings new peoples under its dominion by conquest or loses them by secession).

3. It is not necessary, however, that those over whom power is had consciously defer to the power holders; indeed, they may not be aware who the power holders are.

DF. The *arena* of power is the situation comprised by those who demand power or who are within the domain of power. The *political man* (homo politicus) is one who demands the maximization of his power in relation to all his values, who expects power to determine power, and who identifies with others as a means of enhancing power position and potential.

Note that the arena of power is not necessarily composed of political men, in the sense of the definition. The political man is an idealization; he has been approximated in human history, but never attained. We have no record of anyone, however tyrannous and power seeking, who succeeded in transforming himself wholly into an instrument of power for the sake of power. However, the image of the *machtmensch* receives enough corroboration from the facts of experience to possess an enduring core of scientific and practical utility. From a scientific point of view the *homo politicus* serves the same purpose that the economic man played in the history of serious economic theory. Speculative models of this type have often performed an important role in the history of science, where it is taken for granted that observation will deviate, however slightly, from the theoretical image.[4]

The picture of the arena given in our definition is not strictly comparable with the "pure market" theory of the economists. The "pure arena" would be composed entirely of political men, in the same way that the strictest modes of economic thought relate to a market made up of economic men alone. We use the term "arena" to refer to any situation in which power is sought and persons are brought within the domain of power. It is not postulated that those who demand power pursue power in preference to any other value, like wealth. Hence the "pure arena" is a very special case, and is only approximated in any known historical situations.

A side glance at the postulational structure of economic theory may sharpen the significance of the present concepts. In the most general theory of economic behavior it is assumed that

4. The "economic man" got in the way of economists only when economic thinkers began to have greater confidence in their models than in their data, became purists in scientific inquiry, and refused to explore the possibilities of more-than-economic-models. They studied the pure market in preference to the empirically more significant combinations of market with what we call arena. On political personality see Lasswell, 1930, 1948.

men seek only one value, and that they strive to enjoy as much of it as possible. Cournot used the following words to describe his method: "We shall invoke but a single axiom, or, if you prefer, make but a single hypothesis, i.e., that every one seeks to derive the greatest possible value from his goods and labours." Edgeworth phrased the postulate of the economic man thus: "Economics investigates the arrangements between agents each tending to his own maximum utility." Pigou reworded the idea as "the effort on the part of every agent to maximize his satisfaction." When there is cooperation and exchange there is a "market"; and it has been convenient for economists to begin with a highly simplified picture of the "perfect market." This is defined by Jevons as the situation "when all traders have perfect knowledge of the conditions of supply and demand and the consequent ratio of exchange." In addition to the postulate of perfect knowledge there is complete freedom from coercion.[5] It is evident that some postulates of economic theory, if taken literally, have related to all human behavior rather than behavior pertaining to a selected value. This is one of the recurring ambiguities of economic thought.

To bring our speculative models closer to specific situations it is necessary to introduce an intricate pattern of postulates. For instance, what are the postulated demand ratios for power in relation to any other value or set of values? What are they in relation to specified power positions? What are the postulated relations between increments or decrements of optimism-pessimism and the demand ratios of power and other values? Note, further, that demand and expectation relationships may be postulated to vary according to the various parts of the self (i.e., primary ego and each secondary component of the self).

This rigorous method is not fully attained in the social disciplines, even in economics. The result is a sizable gap between the formal elegance with which a limited number of postulates are elaborated in pure theory, and the way in which new postulates are smuggled into the "institutional" analysis of specific contexts. The "smuggling" consists in failing to

5. The most complete statement of the postulates of classical theory is by Frank Hyneman Knight, *Risk, Uncertainty and Profit,* Houghton Mifflin, 1921. The most ambitious attempt to set up postulates of the homo politicus is by Catlin (1930).

make explicit the point at which postulates are introduced, and the logical consequences of the new postulate system.[6]

We use the term *stage* to designate the situation in which the respect value is involved. The situation specialized to the moral process might be called the *court*, emphasizing the continued process of judgment by which the "righteous man" weighs his conduct. The locus of affection in regard to a given person is often called his *circle*, comprising the pattern of relations not only with intimates, friends, and family, but all those from whom he demands or expects affection.

Among the welfare values, in addition to "market" for wealth, we speak of *habitat*, *shop*, and *forum* as the loci of conduct in relation to well-being, skill, and enlightenment, respectively. Thus the forum in this generalized sense includes any situations of disclosure—the school, the library, or the market place; the shop, in the same way, includes the studio as well as the factory; the habitat comprises the "living conditions" in a biological sense.

DF. An *encounter* is an interaction in the power process.

When states, parties, pressure groups, or political individuals affect one another in the power process, we describe the interaction as an encounter. All may demand power, seeking to bring some or all of the others within their domain; or, where power demands of one of the groups in question is negligible, this group is in the domain of some or all of the others. Manifestly an arena is a pattern of encounters.

The corresponding category in economics is *exchange*, which depends, as Jevons pointed out, upon specialization and cooperation—in short, upon interaction.

In reference to well-being, we speak of *living* when we describe interactions in the habitat. *Occupation* is the interaction that goes on in the shop, *disclosure* in the form, *confrontation* on the stage, *appraisal* in the court, *sociality* in the circle.

DF. The *determination* of the power process is its shaping into a particular pattern.

6. Contrast the formal brilliance of A. C. Pigou, *The Economics of Stationary States*, Macmillan, 1935, for instance, with the haphazard theoretical structure of typical studies in economic history. For an explicit demand for more pertinent theoretical tools in economic analysis, see Milton Friedman, "Lange on Price Flexibility and Employment: A Methodological Criticism," *American Economic Review*, Vol. 36, 1946, 613–31.

An encounter in the arena sets in motion a process of focusing the activities of all concerned to the end of affecting the outcome. The process is equivalent to the *production* of wealth, which is not concluded until the claim to the service is offered for exchange in the market. Power is not completely made available (shaped) until it is involved in fighting, arguing, boycotting, negotiating—all of which may be resorted to in a particular process of power determination.

The corresponding activities in relation to living are called *adaptation.* The perfecting and applying of skill in an occupation is *praxis.* The shaping of enlightenment is *inquiry,* manifested in and affected by disclosure in the forum. *Recognition* is a convenient term to describe the formative features of a respect interaction. When rightness is concerned, the phrase of its "production" is *moralization;* affection proceeds by *bestowal.*

The outcome of the shaping of power in an encounter is a *decision,* in the sense defined at the beginning of §5.1. An encounter can always be characterized in terms of the policies being carried out by the participants in the interaction. Power is shaped in the interaction as severe sanctions are made available to enforce some resultant policy.

A vote, a surrender, a court judgment are all decisions (when they are subsequently made effective). They are decisive phases in the flow of determinative activities during encounters in arenas.

The market equivalent of decision is *transaction,* which is the outcome of production and exchange. *Vitality* is the result of adaptation in living. Similarly, occupation and praxis terminate in *performance,* disclosure and inquiry in *knowledge,* confrontation and recognition in *prestige,* appraisal and moralization in *rightness,* and sociality and bestowal of affection in *cordiality.*

DF. An *alignment* is the power ratio for and against a decision.

Alignments in a voting situation include all the possible combinations of unanimity, exceptional majority, bare majority, plurality. Settlement of a war may involve every gradation from total victory of one side to peace without victory.

Alignments in the arena correspond to *prices* in the market, which are the exchange ratios established in the transaction. We speak of *salubrity* in living as the degree of vitality, *craftsmanship* as the level of performance in an occupation, *informativeness* as the degree of knowledge attained in the process of disclosure, *distinction* as the measure of prestige growing out of confrontation, *morality* as the pattern of rightness emerging by appraisals, and *friendliness* as the level of friendship arising in the course of sociality.

DF. *Ascendancy* is the enjoyment of power.

We have used the term "determination" to refer to the activities concerned with the shaping of power. There is, however, another dimension to the power process, which is the enjoyment of the value. Usage has supplied us with no word with the appropriate connotations, and the term "ascendancy" is in many ways unsatisfactory, since it has many overtones of arrogance, which is not necessarily involved.

Economic analysis provides us with the term *consumption* to characterize the final stage of the wealth process. For the enjoyment of well-being we select the word *consummation,* and for skill enjoyment, *expression.* (Unfortunately both terms are often employed in a far more inclusive sense.) The enjoyment of enlightenment we call *insight*, of respect *repute,* of rectitude *virtue*, and of affection *friendship.*

DF. The doctrine of power is *political doctrine* and the science of power (in the narrowest sense) is *political science.*

Presently we discuss in detail the significance of political doctrine, pointing out that the words refer to the operative demands and expectations of those who seek or hold power, insofar as these perspectives relate to power. For the theoretical analysis of the determinative conditions of power on the basis of disciplined procedures of observation, we speak of political science.

We reiterate that it is often useful to expand the scope of the science of politics to include the study of other values in conjunction with power (especially the deference values as a whole). Later we shall define political science in ways that foster certain normative ends.

The corresponding terms for wealth are *economic doctrine* and *economics.* The doctrine pertaining to the respect process is usually known as the *code of honor*, and the cor esponding science the branch of sociology concerned with *status*. For rectitude, the doctrine is the *moral code* and the science *social ethics* (as an empirical study of moral conduct). Similarly, for affection there is a *code of friendship*, and an inquiry for which we may coin the term *amicology*.

The doctrine pertaining to well-being may be designated as *hygiene* in an extended sense, and the science *social biology*. Skill doctrines are usually referred to as *professional standards*, but there is no common term for the science of the skill process (patterns of acquisition and exercise of skills in society). Doctrines with regard to enlightenment are *standards of disclosure*; the corresponding science is comprised in the *sociology of knowledge*.

§5.2 *Forms of Influence and Power*

DF. The *base value* of an influence relation is that which is the condition for the exercise of the influence in question. The *power base* is the value which is the condition for participation in decision making in the given case.

To exercise influence is to affect the policies of others as to weight, scope, and domain. The "base value" of the influence refers to the causal condition of its exercise: that which gives the influence its effectiveness. Since to have influence is to occupy a high value position, we can describe the conditions for exercise of influence in terms of values. Whenever X has influence over Y, there is some value with regard to which X enjoys a favorable position, and because of which he can exercise influence over Y. This is the base value of the influence relation, or the *influence base*. Note that there can be a chain of values operating as bases in a given relation. X may use wealth to influence power which in turn affects the wealth of Y.

Any of the values of which we have spoken may serve as a base of influence. The exercise of influence may rest on well-being, on the physical strength of the person exercising it, as in the forms of influence known as "intimidation" and "brute force," for example. It may depend on wealth, as in the case of bribery; on skill, as in the influence of the expert; or on enlightenment, the influence of the sage or teacher. Influence may rest on power, as exemplified by indoctrination; or on respect, the influence flowing from reputation. Rectitude is an influence base in the case of moral authority; and affection is the influence exercised by friends and loved ones. In any given influence relation, of course, there may be several base values; and no one of them is necessarily present in every case.

Since power is a type of influence, the definition applies also to the base value for power, or the *power base*.[7] A power holder may owe his power to his wealth, ability, reputation, popularity, or, in general, favorable position with regard to any value.

DF. A *form of influence* is a kind of influence relationship specified as to base value and scope. A *form of power* is a form of influence in which the effect on policy is enforced or expected to be enforced by relatively severe sanctions.

It is useful to differentiate among the various cases of the exercise of influence between influence relations differing in base value, scope, or both. The question, influence over what and on what basis, is answered by a specification of the form of influence so defined.

A form of influence is a *form of power* whenever the effect on policy is enforced by relatively severe sanctions. Any form of influence may be regarded as in fact a power relation if the deprivations imposed by the influential are important enough to those over whom influence is being exercised. This is more likely to be true for some forms of influence than others; the exercise of influence based on well-being or wealth is more likely to involve deprivations severe enough to constitute power than is influence based on rectitude and respect. But this is not necessarily the case, and whether or not it holds depends on the scale of values operative in the culture. In medieval Europe the Church exercised power enforced by the sanction of excommunication, which entailed deprivation in such values as respect, rectitude, and affection. In many contemporary cultures, however, it would be correct to speak only of the influence (not power) of the Church; loss of position in these values is no longer as severe a deprivation. Speaking generally, therefore,

7. This is to be distinguished, in general, from the *power sanction,* the value whose deprivation constitutes the sanction by which the decision is enforced. When policies are not expected to be, and are not in fact, enforced by sufficiently severe sanctions to be decisions, it is also convenient to distinguish the *influence sanction* from the influence base.

any form of influence *may* be a form of power, but is not necessarily such.

Since power is itself a value, forms of influence which include power in their scope are usually themselves forms of power. The king's mistress, though she has only influence, not power, over the king, may have power over his subjects in the degree of that influence. Forms of influence based on power are themselves forms of power only if the scope of the influence is included within that of the power in question. The king may exercise influence over standards of morality, say, by virtue of his power position, but he does not necessarily exercise power over morality.

Political science is concerned with power in general, with all the forms in which it occurs. Failure to recognize that power may rest on various bases, each with a varying scope, has confused and distorted the conception of power itself, and retarded inquiry into the conditions and consequences of its exercise in various ways. As Tawney has observed:

> The discussion of the problems which power presents has been prejudiced . . . by the concentration of interest upon certain of its manifestations to the exclusion of others . . . A realistic treatment of it has suffered, in particular, from the habit of considering it primarily, or even purely, in political terms. Power is identified with political power, and political power is treated as a category by itself.[8]

Political power, on the contrary, is a complex form which presupposes always other forms of power, and though of course it differs from these others in characteristic ways, it has much in common with them as well. The "power of the state" cannot be understood in abstraction from the forms of power manifested in various types of interpersonal relations.

In particular, it is of crucial importance to recognize that power may rest on various bases, differing not only from culture to culture, but also within a culture from one power structure to another. A may be exercising power over B because of his economic position, X over Y because of his control over the instruments of violence, and still another power holder may owe

8. Tawney, 1931, 228–9. We will shortly introduce the concept of "political power" as only one of the special forms of power: that for which power as a value is both base and scope.

his power to particular skills. Tawney (1931, 230–1) concludes:

The foundations of power vary from age to age, with the interests which move men, and the aspects of life to which they attach a preponderant importance. It has had its source in religion, in military prowess and prestige, in the strength of professional organization, in the exclusive control of certain forms of knowledge and skill, such as those of the magician, the medicine man, and the lawyer.[9]

The following table introduces designations for the various forms of influence with the values discussed in §4.1 as scope and base values. As has already been pointed out, any of these forms of influence may in fact constitute power relations. We shall use the word "power" rather than "influence" in the designation wherever the form in question familiarly involves severe deprivations. Neologisms have been avoided wherever possible, though at the cost of introducing distinctions between terms often loosely used as synonyms. For grammatical convenience, the designations are not uniform in reference, some referring to the exercise of power or influence, some to its possession, and some to the condition or results of being subject to it. (In many cases familiar terms already available refer only to the deprivational—or only to the indulgent—aspects of the exercise of the power or influence in question, and we have retained these terms where neutral designations were not convenient.)

The most familiar base of influence and power is power itself: power over some values often constitutes the condition for influence or power over other values. Control, based on power, over power policy is *political power* in the narrow sense (not to be confused with what we shall later define as authority). The veto and appointive powers of the president are typical political powers in this sense: control is exercised over the pat-

9. On the power of the magician, for example, James Frazer points out in his *Golden Bough* (one-vol. ed., Macmillan, 1922, 45 and 61): "The magician ceases to be merely a private practitioner and becomes to some extent a public functionary. The development of such a class of functionaries is of great importance for the political as well as the religious evolution of society. For when the welfare of the tribe is supposed to depend on the performance of these magical rites, the magician rises into a position of much influence and repute, and may readily acquire the rank and authority of a chief or king . . . In savage and barbarous society many chiefs and kings appear to owe their authority in great measure to their reputation as magicians." On other power bases in "primitive" cultures, see G. Landtman, *Origin of the Inequality of the Social Classes*, University of Chicago Press, 1938.

TABLE 2

Forms of Influence and Power

	Scope Values							
Base Values	Power	Respect	Rectitude	Affection	Well-Being	Wealth	Skill	Enlightenment
Power	Political Power	Homage	Inculcation	Fealty	Compulsion	Polinomic Power	Directorship	Indoctrination
Respect	Councilorship	Sponsorship	Suasion	Esteem	Charisma	Credit	Guidance	Authoritativeness
Rectitude	Mentorship	Approbation	Moral Authority	Devotion	Chastisement	Ethonomic Influence	Injunction	Censorship
Affection	Personal Influence	Regard	Moral Influence	Love	Guardianship	Benefaction	Zeal	Edification
Well-Being	Violence	Terror	Discipline	Rape	Brute Force	Brigandage	Forced Labor	Inquisition
Wealth	Ecopolitical Power	Standing	Simony	Venality	Subsistence Power	Economic Influence	Employment	Advertising
Skill	Expertness	Admiration	Casuistry	Ingratiation	Prowess	Productivity	Management	Intelligence
Enlightenment	Advisory Influence	Fame	Wisdom	Sympathy	Regimen	Economic Foresight	Instruction	Education

terns of control themselves, and the condition of control is the possession of power.[10]

The influence over respect which is exercised by power we call *homage;* in the significantly ambiguous phrase, power "commands" respect. Similarly, power may influence the moral process; we speak here of *inculcation* of a moral code. Such inculcation need not proceed by explicit decisions (the power of the Roman censor): morality varies, apart from statutory enactment, according to whether the throne is occupied by a Charles or a Cromwell. The influence of power over affection we designate *fealty.* The relations of the power holder to his domain may exhibit a high degree of personalization; a sentimentalized identification on the part of the followers is a regular component of leadership.

When power is the basis for control over well-being, we speak of *compulsion;* this is the form of power exercised by the army and police. Control over wealth on a power basis constitutes *polinomic* (politico-economic) *power,* exemplified by taxation or the granting of franchises. Power may influence or control the skill process; we speak here of *directorship.* The leaders of a labor union of skilled workers direct the exercise of skills in the present sense. Control over enlightenment based on power is usually called *indoctrination.* This includes political, as distinct from purely moral, censorship, as well as all official propaganda (bureaus of information and so on).

Various forms of influence are based on respect. Influence over power on this basis we refer to as *councilorship.* The councilor affects the decision-making process by virtue of the respect accorded him by those participating in the process. Respect may be the basis of influence over respect itself; this form of influence we designate *sponsorship.* The sponsor evokes respect for his protégé by virtue of the respect he himself commands. *Suasion* is the influence of respect on morality; conduct approved by the most respected members of the community acquires a claim to *rectitude.* Respect may influence affection as well; prestige often evokes a high degree of sentimentaliza-

10. In a wide sense, all the forms of power are "political"; we shall continue to use the word "power" alone for the wider concept, reserving "political power" for the special form just introduced. Where necessary, the wider concept may be referred to as "social power," since it comprises all the forms of control manifested in interpersonal relations.

tion, as in certain types of hero worship. We speak here of *esteem.*

One of the most important forms of influence based on respect is *charisma:* the veneration accorded a leader may give him even the power of life and death over his followers (or indeed, in their expectations, over a universal domain—see Weber, 1925). Influence over wealth based on respect is familiar as *credit,* though the term is used here in a somewhat wider sense than in economics. Respect may affect the skill process —the *guidance* of the apprentice by the master. And it may affect enlightenment as well: the person respected enjoys *authoritativeness.* It is noteworthy that the scope of such authoritativeness is independent of the specific skills or attainments which evoked the respect in the first instance: thus a physicist or novelist may speak authoritatively in this sense on theological or political issues.

Rectitude—moral standing—also serves as an influence (and sometimes a power) base. As it affects the power process, we call such influence *mentorship,* exemplified by the king's confessor (Rasputin). The effect of rectitude on respect we designate *approbation,* illustrated by the shift in perspective involved in the Reformation towards such matters as priestly celibacy. The influence of rectitude on the moral process itself is *moral authority.* Influence over affection based on rectitude we call *devotion.*

When moral standing or considerations are the basis of influence over well-being, we speak of *chastisement,* of which penance is the most familiar exemplification. Moral influence over economic policy we call *ethonomic* (ethico-economic) *influence,* illustrated by doctrines of "usury" and the effect on the economic process of conceptions of honesty, prudence, "fair practices," and the like.[11] For the effect of moral codes on skill we use the term *injunction,* illustrated in the moral imperative prohibiting or impelling the use of certain designs or materials in the arts. Influence over enlightenment on the basis of rectitude constitutes (moral) *censorship.*

Affection is also an influence base, so familiar, indeed, that the word "influence" colloquially refers specifically to the ability to affect policy because of personalized relations with those

11. A richly suggestive study of ethonomic influence on early capitalism is Tawney, *Religion and the Rise of Capitalism,* 1926.

influenced. We call this *personal influence* only when its scope is power. The king's mistress, or the old friends of a newly elected president exercise this form of influence. The respect emerging from personalized relations we designate *regard*, and the effect of such relations on rectitude, *moral influence*. Influence on affection based on affection may be called, for lack of a better term, *love*.

Affection as an influence base over well-being yields *guardianship*, and over wealth, *benefaction*. Both guardian and benefactor affect well-being on the basis of sentimentalized identifications with those influenced. *Zeal* is the effect on skill of affection, *edification* on enlightenment.

The forms of influence based on well-being are almost always power relations: deprivations of physical health and safety are usually regarded as very severe sanctions. When such power is applied to power itself, we speak of *violence;* assassination and the "purge" are typical acts of violence as here defined. We designate as *terror* the control of respect with well-being as the power base. The reign of terror secures respect for the power holders by deprivations of safety. The concentration camp exemplifies violence with regard to a political opposition, terror in relation to the citizenry at large. The effect on the moral process of power based on well-being is *discipline;* and on affection, *rape*, in the generalized sense given the term by Serge Chakotin in his *Rape of the Masses* (G. Routledge, 1940).

When power based on well-being is applied to well-being itself, it is called *brute force*. In the exercise of brute force (struggle for existence), the issue is one of survival, not a redistribution of power, wealth, respect, or other values. Force as here defined is thus a distinct form of power, not power in general, nor is it necessarily a component of all forms of power. *Brigandage* is power over wealth based on well-being: the brigand controls the distribution of wealth by threatened deprivations of health and safety. Power, based on well-being, over the exercise of skill is *forced labor*. Power on this base over enlightenment we term *inquisition*, the historical institution so designated being the most familiar exemplification of this form of power.

Wealth often constitutes an influence (and sometimes power) base. Control over power on the basis of wealth is *ecopolitical* (economic-political) *power*, exemplified in the purchase of votes or office. The effect based on wealth over the distribution of respect is *standing:* it is the position enjoyed by the aristocracy of wealth. When wealth is the basis of influence over rectitude, we use the term *simony* in a somewhat widened sense. Influence over affection based on wealth is *venality:* the distribution of largess may evoke sentimentalized identifications as well as depersonalized support (if, for instance, the ideal of the "magnanimous man" is important in the culture).

Control over well-being based on wealth we call *subsistence power.* "In the general course of human nature," says the *Federalist* (No. LXXIX), "a power over a man's subsistence amounts to a power over his will." It is this form of power for which the Marxists have used the (negative) demand symbol "wage slavery." Influence over the wealth process based on wealth itself we term *economic influence*, and over the skill process, *employment.* The effect of wealth on enlightenment we call *advertising* in a generic sense, comprising subsidized publications, paid publicity, the prevention of publication by economic means, and so on.

Skill is often an influence base. The politicized *expert* exercises influence over power on the basis of skills—in administration, military or economic affairs, propaganda, and so on. Respect evoked by skill is *admiration;* the impact of skill on the moral process we term *casuistry* in its original sense. Skill in evoking affection is *ingratiation*, the influence base of the Iago in politics.

Skill affecting well-being is *prowess*, in many cultures not only an influence but even a power base. The impact of skill on the wealth process is *productivity*, and on skill itself *management.* We use the term *intelligence* (in the sense familiar in the military context) for influence over enlightenment based on skill. The intelligence officer influences policy on the basis of his skills in obtaining and distributing information.

Enlightenment, finally, may also serve as an influence base. As affecting power, it may be designated *advisory influence;* the adviser is thus distinguished from the councilor or mentor as influencing policy on the basis of his knowledge, rather than respect or moral standing. The impact of enlightenment on respect is *fame*, on rectitude, *wisdom*, on affection, *sympathy*.

Influence over well-being on this basis we term a *regimen*,

The impact of enlightenment on the wealth process is referred to as *economic foresight*, and on skill, *instruction*. The influence of enlightenment on enlightenment itself is *education*, to be contrasted with the indoctrination resulting from the exercise of power.

The forms of influence and power just discussed are far from complete in any sense. New forms arise when we consider any other values as either scope or base values. To give but one example, religious values (not to be identified with rectitude as a purely moral value) have sometimes served as an influence base. When the scope of such influence is power, the resultant form is called *theocratic;* and the same base, applied to the various other values as scope, yields other hieratic forms of influence and power.

In short, the concepts of influence and power are extremely general, and have reference to a wide range of interpersonal relations. The analysis can be carried to whatever level of refinement is required by the particular problem at hand.[12] But political phenomena are only obscured by the pseudo simplification attained with any unitary conception of power as being always and everywhere the same (violence or economic power or . . .). What is common to all power and influence relations is only effect on policy. What is affected and on what basis are variables whose specific content in a given situation can be determined only by inquiry into the actual practices of the actors in that situation.

PROP. The forms of power are interdependent: a certain amount of several forms of power is a necessary condition for a great amount of any form.

The purport of the proposition is to exclude attempts to analyze and interpret political situations always in terms of

12. George Cornewall Lewis, in his ***Remarks on the Use and Abuse of Some Political Terms,*** says of the word power that it "appears to signify the possession of the means of influencing the will of another, either by persuasion or threats; or of constraining his person by the application of physical force" (Clarendon Press, 1898, 171). Among recent writers, Russell (1938, 36) follows this classification. "Powers over human beings may be classified by the manner of influencing individuals, or by the type of organization involved. An individual may be influenced: A. by direct physical power over his body, B. by rewards and punishments as inducements, C. by influence on opinion, i.e., propaganda in its broadest sense." The discussion of the present section is intended to indicate the enormous variety of practices necessarily lumped together in any simple classification.

some one form of power only, just as we previously indicated the futility of attempting to deal with all interpersonal relations as concerned only with some one basic value, such as power, wealth, or glory. Each form of power always involves a number of others, to degrees and in ways which must be separately determined, in principle, in each case. The point has been forcefully stated and elaborated by Bertrand Russell (1938, 13–14):

> . . . Power has many forms, such as wealth, armaments, civil authority, influence on opinion. No one of these can be regarded as subordinate to any other, and there is no one form from which the others are derivative.

Most commonly, the various forms of power based on wealth ("economic power") have been assigned an especially fundamental role. Russell writes further (pp. 120, 135):

> It has been customary to accept economic power without analysis, and this has led, in modern times, to an undue emphasis upon economics, as opposed to war and propaganda, in the causal interpretation of history. . . . The actual degree of economic power possessed by an individual or group depends upon military strength and influence through propaganda quite as much as upon the factors usually considered in economics.

Solon's comment on the wealth of Croesus is very much to the point: "If another king come that hath better iron than you, he will be master of all this gold."

That the forms of power are interdependent does not entail, however, that all the forms are always of equal importance. (We shall later consider types of social structures characterized by the predominance of some of the forms rather than others.) In denying the self-sufficiency of economic power, we are not denying the importance which it has in fact had.[13] But to say that wealth does serve as a power base, and that the resultant forms of power are important, is far from saying that economic power is the only form of power, or always the most fundamental. Tawney's position on this point, as on others, avoids the common extremes in both directions:

13. "Money will always have power," as Bryce has observed (1924, II, 488), "because the rich man has something to give which others are glad to receive, so power cannot be dissevered from wealth so long as wealth exists" (and is highly valued).

It is not the case, as is sometimes suggested, that all forms of power are, in the last resort, economic, for men are so constituted as to desire other than temporal goods and to fear other than economic evils. It is true, however, that, since economic interests, if not the most intense, are the most generally operative and continuous in their operation, most forms of power have some economic roots, and produce, in turn, some economic consequences.[14]

The preceding discussion on the alleged self-sufficiency of economic power may be repeated for any of the other forms of power or influence—for instance, those based on enlightenment, rectitude, and respect, and spoken of loosely as the "power of opinion." Russell states once more (1938, 136–7):

It is easy to make out a case for the view that opinion is omnipotent, and that all other forms of power are derived from it. But this would be only a half-truth, since it ignores the forces which cause opinion. . . . In the background, there is usually force in the service of some creed. Per contra, a creed never has force at its command to begin with, and the first steps in the production of a widespread opinion must be taken by means of persuasion alone.

In short, none of the forms of power can stand alone: each requires, for its acquisition as well as maintenance, the simultaneous exercise of other forms of power as well. And none of the forms of power is basic to all the others. As patterns of valuation in a culture are modified, and changes come about in the social order and technology, now one form of power and now another, plays a fundamental role. Political analysis must be contextual, and take account of the power practices actually manifested in the concrete political situation.

PROP. The amount of power tends to increase till limited by other power holders.

14. 1931, 231. Beard has at times overgeneralized the role of economic power—though in justifiable reaction to its frequent neglect. Thus he writes (1934, iii–iv): "Political science with economics left out is an unreal and ghostly formalism. . . . It is impossible to gain any understanding of politics or to make any statesmanlike decision in politics without taking into account, as fully as knowledge will permit, the known economic relevancies." It is tautologous that understanding is impossible if *any* relevancies are ignored. The question is when and in what way economic power *is* more relevant than other forms. To take an example at random, an account of the Islamic empire would be an "unreal and ghostly formalism" if it did not take into account the known religious relevancies as well as the economic.

This is among the most widely recognized characteristics of power; power is, as the *Federalist* puts it, "of an encroaching nature." In modern times, Michels in particular has elaborated and documented the proposition:

> Every human power seeks to enlarge its prerogatives. He who has acquired power will almost always endeavour to consolidate it and to extend it, to multiply the ramparts which defend his position, and to withdraw himself from the control of the masses.[15]

This highly generalized proposition is particularly well adopted to the systematic study of specific contexts, since common experience discloses that power holders seldom act in strict conformity to the ideal type of homo politicus. After observing the degree of deviation from the speculative model, the inquirer can proceed by the orderly introduction of more complicated postulates to account for phenomena such as the sacrifice of power for respect, wealth, or other values. In this way the characteristic value pattern of specific persons and groups can be ascertained. It is not being said that *only* power limits power. Limits to power are also set both by technical factors and by the social order. The domain of power is restricted by available techniques of transportation and communication (a factor illustrated in the continued independence of Switzerland). The weight of any individual's power is limited by his physical and psychological endowments: the vitality of great political leaders is a commonplace. The scope of power may be limited by the technicalities of decision making in the area in question: even a dictator requires experts who in fact exercise power within the scope of their special skills. And of course power holders, like other persons, are occasionally subject to lassitude, inertia, and

15. 1915, 207. The hypothesis is, of course, fundamental to the political theory of Hobbes, who explains the continuing demand for power on the basis of its relation to other values: "I put for a general inclination of all mankind, a perpetual and restless desire of power after power, that ceaseth only in death. And the cause of this, is not always that a man hopes for a more intensive delight, than he has already attained to; or that he cannot be content with a more moderate power: but because he cannot assure the power and means to live well, which he hath present, without the acquisition of more" (*Leviathan*, chap. xi). In fact, however, it is just this pattern of expectation and demand which frequently undermines security. "Power controlled or abridged," the *Federalist* observes (No. XV), "is almost always the rival and enemy of that power by which it is controlled or abridged." Where conflicting demands are sufficiently rigid and intense, such rivalries easily break out into violence.

a reluctance to assume responsibility, all of which operate to limit the weight of power.

The social order is equally important as a limitation on power. The mores at any given time may put outside the scope of power (though not necessarily outside the scope of influence) such practices as those of religion or sex. In some societies (like the Zuni) mores directly concern power itself, sanctions being applied, for example, to any sort of personal ambition or aggressiveness. It seems preferable, in these kinds of cases, not to say (in an attempt to subsume them under the present hypothesis) that society as a whole is the power holder limiting subordinate power holders, but rather to recognize other types of limitation on power than conflicting power holders—though the latter factor remains of extreme importance. To speak of society as a whole as a power holder is to miss the whole point of political analysis. Power is distributive, and the aim of political science is to determine how and on what basis it is distributed.

PROP. Low power position implies low position in the scope values.

Those with least power of a given scope are likely to have the least favorable position in the patterns of the values included in that scope. Those with least control over the economic process will tend to have the lowest incomes. The proposition has been formulated in various ways by Laski, among others: "Classes excluded from a share in power have always been classes excluded from a share in benefits" (1925, 27). And again, "In the long run, in any political community, exclusion from political power is also exclusion from the benefits of its operations" (1935, 54). But the converse of the proposition is not necessarily true: one may exercise power of considerable weight without a correspondingly high value position, as has been pointed out previously. It should be added, however, that the original proposition is not alleged to be necessarily true either. It, like the other propositions formulated here, is to be interpreted as a hypothesis-schema; fruitful hypotheses might be derived from it if suitable qualifying conditions were specified. As an unqualified generalization it fails to account for such obvious cases as, for example, legislation protecting children against their parents. Nevertheless, it indicates what we take to be a promising direction for further inquiry.

PROP. Forms of power and influence are agglutinative: those with some forms tend to acquire other forms also.

The proposition follows from two previously formulated hypotheses: that positions in different value patterns tend to approximate one another, and that the amount of power tends to increase till limited by other power holders. The first implies acquisition of new forms of influence by extension of the influence base, and the second by extension of the scope of influence. Suppose a person or group exercises influence based on a value A over a value X. There will be a tendency toward a favorable position with regard to values B and C as well as A, and on the basis of all three values, a tendency to influence Y and Z as well as X. A person of high wealth position might exercise ecopolitical power, and through it further increase his wealth. Through wealth, he may tend to acquire respect, and thereby councilorship as well. On the basis of both wealth and respect, he may influence other values than power—for instance, enlightenment, and transmit his political perspectives through authoritativeness as well as paid publicity.[16]

§5.3 *Choice and Coercion*

DF. *Constraint* is the exercise of influence by threat of deprivation; *inducement*, by promise of indulgence.

The definition allows to constraint and inducement great variation in degree—from the most mild deprivation to the most severe, from petty to overwhelming indulgence. Further, the deprivation or indulgence is not limited to a particular value, for instance wealth or physical well-being. Constraint is not restricted to brute force, brigandage, violence, or terror—forms of influence based on well-being—nor inducement to such forms of influence as subsistence or economic power. They may consist in mild deprivations or indulgences of, say, respect or affection.

DF. *Coercion* is a high degree of constraint and/or inducement; *choice*, a low degree.

16. Documentation of such patterns of agglutination may be found in G. Myers, *History of the Great American Fortunes*, Modern Library, 1936. Agglutination reaches a maximum in the totalitarian state.

We say that coercion is involved in an influence situation if the alternative courses of action are associated with severe deprivations or indulgences, and choice if they are mild. We do not speak of coercion *wherever* the I:D ratio is near an extreme, but only where the extreme is produced by the exercise of influence over the values in question, that is, where the indulgence or deprivation is promised or threatened in an interpersonal situation. (It is not the "act of God" but the shaman's spell that is coercive.) Similarly, the concept of choice as here defined does not entail that *no* great indulgences or deprivations are involved, but only that they are not involved through having been imposed by someone exercising influence over the actor. Choice in the present sense is not limited by the properties of objects and events, but only by other persons.

Thus in addition to the weight, scope, and domain of influence we may speak of its degree of coerciveness (or, alternatively, of the degree to which it limits choice). This characteristic depends on which values serve as the influence base (and function as positive or negative sanctions), and on the amounts of those values promised or threatened. The degree of coerciveness attaching to specified amounts of a particular value varies, of course, with the standards of the culture (or of the particular groups, such as classes, to which the persons in the domain of influence belong). The culture traits not only determine whether a given object is a value, but also how much of a value it is, that is, how it compares in value with other values. A choice situation in one society might thus constitute coercion in another—the indulgences and deprivations might represent greater values.

The exercise of power is simply the exercise of a high degree of coerciveness.[17] When the values promised or threatened are sufficiently important to those over whom the influence is being exercised, the latter are being coerced: they are subjected to a power relationship. The power situation is always intense—there is a stress toward action evoked by considerable inducements and constraints. The intensity of the situation is thus sometimes useful as an index of whether power is involved or some form of influence of a low degree of coerciveness.

It is to be noted that coercion as here defined includes induce-

17. For the converse of the power and influence relations we may use the terms "submit" and "acquiesce" to connote the presence or absence of coercion.

ment as well as constraint: in terms of the classical discussions, love may play as important a role as fear.[18] Moreover, the conception of power here developed does not exclude or even minimize the element of consent in power relationships. "Coercion by consent," while verbally a paradox, has reference to a familiar and important aspect of the power process—specifically, to the perspectives of those over whom power is being exercised. Identifications, expectations, and demands render power authoritative, and this constitutes consent to the power structure and practices. The fact that power, by definition, rests on coercion does not entail that the power situation itself cannot be the result, in part, of choice. Laws are enforced by deprivations of life or liberty: the element of coercion is certainly present, and we speak therefore of the power, not merely influence, of the legislator and magistrate. Nevertheless, that there be laws (and even these particular laws), and that the laws be enforced, may well be a matter of general consent. The intensity which these perspectives of consent sometimes attain is indicated by the (internalized) demands of the criminal himself for punishment. To be sure, power may be exercised without consent also; we call this "naked power"; but naked power is the exception, not the rule, and certainly cannot be identified with all power merely on the grounds that power always involves coercion. The matter will be discussed throughout the next chapter.

The following table introduces terms for coercive and noncoercive value practices. The terminology refers to patterns near the poles of "perfect" choice or "total" coercion.

TABLE 3

Practices in Choice and Coercion Situations

Value	*Choice*	*Coercion*
Power	Negotiation	Submission
Respect	Consideration	Obeisance
Rectitude	Moral Freedom	Moral Subjection
Affection	Love	Servility
Well-Being	Play	Toil
Wealth	Bargaining	Rationing
Skill	Artistry	Servitude
Enlightenment	Education	Indoctrination

18. See Machiavelli, *Discourses,* III, 21.

Negotiation and *submission* refer to practices with regard to power (encounters) in situations of choice and coercion respectively. Patterns of the distribution and exercise of power may themselves result from the exercise of power; here we speak of submission. Where the power practices are not coercively determined, we say they are the outcome of negotiation. Submission may result from the form of power we call violence, as exemplified by military conquest or assassination. The coercive element may stem from the exercise of ecopolitical power—the financial supporters of a political leader may stipulate changes in his program. Or it may be the exercise of political power which results in submission—a presidential veto, for example.

Respect practices (confrontations) we refer to as *consideration* when freely engaged in, and *obeisance* when they result from coercion. The reign of terror is a typical instance of the coercive evocation of respect. Homage is another type of obeisance, power itself constituting the base of the coercion involved. By contrast, respect in the form of admiration or regard exemplifies consideration: the inducements and constraints operative are ordinarily not sufficiently intense to constitute coercion.

Practices with regard to moral values (moral appraisals) may also be subject to the exercise of power; we speak in this connection of *moral freedom* and *moral subjection*. In the latter case, adherence to specified moral standards is coercively determined. It may result from the imposition of discipline (power over rectitude based on well-being), or take the form of inculcation, where power itself is the base of extreme inducements and constraints to moral behavior. There is moral freedom in the degree to which choice may be exercised with regard to standards of morality. Freedom of religion is a familiar instance of moral freedom in this sense. The regulation of public morals by law (decency, "sexual offenses," and so on) exemplifies moral subjection.[19]

Coercion may be operative in practices concerning affection in the wide sense (sociality). Affection for the ruler evoked

19. The concept of moral responsibility and the contrast between "freedom" and "license" is not involved in the present distinction. The ground of the distinction is not whether there *are* moral standards to which the individual feels himself obliged to, and does, conform, but whether or not these standards and adherence to them is coercively determined.

by the exercise of power is a familiar instance of *servility* as distinguished from noncoercive *love*.

We may speak of *toil* where practices with regard to well-being (work) are controlled by the exercise of power, and *play*, regardless of serious intent, where the activity is free from coercion. The chain gang exemplifies toil coerced by brute force; "wage slavery" is toil where the coercion is in the form of subsistence power; military service is also toil in the present sense, the element of coercion consisting in the form of power designated as compulsion.

Bargaining and *rationing* are practices with regard to wealth (exchanges) in situations of choice and coercion, respectively. We speak of rationing wherever the exercise of power introduces into the market extremes of inducement or constraint; bargaining is the practice in a freely competitive market. Thus rationing in the present wide sense is not limited to exchange involving constraints imposed by polinomic power. Inducements to consume may constitute rationing in the present sense as much as constraints in the way of consumption; and the element of coercion may be introduced by the exercise of subsistence power or brigandage as well as by polinomic power. The requirement that employees purchase only at company stores, for example, is rationing based on subsistence power, as distinguished from the familiar polinomic rationing; and the brigandage of the racketeer forcing sales at the point of a gun also destroys the freely competitive market.

In the same way we speak of the exercise of skill (occupation) as *artistry* where it is free from coercion, and otherwise as *servitude*. Forced labor (the form of power based on well-being whose scope is skill) yields one type of servitude. Skilled labor connoting employee status may also imply an element of coercion in the form of subsistence power. In a statist economy the exercise of skills is servitude subject to the form of power previously designated as "directorship."

Coercive control of the acquisition of enlightenment (disclosure) we refer to in general as *indoctrination*, as contrasted with *education*. Indoctrination includes a variety of practices in addition to the specific form of power designated as such. In particular, it includes interference with the acquisition of knowledge, as well as its enforced dissemination and acceptance. We might speak in this connection of "negative indoctrination." Exclusion of certain groups from the schools, or censorship and suppression of information are instances of negative indoctrination. The institution of the inquisition (secret police and so on) is another example of indoctrination in the present wide sense, the coercive power over enlightenment being based directly on well-being: deprivations of life and liberty for deviational beliefs are also to be included under indoctrination in the present sense. Practices with regard to enlightenment constitute education only when they are free both of extreme inducements and extreme constraints.[20]

20. That is, free of coercion affecting the *content* of the disclosures in question. Compulsory attendance at schools is not in itself indoctrination except in the degree to which what is taught in the schools is subject to power practices. However, the effect on content may often be considerable even though indirect.

VI

SYMBOLS

Symbols are among the perspectives and instrumentalities of power. Distinctions are made between myth, ideology, and utopia; and between political doctrines, formulas, and key symbols. Power itself is classified as formal and effective, into authority and control, according to the role of the symbols (perspectives) with which it is associated.

§6.1 *Political Symbols*

DF. *Political symbols* are symbols that function to a significant extent in power practices.

SYMBOLS HAVE thus far been considered as relevant to the political process in a general way—as expressing and inculcating perspectives. In this respect the study of symbols is equally important for every social science: the conduct investigated consists of practices rather than merely operations, and the subjective factors on which the difference depends may be studied by way of the symbols in which they are expressed.

Political symbols are by definition those which have a peculiar relevance to political science. They function directly in the power process, serving to set up, alter, or maintain power practices. Most familiar, perhaps, are the authoritative or semi-authoritative types of political symbols: constitutions, charters, laws, treaties, and so on. But there are many other sorts as well: party platforms, polemics, and slogans; speeches, editorials, forums on controversial subjects; political theories and philosophies. Merriam calls attention to other forms of political symbolism: memorial days and periods; public places and monumental apparatus; music and songs; artistic designs in flags, decorations, statuary, uniforms; story and history; ceremonials of an elaborate nature; mass demonstrations with parades, oratory, music.[1]

1. Merriam, 1934, 104–5. "The importance of ceremonialism," he writes,

All political symbols, then, have causes and consequences in power relationships. This connection with power practices is not necessarily in terms of what C. W. Morris calls the "designative" meaning of the symbol; the political significance of the symbol may lie in its "appraisive" or "prescriptive" meaning. The bearings of the symbol on power relationships may result from the feelings it arouses or action it incites rather than from the objects or states of affairs symbolized. A place name may function as a political symbol for persons identified with one another on the basis of shared perspectives in regard to that place (the "fatherland," the "jewel of the Empire," "the dagger aimed at our heart," and so on); the significance of the name may be purely designative, however, for the geographer or historian.

The analysis of political symbols often requires as well a distinction between manifest and latent content. The manifest content—the literal, direct, or obvious significance—may be far removed from power practices and relations. The symbol may purport to state a nonsocial fact or express a nonpower demand; but its latent content may be directly political. A statement purportedly about the chemistry of the blood may actually function to reinforce politically important identifications; the significance of a demand for universal education may lie in its relation to a latent demand for a share of power.[2]

DF. Political symbols are *global* or *parochial* according to the territorial range of their significance; *general* or *special* according to the range of practices signified; *universal* or *particular* according to the logical form of their presentation.

Thus when the symbol "worker" is changed to "workers of the world," it has been made global; to "American workers,"

"remains little diminished in our own day. Modern states still retain symbolism as the center of their political system."

2. In calling attention to the fact that symbols may be classed as political in terms of their latent content, we are not saying that all symbols are in fact political, much less that "everything is propaganda." Even when it has been established—by data concerning its functioning in specific situations—that a given symbol can fruitfully be considered a political symbol, it does not follow that it is *ipso facto* propagandistic. It is useful to restrict the term "propaganda" to symbols deliberately manipulated for certain purposes, while many political symbols arise and gain currency spontaneously. Moreover, the purpose of the symbol manipulation which constitutes propaganda is control of public opinion, and this is by no means the only purpose for which symbols—and even political symbols—are manipulated. Propaganda will be discussed in the next section.

parochial. Similarly, "white collar worker" is a specialization of the original general symbol; the transformation of Locke's "Life, liberty and property" to Jefferson's "life, liberty, and the pursuit of happiness" is a generalization of the more specialized phrase. "Peace in our time" is particular in form; "Human nature is unchanging" is universalized.

The terms defined indicate, of course, directions of change rather than sharply demarcated categories; they are polar, that is, comparative concepts rather than absolute specifications. We shall speak of *expansion* and *contraction* of the symbol in referring to changes in the two directions in any of the respects defined.

PROP. The expansion of demand statements varies directly with the extent of conflict with the demand, and inversely with the expected influence of the groups included by the expansion and the expected internal conflict among these groups.

When a demand is challenged, and conflict arises in the process of satisfying it, there is a tendency to expansion with regard both to the values demanded and to the groups in whose name the demand is being made. The demand tends to be presented as subsumable under a more general perspective already accepted, and the symbol of identification to include a far larger aggregate than would actually be indulged by attainment of the demand. Thus "democracy" might be alleged to be at stake in, say, jurisdictional disputes between rival unions, and "freedom of the press" in controversies concerning advertising—extreme instances exemplifying a *trivialization of ideology*. The demand may even be universalized, and presented as the inevitable consequence of the workings of natural law and logical necessity.[3]

In the same way, the symbols of identification tend to be expanded beyond the group actually making the demand. The individual is acting in behalf of a group: not "I" but "we" want this or that. A demand group presents itself as speak-

3. The Marxist critique of "ideology" has especially emphasized the universalization of systems of demands: "The selfish misconception that induces you to transform into eternal laws of nature and of reason, the social forms springing from your present mode of production and form of property—historical relations that rise and disappear in the progress of production—this misconception you share with every ruling class that has preceded you" (*Communist Manifesto*, II).

ing for some larger grouping—a class, or some wide functional or territorial group ("Labor demands . . . ," "We of the South want . . ."). Such groups in turn invoke still more expanded identifications: "the nation," "all right thinking men," or even "mankind." [4] The conflicts evoking such expansion of the demand may have been internalized—the demand may have been challenged by the self in search of self-justification, which is provided by the wider identifications and the generalization of the value.

Expansion of the demand as it arouses conflict serves the obvious purpose of evoking wider and more intense support of the demand. Support is forthcoming not only because the demand is presented as a valid interest of the groups appealed to, but also because the expansion of the demand at the same time provides a justification for it: the effects aroused by the generalized identification and demand symbols are attached to the specific demands involved.[5]

Expansion is limited, however, by the expected influence of the groups included in the expansion, for such inclusion may involve a commitment to share with them the demanded redistribution of value; and the more influential the group, the more difficult a subsequent evasion of the commitment. (Hence we can also expect that the expansion will be by way of general symbols rather than by enumeration of many more specific and parochial symbols, for the former do not designate actually influential groups. The demand will more often purport to benefit "mankind" or the "nation" than specified parts of them.)

4. Compare Laski, 1935, 95: "Groups produce value-systems which are a function of their social relations. Those value-systems will always claim universality; they will represent themselves as valid for persons beyond the group. But, in fact, the values will always be limited by the width of the actual experiences from which they arise. And the values which go into actual operation will always be those of the group which, at some given time, control the machinery of the state." Compare also Pareto, 1935, 1498.

5. Compare Lasswell, 1930, 184: "Ambiguity of reference, combined with universality of use, renders the words which signify parties, classes, nations, institutions, policies, and modes of political participation readily available for the displacement of private affects . . . The private motives are readily rationalized in terms of collective advantage." Machiavelli states the point with characteristic directness and practical intent (*Discourses,* I, 47): "Men are apt to deceive themselves upon general matters, but not so much so when they come to particulars. . . . The quickest way of opening the eyes of the people is to find the means of making them descend to particulars, seeing that to look at things only in a general way deceives them."

But in spite of the "expense" of commitments to share in the redistribution of values, the overall tendency is toward expansion rather than contraction. Limitation can be imposed in the actual redistribution of the value, regardless of the expanded symbols, whereas a redistribution wider than that specified in the symbols of identification would have failed to take advantage of all the potential support.[6]

A further factor limiting expansion is the possibility of internal conflict among those appealed to. Expansion cannot go so far as to cut across major lines of group conflict, or as to betray the disparity between those who would be indulged by satisfaction of the demand and those in whose name the demand is made. Ignoring heterogeneities of perspective among potential supporters weakens the solidarity of those actually making and supporting the demand.

A corollary of the hypothesis is that opposition to a demand proceeds by contraction of its symbols: the groups in whose name and for whose benefit the demand is made are alleged to be as narrow as possible, and the values demanded are formulated in specific and particular terms, dissociated from the general and universal perspectives under which they have been subsumed. Limiting the identifications directly minimizes support for the demand; and by counteracting the values the opposition can accept the "principles" invoked, and indeed oppose the specific demand on the basis of those very "principles." [7]

PROP. The I:D ratio publicly expected by a group (optimism-pessimism) varies with:

6. Pareto discusses the problem of expansion and its limitation in terms of what we have referred to as the maximization of the I:D ratio (1935, 1221): "On the one hand there is a tendency to make the largest possible number of persons share in the advantages that the individual asks for himself. On the other, there is a tendency to restrict that number as far as possible. The contradiction disappears the moment we consider that the tendency is to admit to the advantages all whose cooperation helps toward obtaining them, so that their introduction yields more profits than it costs; and to exclude all who do not help, or help less effectively, so that their participation costs more than it yields." Of course the important question, empirically, concerns the conditions under which expansion is not economical; the hypothesis under discussion formulates one of these conditions. But there are others as well—for instance, the initial intensity of the demand.

7. The opposition may also invoke rival expanded symbols if the original ones appeal to members of the opposition groups or their potential allies, and the rival symbols can be made to appeal to the supporters (or potential supporters) of the demand.

a. The evidence, relevant to the expectation, available to those controlling the symbols of expectation
b. The morale of the group
c. Perspectives of potential supporters within and external to the group
d. The power position of the subgroup controlling the symbols in relation to rival subgroups
e. The intensity of antecedent indulgence or deprivation of the self by the self

As another example of the type of problem that may be investigated concerning political symbols, we select their optimistic-pessimistic character. The factors listed in the hypothesis are of course not exhaustive, but they indicate the sort of consideration generally relevant to the public presentation of political symbols.

a. Optimism is more likely to characterize political symbols when the facts warrant expectations of indulgence than when they do not. If, however, the absolute amount of deprivation is expected to be great, regardless of the I:D ratio, ultimate indulgence is emphasized in order to justify the expected sacrifices. Great expenditure must be compensated not only by great reward, but by certainty of the reward.[8] When the facts, as brought to the focus of attention of those manipulating the symbols, warrant pessimistic expectations, these may be publicly formulated so as to preserve the power position—realism may help to retain confidence, credibility, and support when the expected deprivation does in fact occur. Identifications, and with them faiths and loyalties, are less shaken by expected than by unexpected deprivations.

b. A reality basis for optimism or pessimism is, however, neither a necessary nor a sufficient condition for the circulation of corresponding types of symbols: another important factor is the morale of the group. Morale has been defined as intensity of participation in the group, and thus, in effect, as the ability of the group to withstand deprivation. Where morale is low and deprivation especially to be avoided, symbols of expectation of deprivation are avoided as well. For the expecta-

8. Compare Machiavelli, *Discourses,* I, 60: "Men cannot be made to bear labor and privations without the inducement of a corresponding reward, nor can they be deprived of such hope of reward without danger."

tion of deprivation is itself deprivational; pessimism under such conditions may destroy first solidarity and then cooperation. Only a group with high morale can afford to be fully realistic. The group acts may be falling short of the intensity of its demands—the group is prepared to put forth more effort if the necessity for it is accepted. Under such conditions pessimism may characterize the public symbols: expectations of deprivations serve here to prepare for and possibly forestall them.

c. The perspectives of potential supporters are relevant in terms of the "bandwagon" mechanism—the taking up of identifications in the expectation of ensuing indulgence. Thus optimism may recruit support by symbolizing such support as alignment with the winning side—an obvious element in the symbols of election campaigns, for example. (Of course, optimism as to the self may take the form of pessimism as to the other, so as to undermine enemy support by the same mechanism.) Analogous considerations lead to pessimistic symbols where the immediate expectations are of deprivation. Those of least faith and loyalty, and weakest identifications, may withdraw support in the face of deprivation, and thereby affect the morale of the entire group. Pessimistic symbols serve to exclude the "bandwagon" supporters in critical situations without serious injury to group morale as a whole. (The technique of calling for volunteers for especially dangerous tasks is another application of the same principle.)

d. Power position vis-à-vis rival claimants for group control is another factor determinative of symbols of expectation. Optimism may serve the function of maintaining faith in and loyalty to the leadership. Where expectations of deprivation are already widely disseminated, however, pessimistic symbols are invoked to point to the necessity of complete solidarity and cooperation.

e. Finally, favorable expectations may be welcomed because of long continued deprivation of the self by the self (for instance, self-contempt or humiliation). The working of this factor is exemplified in early Nazi propaganda. And conversely, antecedent indulgence of the self by the self may lead to pessimism as an expression of a sense of guilt for unwarranted self-indulgence (complacency), or out of a desire to forestall, by a propitiatory device, real deprivation.

PROP. Political symbols circulating among the power holders correspond more closely to the power facts than do symbols presented to the domain.

The point is not simply that standards of disclosure are markedly different for the powerful and powerless, but the more general one that the milieu of the powerful embodies fuller and more accurate symbolizations of power relations and practices. In terms of our definition of enlightenment as knowledge of the direction and instruments of policy, we may reformulate the hypothesis: the distribution of enlightenment corresponds to the power pattern.

The assumption is that knowledge of the power facts is an important condition for the acquisition and maintenance of power. Realistic perspectives are necessary for continued exercise of power, but not for submission to it. Speaking generally, those who have power know they have it and how it is being used; the powerless are more likely to be deceived as to their power position—particularly since enlightenment itself may be subjected to power practices.

The hypothesis is not to be misconstrued in terms of the pernicious dualism between "reason" and "emotion." Possession of enlightenment in the present sense in no way implies the absence of sentimentalized identifications or demands, or loyalties and interests impregnated with emotion. It is not being said that the powerful have no faith in the symbols of justification of the power structure, but only that it has knowledge of this structure and the way it functions. On the contrary —as will be indicated later in the chapter—such faith is likely to be strongest among those exercising power on the basis of such symbols.[9]

There are, of course, conditions under which the milieu of the powerful deviates significantly from the power facts. Among these may be mentioned: a gradual change in technology has altered the important base values of power; the skills appropri-

9. Pareto's concept of "sentiments" is sometimes applied in the dualistic sense being criticized, as in the following formulation of a hypothesis similar to the present one (1935, 2250): "One may say, in general and speaking very roughly, that the governing class has a clearer view of its own interests because its vision is less obscured by sentiments, whereas the subject class is less aware of its interests because its vision is more clouded by sentiments." But sentiment does not necessarily becloud vision, nor does its distribution necessarily follow the power pattern.

ate to the powerful are ceremonial (skills in the manipulation of internalized symbols); the practices of education of the young, and the principles of recruitment for the exercise of power conflict with the acquisition of enlightenment (because, for example, it violates standards of propriety); rival factions among the powerful are in conflict sufficiently intense to interfere with the process by which power facts are brought to their focus of attention.

§6.2 *Propaganda*

DF. (Political) *propaganda* consists of political symbols manipulated for the control of public opinion.[10]

Only political symbols are characterized as propaganda in this definition. The use of symbols to gain acceptance or rejection of, say, a scientific hypothesis is not an instance of propaganda (regardless of the illogicality or emotional appeal of the arguments invoked). Similarly, advertising—even in the wide sense of any influence of wealth over enlightenment—is not necessarily propaganda: its symbols may be functioning in the market rather than the political arena.

Propaganda concerns opinion, not consensus. On the present definition, propaganda relates only to controversial matters, not to those on which disagreement is excluded by the group. To be sure, political symbols may deal with matters of consensus as well—such symbols (ideology) are extremely important and will be discussed in the next section; but it is useful not to classify them with propaganda concerning debatable issues.

The definition requires further that the symbols be manipulated, that is, specifically introduced for their effect on public opinion. (The term would otherwise be far too inclusive, since almost all symbols—and especially political symbols—have an effect to some degree on public opinion.) Strictly speaking, of course, no symbols are spontaneous: there is always a person or group bringing the symbol to the focus of attention of other

10. Many of the confusions involved in the concept of propaganda result from the fact that the term is normatively ambiguous to a high degree. As here defined, the term is used purely descriptively, not as a negative demand symbol. Political symbols are being classified as propaganda on the basis of specific characteristics of their use; but the classification is not to be taken as expressing a valuation of such symbols.

persons for specific reasons. The point is that a symbol is not to be regarded as propagandistic on the basis of merely incidental effects; it is required that the effects on public opinion be one of the major intentions.

It is to be observed, finally, that nothing is said in the present definition about the properties of the symbols themselves, but only about their function. The symbols may be (and of course frequently are) sentimentalized, fallacious, irrational, and so on. But it is not required by the definition that they be of this sort. Indeed, among the important questions about propaganda to be investigated is that of the conditions under which propaganda symbols have characteristics of this kind, and the conditions under which such characteristics are more or less effective than their contraries.

Symbols, then, are classified as propaganda in terms of their intended effect on public opinion. We may divide the successive phases of the total effect into: attention, comprehension, enjoyment, evaluation, and action.

1. The symbol impinges on attention. The mere shift in focus of attention from one set of symbols to another may itself effect a change in opinion. Frequent and emphatic repetition of the symbol may be sufficient to evoke the desired response—changes in the identifications, demands, and expectations elaborated in terms of the symbol, and in the externalized responses based on the perspectives involved.

2. The symbol is understood. Ordinarily, effectiveness of propaganda depends on the significance of the symbols, not on the signs alone. (The hypotheses of the preceding section, for instance, deal with the effects of varying sorts of content in varying conditions.) But it is to be emphasized that the symbol need not be regarded as having beforehand a fixed and definite meaning. This phase of the propaganda process might in fact be designated as "interpretation" rather than "comprehension." Indeed, much of the effectiveness of propaganda rests on its susceptibility to varying interpretations, a characteristic often deliberately sought for by the propagandist, so as to make a simultaneous appeal to heterogeneous predispositions.[11]

11. See Lasswell, 1930, 189–90: "The problem of him who would manipulate the concentration of affect about a particular symbol is to reinforce its competitive power by leading as many elements as possible in society to read their private meanings into it. . . ."

3. The symbol itself is enjoyed, positively or negatively. Here esthetic factors in a wide sense become relevant. The speech or article is reacted to in terms of the style, structure, emotional appeal, and so on—in some degree of independence of its propaganda content. This factor is of especial importance where attitudes toward the propagandist himself are among those to be controlled. When the leader propagandizes, for example, it is not enough that he say the right things; he must say them in a way that will evoke favorable responses to himself as well as to the policies for which he is propagandizing.

4. The referent of the symbol is revaluated in terms of the identifications, demands, and expectations formulated by the symbol. Here we have modification of opinion in the narrow sense—those exposed to the symbol react in new perspectives to the persons, policies, and situations to which the symbol refers.

5. Action is finally brought about. The response in the given circumstances may be internalized. But the effect of the symbol is not limited to the spatio-temporal region of its occurrence. It extends into the environment not only by way of externalized response, but also by modifying predispositions so as to alter future responses.

PROP. Propaganda in accord with predispositions stengthens them; propaganda counter to predispositions weakens them only if supported by factors other than propaganda.

The hypothesis is a rejection of the view that propaganda "creates" opinion, and insists rather that propaganda operates only on given predispositions. It is a familiar fact that propaganda counter to predispositions can even have the effect of strengthening rather than overcoming them. As MacIver puts it (1926, 308):

> The great organs of opinion may exploit prejudices of the people, but they cannot run counter to them. A body of opinion creates a newspaper rather than a newspaper a body of opinion. The press can confirm and strengthen trends of opinion already formed.

This is not to deny the effectiveness of propaganda, but to formulate limits and conditions of its effectiveness. It can strengthen predispositions and, in particular, give them specific direction; and it can contribute to weakening them if this process is supported by direct experience, or by nonpropaganda symbols.

The hypothesis thus has important bearings on the role of propaganda in the political process. Propaganda cannot operate to alter the power structure except in directions to which the participants in the power process are already predisposed. Michels writes (1915, 244–5):

> The force of persuasion has a natural limit imposed by social relationships. Where it is used to influence the convictions of the popular masses or of social classes to induce them to take part in a movement which is directed towards their own liberation, it is easy, under normal conditions, to attain to positive results. But attempts at persuasion fail miserably, as we learn again and again from the history of social struggles, when they are addressed to the privileged classes, in order to induce these to abandon, to their own disadvantage, as a class and as individuals, the leading positions they occupy in society.[12]

It is irrelevant to urge against the hypothesis that there is such a thing as "the political lie," and that falsehood, distortion, and misrepresentation are effective propaganda techniques. There is such a thing as an unpalatable falsehood as well as an unpleasant truth. The point being made is precisely that propaganda, whether true or false, must be formulated to conform to predispositions; where this is impossible or unsuccessfully accomplished, propaganda is of no avail. And conversely, education is a safeguard against propaganda only insofar as it deals with perspectives as a whole, not merely expectations ("facts"), and with predispositions to action as well as expectations about action. It is the values of a person—integrated perspectives, including identifications and demands—and not merely his knowledge of matters of fact (expectations) which is chiefly determinative of his response to propaganda.

PROP. Propaganda pushes the intensity of the situation to extremes: facilitates catharsis if the intensity is low, and precipitates crisis if the intensity is high.

12. Our hypothesis does not entail the impossibility of Laski's "revolution by consent," but rather that this can occur only when the predispositions have a certain direction—skepticism and pessimistic expectations of the ruling group, vigorous demands and optimism characterizing the rival claimants of power. But see p. 261 below.

The contradiction is ascribing to propaganda, as is frequently done, the effects of both producing and reducing tension is resolved by specifying the situation in which the propaganda functions. In accord with the preceding proposition, propaganda is never a self-sufficient source of anxiety or security, but may contribute to either under appropriate conditions. Crisis is not brought about by the agitator's fiat, but a preexistent stress toward action may be exacerbated, even to the point of violence, by the manipulation of symbols. Contrariwise, if the initial situation involves only lesser tensions, the diffused restlessness and discontent may find adequate expression in the symbols alone, with minimal externalized response.

PROP. Quantity of propaganda is a function of:

a. The heterogeneity of public opinion
b. The disparity of the desired effect with the predispositions
c. Technics and techniques of communication

More propaganda is needed the more heterogeneous is the public whose opinion is to be controlled, and the more the desired opinion deviates from the established perspectives. (Thus the early phases of a revolutionary regime always involve an enormous quantity of propaganda.) Technics of communication are relevant in terms of such factors as the size of the public and the ease with which the propaganda can be brought to its focus of attention. Various culture traits determining techniques of communication also have a bearing on quantity of propaganda. Attitudes toward language may discount too great a multiplicity and frequency of symbol manipulation, or on the contrary expect it as a measure of earnestness of purpose or reliability of commitment. In general, any large and rapid social change will be accompanied by considerable propaganda; hence its extensiveness in modern society.

Quantity of propaganda, on the hypothesis, is not a function of dictatorship or democracy—that is, of the character of power relationships and practices—except insofar as these affect factors like the above. The significant difference in the propagandas of these political patterns is not as to quantity, but variety, and appeal to valid or merely assumed interests.

DF. *Agitational propaganda* is propaganda of great intensity; *persuasive propaganda,* of lesser intensity.

Agitation is the manipulation of symbols for control of response in situations involving great stress toward action, and operating to increase that stress.[13] Agitational symbols are thus more highly sentimentalized, and include more direct and prominent reference to externalized responses. Emphasis is on the operational rather than symbol elaboration of the opinion; rather than presenting grounds for the opinion called for, agitational propaganda concentrates on specifying the demanded action. It is thus characterized by slogans, lack of variety, dynamic style, and so on.

PROP. Agitational rather than persuasive propaganda tends to be invoked where the effect is desired in a short time, or where those with power over symbols are unwilling to distribute enlightenment throughout the domain of their power.

Perspectives are more rapidly and intensely induced by agitation, but less fully integrated with the other perspectives of the person. Interests appealed to, even though valid, are not known to be such by those accepting them; demands based on them reach expression in externalized response with minimal subjectivity. Thus one would expect agitational propaganda rather than persuasion in the case of demands pertaining to an immediate future made by special interest groups (since distribution of enlightenment would expose the limited interest served). But pressure of time or difficulties in the way of distribution of enlightenment may motivate the use of agitation even for action in the general interest.

When quick results are imperative, the manipulation of masses through symbols may be the only quick way of having a critical thing done. It is often more important to act than to understand. It is sometimes true that action would fail if everyone understood it (Lippmann, 1922, 236).

§6.3 *The Political Myth*

DF. The *political myth* is the pattern of the basic political symbols current in a society.

13. Compare Lenin's distinction between agitation and propaganda, the latter constituting the dissemination of doctrine, the former being the manipulation of symbols to intensify and externalize discontent. As defined above, agitation can be used in crowds and publics, and is propaganda in the latter case.

The basic symbols are those having a bearing on the social structure, not merely on some one particular power relationship or practice. They formulate the most general perspectives concerning interpersonal relations in the society; specific power facts are responded to in these perspectives. The political myth consists of the political perspectives most firmly accepted.

The whole body of beliefs existing in any given age may generally be traced to certain fundamental assumptions which at the time, whether they be actually true or false, are believed by the mass of the world to be true with such confidence that they hardly appear to bear the character of assumptions (Dicey, 1926, 20).

The political myth comprises these "fundamental assumptions" about political affairs. It consists of the symbols invoked not only to explain but also to justify specific power practices.

The term "myth" is not to be interpreted as necessarily imputing a fictional, false, or irrational character to the symbols—though, as we shall see, such an imputation is often correct. As before, we characterize symbols in terms of their functioning, not directly by their properties.

The present concept is close to a number of others which have played an important part in the classical literature: Marx's "ideology," Sorel's "myth," Mosca's "political formula," Pareto's "derivations," Mannheim's "ideology" and "utopia," and others.[14] Some of these terms will be introduced by explicit definition in this and the following sections.

DF. The *political doctrine* is the part of the political myth that formulates basic expectations and demands; the *miranda*, the part consisting of basic symbols of sentiment and identification.

The political doctrine consists of the basic expectations and demands concerning power relations and practices in the society. Merriam (1934, 113) refers to these as "credenda"—things to be believed—as distinguished from the "miranda"—things to be admired.

The credenda of power . . . contain the reasons which oblige the intellect to give assent to the continuance of authority. And this assent may be due to government in general, or to particular holders

14. For further discussion of such concepts, see R. M. MacIver, 1947, 4.

of power, or to the special system of authority in vogue at any given moment in a particular unit of power.

The political doctrine is authoritatively set forth in constitutions (especially preambles), charters, formal declarations, and so on (see Friedrich, 1937, 135).

Frequently political theory serves chiefly to embody political doctrine. No clear separation is made between hypotheses of political science and the demands and expectations of political philosophy. Political theory is normatively ambiguous to a high degree—statements purporting to be scientific generalizations often serve instead to express and justify political preferences.[15] Rousseau's remark, "I always feel happy, whenever I meditate on governments, always to discover in my researches new reasons for loving that of my country," is suggestive, to say the least. The matter is forcibly put by Merriam (1931, xiv) in the view that theories of the state "have been in large measure justifications or rationalizations of groups in power or seeking power—the special pleadings of races, religions, classes, in behalf of their special situation." Theories of the state have often been, in short, enunciations of political doctrine.

In the same way, legal and economic theories have often served as formulations of political doctrine, apart from whatever scientific purport they may have had. Indeed, scientific propositions in the strict sense may at the same time be functioning as political symbols, and especially is this true of the social sciences. As Louis Wirth has pointed out, "Every assertion of a 'fact' about the social world touches the interests of some individual or group." [16] This need not impugn the objectivity of the assertion, but calls attention to its possible functioning in the political process as well as the process of inquiry.

Another important component of the political myth, embodying (at least in its latent content) many elements of political doctrine, are the various elaborations of social norms, the theories of what is right, good, proper—symbols included in

15. A rough classification of a sample of 300 sentences from each of the following yielded these proportions of political philosophy (demand statements and valuations) to political science (statements of fact and empirical hypotheses): Aristotle's *Politics,* 25 to 75; Rousseau's *Social Contract,* 45 to 55; Laski's *Grammar,* 20 to 80. Machiavelli's *Prince,* by contrast, consisted entirely (in the sample) of statements of political science in the present sense.

16. Introduction to Mannheim, 1936, xvii.

what Pareto calls "derivations." Mill observed in his essay on liberty that "wherever there is an ascendant class, a large portion of the morality of the country emanates from its class interests, and its feelings of class superiority." And not only does it "emanate" from the social structure, but it may serve also to formulate fundamental justifications for that structure. A similar relation between standards of taste and the social structure has been emphasized by Veblen and others.

The miranda are the symbols of sentiment and identification in the political myth. They are those whose function is to arouse admiration and enthusiasm, setting forth and strengthening faiths and loyalties. They not only arouse emotions indulgent to the social structure, but also heighten awareness of the sharing of these emotions by others, thereby promoting mutual identification and providing a basis for solidarity.

> The emblem or shibboleth not only calls the attention of an individual who sees or hears it to the object or fact that it symbolizes, and awakens in him certain feelings; it also fixes his attention upon the feelings that it arouses and the conduct that it incites in others. The emotions and conduct of others, of which he is thus made aware, at once begin to act upon himself as an influence that merges with the original effect of the emblem or shibboleth.[17]

Flags and anthems, ceremonials and demonstrations, group heroes and the legends surrounding them—these exemplify the importance of miranda in the political process.[18]

PROP. The content of the political doctrine is determined by its political function rather than by the matters of fact which it purports to describe.

That is, the content of the political doctrine is determined by its role in the political process, not in the process of inquiry. It consists of political, not scientific symbols, with characteristics appropriate to their function. Their purport is primarily valuative and incitive, not informative.

Hence it comes about that, as Russell has observed (1938, 98), "Beliefs which have been successful in inspiring respect for the existing distribution of power have usually been such as

17. F. H. Giddings, *Inductive Sociology,* Macmillan, 1901, 138.

18. See Arnold van Gennep, *Traité comparatif des nationalités,* Payot, 1922, for a detailed analysis by an anthropologist of an important type of miranda.

cannot stand against intellectual criticism." But it is to be added that "intellectual criticism" finds its most fruitful application to scientific discourse. We need no more expect political discourse to withstand it than the discourse of poetry or prayer. (We are speaking, of course, of political doctrine, not political science.) Whether a statement is true or false, validly or invalidly deduced from others, and so on, are questions important only with regard to those statements whose successful functioning requires these characteristics. There is a considerable tendency to misunderstand semantics as requiring of all symbols the properties essential to scientific discourse. The mistake is made of supposing that symbols lacking these properties are to be rejected as "nonsense" rather than analyzed in terms of functions other than that of conveying knowledge.[19]

The importance of avoiding this misconception, as applied to political doctrines, has been emphasized by Mosca, among others (1939, 71): Although they

> do not correspond to scientific truths, that does not mean that they are mere quackeries invented to trick the masses into obedience. They answer a real need in man's social nature; and this need, so universally felt, of knowing that one is governed not on the basis of mere material or intellectual force, but on the basis of a moral principle, has beyond any doubt a practical and real importance.

This need has a "practical and real importance" for those exercising power as well as for those subject to it. Continued reliance on violence only has obvious disadvantages for the powerful; and scientific discourse is often inexpedient and ineffective. Rousseau discusses the point fully:

> There are a thousand kinds of ideas which it is impossible to translate into the language of the people. Views very general and objects very remote are alike beyond its reach; and each individual, approving of no other plan of government than that which promotes his own interests, does not readily perceive the benefits that he is to derive from the continual deprivations which good laws impose . . . Since the legislator cannot employ either force or reasoning, he must needs have recourse to an authority of a different order, which can compel without violence and persuade without convincing. It is

19. For a full discussion of the characteristics and functions of the various types of discourse, see C. W. Morris, *Signs, Language and Behavior*, Prentice-Hall, 1946.

this which in all ages has constrained the founders of nations to resort to the intervention of heaven. . . .[20]

The preceding discussion is in no way to be construed as a defense of falsehood and distortion as a political technique. It is rather an insistence that a clear understanding of political doctrine requires its interpretation in terms of other categories and standards than those appropriate to the analysis of a scientific account of political structures and practices. It is not to our present purpose to make value judgments of the characteristics typically exhibited by political doctrines. What is being asserted is simply that the symbols have certain nonscientific (not necessarily *un*scientific) characteristics, and that these are derivative from the functions they perform.

PROP. Maintenance of power depends on adherence in the domain of power to the political doctrine under which the power is being exercised.

The hypothesis calls attention to the inadequacy of violence alone as a stable base for the possession and exercise of power. Merriam observes (1934, 102):

No power could stand if it relied upon violence alone, for force is not strong enough to maintain itself against the accidents of rivalry and discontent. The might that makes right must be a different might from that of the right arm. It must be a might deep-rooted in emotion, embedded in feelings and aspiration, in morality, in sage maxims, in forms of rationalization among the higher levels of cultural groups.

Or, as Rousseau puts it more simply, "The strongest man is never strong enough to be always master, unless he transforms his power into right and obedience into duty." And Hobbes still more concisely: "Even the tyrant must sleep."

This transformation from might to right is effected by the political doctrine. Power distributed and exercised in accord with the political doctrine is right, and submission to it is a duty. Outside of or contrary to the doctrine, power is "tyranny," and

20. Rousseau, *Social Contract,* II, 7. Compare also Edward Gibbon's observation (*Decline and Fall,* chap. ii) on religion in Rome: "The various modes of worship which prevailed in the Roman world, were all considered by the people as equally true; by the philosopher, as equally false; and by the magistrate, as equally useful."

not only does not obligate submission, but may even obligate resistance. The political doctrine thus provides the key symbols and unquestioned axioms on which the justification of the social structure rests. This is essentially the function attributed to it by Mosca (1939, 70 and 97):

> Ruling classes do not justify their power exclusively by *de facto* possession of it, but try to find a moral and legal basis for it, representing it as the logical and necessary consequence of doctrines and beliefs that are generally recognized and accepted. . . . The majority of a people consents to a given governmental system solely because the system is based upon religious or philosophical beliefs that are universally accepted by them. The amount of consent depends upon the extent to which, and the ardor with which, the class that is ruled believes in the political formula by which the ruling class justifies its rule.

PROP. Dependence of a power structure on acceptance of the political doctrine varies inversely with the weight and scope of the power in question.

The inadequacy of violence as a stable base for the exercise of power is, of course, not an absolute, but depends on certain features of the power situation. The hypothesis directs attention to two of these features. Where the power in question is of great weight—approaching absolutism—dependence on doctrine is less than it otherwise would be. For even if opposition did arise, it would be, by hypothesis, relatively powerless. Conversely, dependence on doctrine is greatest where power is shared to a considerable extent. But even in the extreme case of absolutism, there is still a political doctrine and exercise of power in accord with it. "Even in despotic states we never see arbitrary power raised to the height of a principle. Even the despot is regarded as acting according to the requirements of justice." [21] Political doctrine not only serves to keep the domain in subjection; it also provides self-justification for the power holders.

Similarly, power of great scope—one approaching totalitarianism—is less dependent on acceptance of the political doctrine than otherwise. For the greater the scope of power, the greater the control exercised by the powerful over what will be accepted. The function of propaganda in stabilizing a totali-

21. N. M. Korkunov, 1922, 141.

tarian regime, to mention only the most direct technique, is a commonplace. Where power is so limited in scope as to exclude control over symbols, accepted doctrine must be relied upon to minimize the threat from conflicting power holders.

DF. The *ideology* is the political myth functioning to preserve the social structure; the *utopia*, to supplant it.

The terms are taken over from Mannheim (1936); a utopia as here defined need not be "utopian" in the sense of either impracticability or perfection.[22] We call a pattern of political symbols a utopia if their function in the political process is to induce fundamental changes in power relationships or practices; an ideology, if they serve to maintain the given power patterns. Thus counterrevolutionary symbols are as utopian in the present sense as those of a revolutionary movement, and with the seizure of power utopian symbols become ideology. There is not involved here any concept of direction of social change, or any standard of valuation of social structures.

The definitions are based on the way the symbols function, not on characteristics of the symbols themselves. Symbols functioning at one time as utopias may at another serve as ideology, as indeed usually happens in the case of successful revolution —utopian symbols are retained regardless of their increasing divergence from the power facts. And the same individual symbols may simultaneously appear as elements in both an ideology and a utopia (for example, "Americanism" in the slogan "Communism is twentieth century Americanism"). As with other symbol categories previously introduced, the classification cannot be made in abstraction from the concrete situation in which the symbols function.

PROP. In a society with a stable social structure, the ideology is a matter of consensus, not opinion.

That is, the ideology is noncontroversial; disagreements occur only in regard to "applications" of the ideological principles to specific cases. The degree to which the ideology *is* a subject of disagreement and debate may be taken as an index of instability of the social structure supported by the ideology. Under conditions of stability, elaboration of the ideology is in

22. A less misleading term might be *countermyth;* we retain "utopia," however, because of its familiarity in technical contexts in its present sense.

the direction of ceremonialization and glorifications, not explanation and justification.

Spontaneous (nonpropaganda) formulations of the ideology will be frequent and highly elaborated if the ideology is widely and intensely adhered to. Manipulated expressions of ideological faith and loyalty indicate the existence of at least strong predispositions to bring the ideology into question.

A well-established ideology perpetuates itself with little planned propaganda by those whom it benefits most. When thought is taken about ways and means of sowing conviction, conviction has already languished, the basic outlook of society has decayed, or a new, triumphant outlook has not yet gripped the loyalties of old and young (Lasswell, 1936, 29–30).

PROP. Uniformity of ideology—in formulation, promulgation, and acceptance—is a function of other perspectives and of nonsymbolic ("material") uniformities.

The perspectives adopted by persons in given situations depend not merely on the symbols brought to their focus of attention, but also on the relation of these symbols to the predispositions and practices already adopted, both elements varying with the material situation. From the viewpoint of the power holders, the ideology put forward will clearly depend on the base values of their power, on the principles of recruitment to power position, on the characteristic power practices, and in general on the relations of the power holders to their domain.

Thus changes in the division of labor or other nonsymbolic conditions will effect changes in ideology.[23] Conversely, it is difficult to impose a uniform ideology where the conditions set up heterogeneous predispositions and practices.

A common culture cannot be created merely by desiring it. It rests upon economic foundations. It is incompatible with the existence of too violent a contrast between the economic standards and educational opportunities of different classes . . . (Tawney, 1931, 41).

23. Compare the *Communist Manifesto,* II: "Does it require deep intuition to comprehend that man's ideas, views, and conceptions, in one word, man's consciousness, changes with every change in the conditions of his material existence, in his social relations and in his social life? What else does the history of ideas prove, than that intellectual production changes its character in proportion as material production is changed? The ruling ideas of each age have ever been the ideas of its ruling class."

PROP. Every utopia is elaborated into a political doctrine.

Opposition to a social structure is never formulated as a demand merely for the substitution of one set of power holders for another (though this may indeed be the latent content of the demand). It is formulated, rather, in terms of a new "principle" of political organization. A different basis for power is put forward, with concomitant differences in power practices, and only incidentally, as it were, changes in personnel. Michels (1915, 15) has been especially concerned with the utopian elaboration of political doctrine:

> In the modern life of the classes and of the nations, moral considerations have become an accessory, a necessary fiction. Every government endeavours to support its power by a general ethical principle. The political forms in which the various social movements become crystallized also assume a philanthropic mask. There is not a single one among the young class-parties which fails, before starting on its march for the conquest of power, to declare solemnly to the world that its aim is to redeem, not so much itself as the whole of humanity, from the yoke of a tyrannical minority, and to substitute for the old and inequitable regime a new reign of justice.

The doctrine brought forward by the utopia need not always be a new one, however. Opposition may take the form of alleging that the social structure actually obtaining deviates in fact from the doctrine invoked to justify it, and that a change in the social structure is demanded by that doctrine itself. This is a technique to which Pareto, among others, has called attention (1935, par. 1879):

> Assailants of the social order, the better to destroy it, try to take advantage of the forces engendered by that order and therefore make every effort to show that acts which are undoubtedly acts of revolt are legal and therefore ought not to and cannot be punished by the defenders of the order.

Even in such cases, the actual transformation of the social structure involves also changes in the political doctrine. A utopia does not consist simply of rival miranda, though it may begin with such symbols, and certainly will include them; demands and expectations are elaborated to make explicit a justification of the proposed changes in the social structure.

§6.4 *The Political Formula*

DF. The *political formula* is the part of the political myth describing and prescribing in detail the social structure.

The term is adopted from Mosca, who uses it, however, to comprise also what we have called political doctrine. (We have given the term its present meaning because of the connection of the concept with that of political "forms" and the "formal" character of certain political arrangements—concepts which will shortly be made explicit.) While the political doctrine is the "philosophy" of state and government, the political formula embodies the basic public law of the society. The doctrine constitutes the postulates, so to speak, of the formula; hence its frequent formulation in preambles to constitutions, the latter being an important expression of the formula. The political formula, in other words, elaborates in specific and more or less concrete power patterns the content of the political doctrine. (For example, the political doctrine of the divine right of kings may be elaborated in the political formula into a system of royal prerogatives, rules for succession to the throne, power patterns for a subordinate nobility, and so on.)

The political formula is both prescriptive and descriptive—it is normatively ambiguous in a characteristic way. It is prescriptive in inducing conformity to its specifications, and providing the symbols invoked in the detailed justification or crimination of particular power practices. But it is also descriptive—actually, in the degree to which there is in fact conformity to its requirements, and purportedly in that the formula is widely accepted as correctly describing power patterns and practices.

PROP. Maintenance of power depends on apparent conformity by the power holders to the political formula.

We have already spoken of the dependence of the powerful on adherence to the political doctrine by which their possession and exercise of power is justified. There is a corresponding dependence, though not so great, on the political formula—not so great since various formulas may be "derived" from the same doctrine: the constitution can be amended to a considerable degree, for example. But once a particular formula has been elaborated on the basis of the doctrine, it is essential that the holders of power conform (or appear to conform) to it. They otherwise not only rob themselves of justification for the particular deviant practice, but undermine the basis of consent to the power structure altogether. The former is not always important, for there is a tendency to extend to particular practices the justification ordinarily ascribed to the rest of the power practices, even if the particular practice in fact deviates from the basis of justification. But unless the practice is at least *post facto* presented as conforming to the political formula, the effectiveness of the latter—and derivatively the position of those exercising power under the formula —is significantly weakened.

The point is that complex power relations subsisting on a basis that is not altogether coercive depend upon what has been called a "transpersonal principle of domination," that is, a pattern of demands and expectations justifying power on some basis other than its possession by the particular persons who in fact exercise it.

> In a transpersonal power structure the rulers have to act in a manner adapted to its "principle." In some cases they themselves believe in the principle and act in conformity with this belief; in other cases they do not believe in the principle, but nevertheless have to act as if they did believe, because if they acted otherwise they would gradually destroy the principle upon which their power is based and at the same time their own situation as dominators.[24]

The powerful, in short, try to present their possession and exercise of power as legal; and "legal" *means* in accord with the political formula.

24. Timasheff, 1939, 207–8. Compare also N. M. Korkunov, 1922, 345–6: "Submission to political authority cannot be explained on the basis of the personal power of those who govern. Political history shows us by numerous examples that thousands of persons are obedient to the orders of one, and that one often destitute of intelligence, simply because that one person was recognized as representing the state's authority; and celebrated statesmen, on the other hand, have been compelled to shelter themselves behind a ruler who was of no importance from the intellectual point of view, but was the bearer of governmental authority. . . . Submission to rulers is never absolute. They are obeyed only so far as they are recognized as representing something higher than their own personal will. If public opinion pronounces the activity of those who are at the head of the state to be arbitrary, obedience falls off very quickly, and a revolution becomes inevitable."

Without legality, that is, without at least apparent conformity to the political formula, power assumes directly the form of violence. For this reason conformity is maintained in spite of the disparity which may develop between the actual power structure and that symbolized in the formula. Merriam asks (1934, 33):

> Why do not the real leaders overturn the nominal and substitute themselves for their dummies? This ignores the whole basis of power which lies in a social situation, conditioning the actions of the leaders, and making it difficult or impossible for them to operate against the very basis of their own authority. They are not merely leaders *per se*, but they function in a total situation of which they are parts. As servants of the crown they may largely direct the crown, but as claimants of the crown they may become traitors.

We shall return shortly to a consideration of this disparity between effective and purely formal power.

PROP. The interpretation of the political formula is determined largely by the holders of power.

The political formula is, to start with, elaborated chiefly in terms of the identifications, demands, and expectations of the powerful:

> The political formula must be based upon the special beliefs and the strongest sentiments of the social group in which it is current, or at least upon the beliefs and sentiments of the particular portion of that group which holds political preeminence (Mosca, 1939, 72).

Beard's *Economic Interpretation of the Constitution* provides full documentation of this point applied to a particular political formula. The need to conform to the political formula thus cannot be construed as conflicting with the demands and expectations which would otherwise direct power practices; the formula, by and large, is an embodiment of the perspectives of the holders of power.

The hypothesis goes further, however. The formula functions in a political process, and with changing situations the formula requires continued interpretation to continue to be applicable to these situations. The hypothesis is that the interpretation of the formula is determined largely by those with power in the society, so as to continue the satisfaction of their interests. What is being challenged is the conception of "law" as an abstraction exercising a determinate and autonomous control over the political process, independently of concrete power structures and relations. It is this conception which Laski has repeatedly criticized in his treatment of the distinction between "state" and "government" (a distinction which we shall later make on a different basis). "The will of the state," he writes, "is in its laws; but it is the government which gives substance and effect to their content." And again, "Principles may be invalidated by the method of their application, and it is governments which have the actual administration of them."[25] Terms like "state" and "law," that is, are often dealt with as nonempirical abstractions—abstractions altogether cut off from directly observable features of interpersonal relations. When they are given empirical content, they have reference to processes (including symbol processes) in which the distribution and exercise of power are of central importance. The political formula, like any other set of symbols, has significance only in a process in which it is interpreted and applied; in this process, those with most power play the most important role.

The hypothesis is often formulated with specific reference to an economic basis of power, or at any rate to economic interests of the powerful. Oliver Goldsmith's "Laws grind the poor, and rich men rule the law" is proverbial. Laski has frequently stated the hypothesis in this form, as in his observation that "the legal doctrines of a court mainly take their color from the character of the prevailing economic order."[26] Gustavus Myers's *History of the Supreme Court* is an extensive documentation of this form of the hypothesis. But the hypothesis need not be limited to economic power or interests; it is stated so as to be applicable to any power holders, regardless of the base value of their power. Where economic power is the most important form, the interpretation of the political for-

25. Laski, 1935, 12; 1925, 145; and throughout these works. Compare also Anatole France's observation that "The law in its majestic equality forbids the rich as well as the poor to sleep under bridges, to beg in the streets and to steal bread."

26. Article on "Democracy" in *ESS*. Compare also the observation in Aristotle's *Politics*, IV, 6: "The stronger the men of property are, the more power they claim. . . but, not being as yet strong enough to rule without the law, they make the law represent their wishes." That is, they conform to the political formula, but interpret it in accord with their own interests.

mula will be in terms of economic considerations; but where the power holders constitute a military or priestly caste, the interpretation, on the hypothesis, will be determined by considerations of corresponding interests.

Certain interests are common to all power holders—interests in power as a value—and these are of special importance as determinants of the interpretation of the political formula. Where the political formula is expected by the powerful to be deprivational to their power position or potential, it is reinterpreted so as to remove this threat—often even at the expense of more specialized interests (for instance, the economic). As Michels has found from a study of power relationships in political parties (1915, 406), "If laws are passed to control the dominion of the leaders, it is the laws which gradually weaken, and not the leaders."

It is not to be supposed that the political formula is altogether without effect as a restraint on power practices. Power holders vary in the weight of control they exercise over political symbols in general, and over the formula in particular. A recognition of the existence and importance of such control, emphasized in the hypothesis, does not make it impossible to speak of a more or less independent judiciary; the matter is one of degree. Moreover, the interpretation itself is confined to certain limits. What these limits are becomes apparent at least when they are transgressed. As Merriam points out (1934, 213),

> Power without justice rests upon an uncertain basis, and its days are numbered. If we ask what is this justice, the answer is not ready; but the sense of justice in the community is easy to find. It is only necessary to outrage or violate it, and the intangible becomes real, the indefinable evident and effective in terms of authority and morale.

DF. *Formal* is pertaining to the political formula. A *political form* is a pattern of formal practices. The *regime* is the structure of political forms.

The term "formal" as applied to a practice or institution conveys two ideas, both deriving from the political formula: the idea of legitimacy (legality, authority, and so on) and the idea of a symbolic status. A formal practice is one that has been legitimized, by its relation to the political formula; and the operations of which it consists have a significance assigned to them by the formula, regardless of whether or not in fact they have the characteristics ascribed. Voting is a formal practice when it takes place in accord with the shared demands and expectations concerning power relations which we have designated a political formula; and to call it formal is to emphasize, further, that the voting may or may not actually constitute the making of a decision.

It is to be noted that formalities may occur in any politically organized group, and not only the "state." A group is politically organized when there is a certain degree of solidarity and cooperation with regard to power practices. In every such group there is a political doctrine and a political formula, whether or not these are fully explicit in symbols circulating in the group. We may therefore distinguish between formal and informal practices in such groups; the appointment of a committee to make specified decisions for the group is a typical formal practice. (No metaphor is involved in speaking of lesser groups than the state in this way. All of the concepts so far introduced apply to any groups satisfying the general conditions specified in the definitions. Interpersonal relations are the fundamental facts with which political science deals; "state" and "government" have reference to special cases of such relations, and are not the basic concepts from which all others are derived, or in relation to which they must be defined.)

A political form is a pattern of practices specified by the political formula (or elaborated in accord with it). That is, the formula specifies certain operations, and these appear in certain perspectives (of legality and so on) because it is there that they are specified. Patterns such as the bicameral legislature or trial by jury are political forms. The practices of which they consist are formal in that they are warranted by the formula, and because, though power is putatively involved, it remains to be empirically determined whether, how, and to what extent control is actually being exercised.

It is to be noted that only formal power practices constitute political forms in the present definition. The political machine with its boss is not a political form in the present sense, though it may be a common or even invariable pattern of power practices. It is not a political form because it is not formal; little attempt is made to explain or justify it in terms of the political formula; the perspectives in which it appears are not those of legality, but of "necessary evil." Such patterns are in fact political institutions which have not been formalized.

The regime ("frame of government," "political order," and so on) is, then, the pattern of the political forms. It may be distinguished from the *control structure*, the pattern of effective (rather than merely formal) power practices. The two may of course deviate from one another to a considerable degree—power may actually lie in quite different hands and be exercised in quite different ways than is indicated by the formal patterns. In this sense the regime may be fictive, but this does not necessarily diminish its political importance (often the contrary, as we shall see below). The political doctrine and formula have an importance and usefulness which is in general independent of their descriptive truth or falsehood. The regime—the externalization of the political doctrine and formula—functions to minimize the element of coercion in the political process. "To government by opinion there is no other alternative except government by violence," Charles Beard has observed.[27] The regime is in the relevant sense the government by opinion. It is the expected and demanded distribution and exercise of power.

PROP. The regime tends to be supplemented by informal practices not openly counter to the political formula.

Like the political formula, the regime is part of a political process; the patterns are not rigidly fixed but alter with various features of the political situation. The point made in the hypothesis is that this adjustment to changing conditions and considerations takes place to a considerable degree without basic changes in the political formula.

In any country we shall generally find a number of particular constitutional "conventions" or "understandings" which are distinct from the formal "law of the constitution," but are yet inextricably connected with it, and indispensable for its operation.[28]

27. Introduction to J. B. Bury, *Idea of Progress,* Macmillan, 1921.

28. Barker, 1942, 71. Compare also Ostrogorski, 1926, I: "Extra-constitutional forms developed, which have frequently superseded or encroached upon the constitutional order. It is impossible to understand the American government unless

The regime is thereby adapted to changing conditions without straining either the processes of interpretation of the political formula, or the formal basis of power itself. The substitution of the party mechanism for the electoral college in American political practice exemplifies this process (though in many respects the party mechanism has been subsequently formalized).

§6.5 *Authority*

DF. *Authority* is formal power.

Authority is thus the expected and legitimate possession of power. We say "expected" because the actual power structure does not necessarily coincide with that described in the political formula; and "legitimate" because the formula is the source and basis of legitimacy. To say that a person has authority is to say not that he actually has power but that the political formula assigns him power, and that those who adhere to the formula expect him to have power and regard his exercise of it as just and proper.[29] The regime may now be described as the structures of authority and authority practices.

Thus ascription of authority always involves a reference to persons accepting it as such. While X may be said to have effective power over Y independently of Y's perspectives—or anyone else's—X may be said to have authority over Y only from the standpoint of some Z (usually, though not necessarily identical with Y) adhering to the political formula from which the authority derives. Authority is in this sense "subjective": its existence depends on someone's think-so, though not, to be sure, simply on the think-so of the person having the authority. This subjectivity results from the symbolic status characteristic of the formal as such, and may be ascribed to other formal concepts, for example, law, as well as authority.

> Law is much less an objectively established subjection of the person to society than it is a subjective conception by the person himself

one has studied well those extra-constitutional forms. Nor is such study necessary only for more accurate knowledge. The constitutional mechanism itself would work in the wrong way or would revolve in empty space if the extra-constitutional machinery superimposed on it were ignored."

29. On authority as the right to power, see R. M. MacIver, 1947, 83.

of a necessary order of social relations. . . . Authority depends not on the will of the ruler, but upon the consciousness of the subject (Korkunov, 1922, 325, 350).

If we define *allegiance* as formal loyalty (Locke: "an obedience according to law"), we may say that authority is created by allegiance, rather than that allegiance results from the recognition of authority. Authority does not exist antecedently to its recognition (though effective power may and often does), but is brought into being by identifications, demands, and expectations relating to the political formula. (The point is clearly brought out in the sense of the word "recognize" appropriate to diplomacy.)

PROP. Authority alone is power of low weight, increasing with the intensity of the political situation.

Since authority has been defined in terms of power, we may speak of the weight, scope, and domain of authority under the same conditions as previously specified. But these are to be distinguished from the corresponding dimensions of the effective power which may be associated with the authority. For example, the king may have sole authority over the economic and religious practices of all his subjects, but in fact have a voice in the making of decisions concerning only the religious practices of some of his subjects.

The hypothesis states that the possession of authority is itself effective power, whose weight varies with the intensity of the situation in which it is exercised. Possession of authority is itself a basis for participation in the making of decisions —authority is never completely powerless—but the weight of power which it commands depends on the stress toward political action in the domain of power. In situations of minimal conflict the Crown does not exercise effective power *merely* because it is the Crown; as tension mounts, however, authoritativeness itself comes to have more and more weight. Merriam (1934, 12) discusses the matter in terms of "legality" for what we here call "authority":

There is in "legality" a symbolic value of high importance in social relations. To be "legal" is to bear the proud banner which rallies to its support great numbers of almost any community or tends to do so. To be "illegal" is to deter many from support of a position or personality otherwise acceptable or expedient. The legal is likely to emerge with the crown of victory, other things being equal. Thus in transition or tension periods the symbolic value of legality which in some ways seems so vague and empty becomes rich and full of meaning and power.[30]

PROP. Weight of authority varies with the prestige of the authorities.

"Even a nod from a person who is esteemed," says Plutarch, "is of more force than a thousand arguments or studied sentences from others."[31] The respect enjoyed independently of authority status is, in other words, an important factor in determining the weight of authority exercised. Mosca's characterization of the ruling class (1939, 53) follows as a consequence: "Members of a ruling minority regularly have some attribute, real or apparent, which is highly esteemed and very influential in the society in which they live." It may be descent, wealth, prowess, or special skills; it is, in any case, an attribute whose possession confers prestige. The maintenance, if not the acquisition, of authority depends on such prestige: authority replacements are recruited for the most part from those enjoying a high respect position.

Now prestige diminishes with increasing contact with those outside the select (abstinence from such contact is called the maintenance of *distance*). It follows that "authority can neither arise nor be preserved without the establishment and maintenance of distance between those who command and those who

30. Compare also Tawney, 1931, 229–30: "Political authority is a genuine form of power, and is often, both for good and evil, an important form. But it is one form, not the only form. . . . In reality, it is one species of a larger genus. Its special characteristic is that it can set in motion the forces of law, so that it ceases to be merely a fact, and both becomes a right in itself and confers rights on others. But, if scrofula is not cured by the king's touch, neither is power conferred by kissing the king's hands. It is not the legal recognition which makes the power, but the power which secures legal recognition. . . . The river exists before it is canalized, so as to carry the barge and drive the mill. The fact of power exists independently of the right to power. Sometimes, indeed, it exists in spite of it."

31. Compare the more recent observation by Ernest Barker (1942, 111): "A little experience of life is sufficient to teach us that the opinions of those who command prestige—whether the prestige be derived from official position, or from birth or from wealth—have an influence which is out of proportion to their inherent value."

obey."[32] Thus authority is characteristically accompanied by pomp and ceremony; the exercise of authority does not rest on doctrinal symbols alone but makes use of miranda as well. That the word "authority" designates both the person and the formal power he possesses is significant: the person exercising it is responded to, not as a person, but as the embodiment of authority. As was previously pointed out, the relation of authority to its domain is "transpersonal."

Nevertheless, authority cannot hold itself so far distant from its domain as to strain identifications or otherwise weaken solidarity; and of course the exercise of authority necessarily involves some degree of contact with those over whom it is being exercised. Machiavelli advises the Prince to minimize distance in a literal sense—to reside in newly acquired territories, so as to strengthen loyalty to and respect for the new authority. More commonly, authority relies on symbols to make possible "action at a distance." Either he acts through representatives, to whom partial authority has been delegated, or his direct contacts are formalized by ritualistic and other symbols.[33]

The hypothesis under discussion is to be qualified by a recognition that authority itself evokes respect, so that if authority can be acquired by any means, the respect on which its maintenance rests is likely to be forthcoming. Certain symbols, as we have just seen, tend to become intimately associated with the possession and exercises of authority—crown, throne, and scepter—and often possession of the symbol is itself sufficient to induce respect and authority.

> It is common to accept the authority of a person who has, or presumes to have, some real or imaginary symbol of superiority. . . . The sentiment of authority may to a greater or lesser extent become disengaged from the person and attached to the symbol, real or presumed, of authority (Pareto, 1935, 456–70).[34]

32. Michels, article on "Authority" in *ESS*. But if prestige is widely distributed in the society (or there exists a high demand for equality in respect), this factor is severely limited in effect. Authority manifests under these circumstances personalization as well as distance, as exemplified in the "democratic" personal relations of many American authorities.

33. Compare Michels in the article cited in the footnote above: "Authority is preserved by symbols which link the masses with the distant personal or impersonal authority they represent."

34. Psychological investigations in the last decades have accumulated con-

PROP. Every power group seeks to acquire authority or to exercise effective power over authorities.

Whether the attempt is to acquire authority or to exercise power over it depends, as always, on the I:D ratio expected. Where authority itself constitutes power of considerable weight (there is intense faith in and loyalty to symbols of authority), the attempt would probably be to acquire authority. On the other hand, if the power group has special interests which would make widespread acceptance of its authority unlikely, or if existent authorities are themselves predisposed in favor of these interests, control over authority would perhaps be more expedient. The point of the hypothesis is that in any case power does not ignore authority, nor flout it except as a last resort. Power is formalized or given formal sanction wherever possible.

PROP. Nonauthoritative power practices are rendered authoritative by changes in or reinterpretations of the political formula; such practices are not abandoned because they are nonauthoritative.

This follows from the preceding hypothesis together with the earlier proposition concerning the interpretation of the formula by the holders of power. When power practices come into conflict with authority it is the latter which gives way—not, to be sure, by abandoning its claims, but by a transformation of its content. Where modifications in power practices would involve greater deprivations than changes in the political formula (to whatever extent is required) the latter takes place. Laski has often applied the hypothesis to economic power and practices:

> Political forms have always been a mask behind which an owning class has sought to protect from invasion the authority which ownership confers; and, when the political forms have endangered the rights of ownership, the class in possession has always sought to adjust them to its needs.[35]

---

siderable data on the predispositional basis for acceptance of authority in the structure of the family and the biological dependencies of the infant. On the application of such psychogenetic considerations to politics see, for instance, Lasswell (1930) and Erich Fromm, *Escape from Freedom,* Farrar & Rinehart, 1941.

35. Laski, 1935, 293. On the relation between the political formula and power practices compare also Pareto's characteristically unrestrained observation

DF. A regime is *formalistic* in the degree that it diverges from the control structure.

We call "formalistic" any power structure in which authority is divorced from effective power. In such a structure, those whose exercise of power is legitimate and expected—the authorities—do not in fact make the decisions. Their participation in the decision-making process is limited to the purely formal—it is ceremonial and ritualistic. The British monarchy, for example, is formalistic: "the king governs but does not rule." The office of the presidency in the Soviet Union is formalistic in the same sense.

PROP. Increase in the formalism of a regime is slow and gradual; decrease, rapid and sudden.

The proposition relates the correspondence of formal and effective power to revolution. In setting up the hypothesis of a lag between political forms and structures of effective power, it lays the basis for a theory of revolution as an integral feature of the political process. The matter will be fully discussed in Chapter 10.

It is not being said that changes in the correspondence of formal and effective power *must* occur—stability might be attained at any level. The hypothesis is that *if* there is change, that in the direction of further disparity is slow and cumulative, while closer correspondence tends to be brought about with comparative discontinuity. As will be seen below, changes in the division of labor are especially likely to increase formalism: they alter effective power relationships without modifying, immediately, at least, formal relationships. However, the previously discussed reinterpretations and supplementations of the political formula contribute to a gradual decrease of formalism.

PROP. Where control and authority (effective and formal power) are in the same hands, a weakening of one leads to a weakening of the other.

Authority is undermined if it appears more and more formalistic in the perspectives of those over whom it is exercised.

(1935, 466): "It is quite a serious error to assume that court decisions in a given country are made in accord with its written laws. . . . We need say nothing of constitutional law. There is no relation whatever between theory and practice, except in the minds of a few silly theorists."

An authority of whom it is widely known that in fact he exercises no control tends to lose his authority as well. But the disclosure of lack of real power must be particularly emphatic to result in a diminution of authority, in order to overcome the predispositions set up by the presumed equivalence of authority and effective power. The converse loss of power when authority is weakened was discussed in the previous hypotheses concerning the necessity for power to conform (or appear to conform) to the political formula.

The present hypothesis thus makes clear the function of formalism in the political process. The disparity between control and authority makes it possible for the powerful to sacrifice some degree of either formal or effective power in order to maintain the other. Hostility against the power structure is countered with redistributions of authority or changes in formal power practices, leaving the structure of effective power intact. In some cases, concessions may be made with regard to control, so as to preserve the main features of the structure of authority on which power rests. In short, formalism makes possible the resolution of political conflict without revolution, that is, basic changes in the regime or social structure. "Political shams," as Lowell (1913, 3–4) has observed with regard to England, "have done for English government what fictions have done for English law. They have promoted growth without revolutionary change."

The remark of Tacitus (quoted with approval by Machiavelli), that nothing is so weak and unstable as a reputation for power which is not based on force, needs qualification, therefore. The reputation for power without an actual power basis may make the authority useful to the effectively powerful while the latter in turn are secure from his interference in the making of decisions. At the extreme of formalism, authority is ceremonial, and as such is often very stable. Purely ceremonial authority may be politically important as a focus of loyalty, and function in other ways to maintain adherence to the political formula—as is exemplified by a child monarch during a regency.

DF. *Naked power* is nonauthoritative power openly exercised.

It is power not accepted as authoritative by those over whom it is exercised, but nevertheless submitted to. Nonrecognition of power by an external group does not make the power naked, nor does *de facto* deviation from the political formula if there is apparent conformity. Usually, though not necessarily, naked power takes the form of violence. It may be some other form, if the sanctions imposed are important enough to the subjects to bring about submission to it without a recognition of its legitimacy. (There may be threats against the welfare of other persons for whom the subject feels affection.)

PROP. Naked power tends to be exercised in situations where current political myths tend to be widely rejected.

In such situations a claim to authority cannot easily be established; and the exercise of power does not wait on its formalization. Russell puts the point very clearly (1938, 97):

Power is naked when its subjects respect it solely because it is power, and not for any other reason. Thus a form of power which has been traditional becomes naked as soon as the tradition ceases to be accepted. It follows that periods of free thought and vigorous criticism tend to develop into periods of naked power.

PROP. Naked power tends to be formalized as it increases in weight, scope, and domain.

We have stated in a previous hypothesis that power attempts to acquire or control authority. The point being made here is that the likelihood of acquisition of authority by naked power varies with the amount of power.[36] Any competing authority must from the nature of the case remain formalistic, and hence unstable. Authority cannot subsist indefinitely in conflict with effective power; the preservation of the authority of the legitimate governments during foreign occupation, for example, depends on the expectation of their exercise of effective power in a foreseeable future. Without such expectations, power by conquest gradually becomes legitimized. In general, the more effective the control over certain practices, the more likely is formalization of those practices (as illustrated by the dictum that "possession is nine points of the law"). Moreover, vari-

36. Compare Locke's remark in his *Civil Government*, 176: "Great robbers punish little ones to keep them in obedience, but the great ones are rewarded with laurels and triumphs, because they are too big for the weak hands of justice in this world, and have the power in their possession which should punish offenders."

ous values, such as prestige, correlate more or less directly with the amount of power, and these values also facilitate the recognition of authority. In short, "the higher the scale and wider the scope of coercion, the more likely is it to acquire authority and/or sanction." [37]

37. H. M. Kallen, article on "Coercion" in *ESS.*

VII

PRACTICES

Perspectives and operations are patterned in political practices. When power perspectives are operative, conduct is politicized. Fundamental practices in such conduct include patterns of relationship between leaders and led, and the distribution of responsibility in relations of representative and constituent.

§7.1 *Considerations and Conditions*

DF. *Considerations* are the perspectives in which influence is exercised; *conditions,* the factors necessary and/or sufficient for its exercise.

ANALYSIS OF the decision-making process—and, more generally, of the influence process—requires investigation of two sorts of factors: the symbols entering into the focus of attention of those exercising the influence, and the situations in which it is exercised. The latter, from the standpoint of such an analysis, we term "conditions": a condition is a determinant or effect of policy. A consideration is a symbol, referring to conditions, which enters into policy formation. Not all conditions, of course, are always considered; policy may be more or less realistic, more or less enlightened.

Conditions may include the self as well as the environment. A certain degree of solidarity and cooperation is a condition for waging war; whether or not these conditions obtain may be an important consideration in deciding on a warlike policy. Similarly, considerations may be determined by the environment as well as by predisposition. On the basis of the flow of comment and interpretation from the environment, decision makers are able to estimate the applicability of considerations toward which they are predisposed. Those Japanese predisposed toward an imperialist policy timed their attack on the United States in view of intelligence about the progress and prospects of Nazis and Fascists in the world military-political situation in 1941.

PROP. Solidarity in relation to given policies varies with the degree to which considerations favorable to those policies are brought to the focus of attention of the group.

Advancing of considerations acts in a twofold way to solidify the group behind the policy. Over and above the favorable expectations aroused by the considerations advanced is the effect on solidarity of their having been advanced at all. The group participates in this way in the process of decision making (though in fact such participation may be of minimal weight), and the deference thereby extended further predisposes the members in favor of the policy. It may be unnecessary, therefore, to make available the considerations actually decisive for the policy makers. The mere fact that the policy is "explained" and "justified" itself acts in favor of the policy, and if the considerations in addition evoke favorable expectations, they are doubly effective. The sale of war bonds may be promoted by linking them with expectations of shortening the war, rather than preventing or controlling inflation.

The hypothesis, of course, does not deal with *all* the factors relevant to solidarity. Solidarity may be heightened by the enunciation of policy without advancement of considerations, if, for example, the policy is one which the group is demanding or to which it is already predisposed, or if group practices have set up strong predispositions of unquestioning obedience and blind faith. (In the latter case, to put forward considerations in behalf of policy may even weaken solidarity, by shaking confidence in or respect for the leadership.) [1] It follows that support will be most easily secured for policies that can be symbolized as comprised in preexistent demands of the group. It follows, too, that where considerations *are* advanced, they need not

1. Thus it would be a mistake to suppose that prosecution of a war always requires active propagandizing to secure widespread support. Many times the war policy is one demanded by the group before its adoption by the leadership. As the *Federalist* puts it (No. VI), "There have been . . . almost as many popular as royal wars. The cries of the nation and the importunities of their representatives have, upon various occasions, dragged their monarchs into war, or continued them in it, contrary to their inclinations, and sometimes contrary to the real interests of the state." Of course, these perspectives may be the result of previous propagandizing; but the point is that at this stage the advancing of considerations on behalf of the policy is a superfluity.

be the same for the whole group, but may differ to suit the varying predispositions of influential subgroups.

DF. Conduct is *socialized* in the degree that it is determined by considerations of interpersonal relations; otherwise *privatized.*

We use the term "social," here as elsewhere, only in the sense of interpersonal, not in the many narrower senses in which the interpersonal is qualified by relations of cooperation, integration, mutuality, and so on. That conduct is socialized in the present sense does not necessarily imply that it is sociable.[2] It is required only that the conduct involve expectations, demands, and identifications concerning other persons. Thus Hobbes's war of each against all represents a high degree of socialization, in that each determines his own conduct by considerations (fear, rivalry, and so on) of other persons.[3] Indeed, it might be said that one of the purposes of the social contract, in Hobbes's theory, is to permit some conduct to be at least partially privatized.

The scope of privatization varies, of course, from culture to culture. It is determined not only by the social order (standards of propriety, and so on), but also by the political structure of both authority and control. (In the latter regard, the *zone of privacy* appears as one aspect of what is called "individual" or "personal" liberty.) Similarly, there are variations from person to person in the extent to which conduct is socialized or privatized; the stereotypes of the "hermit" and the "politician" represent two extremes. But the tendency to socialization or privatization is not conveniently dealt with in terms of such categories as "extrovert" and "introvert." In many usages, the latter may refer to a high degree of socialization, in that the emphasis of noninterpersonal externalized conduct may in fact be expressive of great internalized emphasis on considerations of others—withdrawal is a form of taking others into account. Of course, since the self, as distinct from the ego, is a social concept, privatization is only a pole of

2. For a recent discussion of the distinction between the sociable, the gregarious, and the political, see John Laird, *The Device of Government,* Cambridge University Press, 1944, chap. i.

3. "For war consisteth not in battle only, or the act of fighting, but in a tract of time wherein the will to contend by battle is sufficiently known . . ." (*Leviathan,* chap. xiii).

conduct to which there can be no more than an approximation.[4]

The concepts of privatized and socialized conduct may easily be extended to groups. Group conduct is socialized in the degree that it is determined by considerations of persons outside the group.[5] Endogamy, for instance, is group privatization with regard to marriage practices. We may refer to a group as *insular* ("isolationist") in the degree to which such privatization applies to a wide range of practices. (The more familiar phrase "closed group" is ambiguous, since it sometimes refers to impermeability or solidarity as well as the insular character. A group may be insular and nevertheless exhibit high permeability: it is easy to become a member of the group, but only members are taken into account in group practices.) Where a group is socialized only with regard to perspectives, but privatized in all its operations, it may be characterized as *self-sufficient.*

DF. Conduct is *politicized* in the degree that it is determined by considerations of power indulgence or deprivation of the self by the other.

Politicization is thus a special instance of socialization, where interpersonal relations are considered in their bearing on power. Demands and expectations concerning power position and potential are important considerations of policy; conduct is determined by the expected I:D ratio in power status. Politicization is a characteristic which may apply to conduct in varying degrees. It is always an empirical problem to determine the conditions under which politicization tends to a minimum or maximum. (One hypothesis concerning these conditions will be formulated immediately below.)

A low degree of politicization may occur in several different forms, to which it is convenient to assign different designations. Perspectives may be nonpolitical because of disillusionment with power as a value, or with the power process.

4. The present concept of privatization is close to that of "emancipation" as developed, for example, by Erich Fromm and Karen Horney.

5. This is not to be confused with the distinction in §1.2 between externalized and internalized responses, according to whether there are environmental changes or only manipulation of symbols. The war dance is an internalized practice, yet socialized insofar as it involves reference to the enemy; implementation of a "five-year plan," though altering the environment, may be privatized insofar as only the group itself, not its relations to others, enters into the perspectives of the plan.

We characterize such a person as *depolitical:* there has been a decrease in the politicization of his conduct due to a failure to satisfy demands or fulfill expectations with regard to the distribution and exercise of power. Disinterest in power may result from its depreciation as compared with the enhanced value of other practices, for instance, those of the arts or sciences. Here we may speak of an *apolitical* characteristic. Politicization, finally, may be actively opposed on the basis of the expectation that it conflicts with other values adhered to, as in the perspectives of the anarchist or religious mystic, for example. Here the characteristic is *antipolitical.*

A person whose conduct is politicized to a high degree is a *politician.* The term has reference, therefore, not merely to the holding or striving for political office, but to the tendency to consider always the effect on influence or power position of projected lines of conduct. A *statesman* is distinguished from other politicians (if the term is used descriptively, rather than normatively) by the wide range of his identifications and expectations: the self which he takes into consideration comprises the entire body politic, and his expectations include the more distant as well as the immediate future.

PROP. The politicization of conduct varies with the amount of power exercised.

The hypothesis is that the powerful are more likely to determine policy by power considerations than are the relatively powerless. Those who already have a comparatively large amount of power act so as to maintain and improve their power position; those with little power give power little consideration.[6]

The proposition is of obvious importance for democratic theory, insofar as democracy involves wide distribution of power. For on the hypothesis, inequalities of power distribution acquire some measure of stability from that very inequality. Considerations of the distribution will be most effective

6. The hypothesis might be generalized to apply to all deference values: respect, rectitude, and affection receive most consideration from the most respected, moral, and popular members of the group. But this does not hold to nearly the same extent with regard to welfare values. For example, the most healthy are not necessarily most concerned about health; and the most wealthy are often the most extravagant, whereas the powerful seldom act in a manner expected to dissipate their power.

on the policies of those concerned to maintain the inequality.

It may be suggested further that power considerations are the most important ones determining policy of power holders. They override principled interests which may be operative, if these conflict with the power interests. Often, however, the latter coincide—in the perspectives of the power group—with their principled interests.

Men come easily to believe that arrangements agreeable to themselves are beneficial to others. A man's interest gives a bias to his judgment far oftener than it corrupts his heart. . . . His "sinister interest" (to us a favorite term of Bentham's) affects him with stupidity rather than with selfishness (Dicey, 1926, 14–15).

Thus the possession of power may be influential apart from its coercive base. It affects the policies of others (by entering into their considerations) without coming to a showdown—that is, without the actual exercise of violence. It is power potential, rather than power position directly, which is crucial in the political process. The players do not always pay to see the winning hand.

DF. A value of a person or group is *considered* in the degree to which realistic considerations of conditions enter into the value practices of the person or group.

Expectations and demands have been defined as realistic (§4.2) in terms of their correspondence to the value potentials in the situation. A value is considered, therefore, when conditions are so taken into account as to lead to perspectives conforming to the possibilities actually available. Thus two types of value practices are excluded: those in which, in Dewey's terms, the value is prized without being appraised; and those in which, though the value is not merely an end but an end-in-view, the considerations are unrealistic. In the former case, the value is unconsidered in that no thought has been taken; in the latter case, the process of deliberation was uncontrolled by the actual data.

In the political process, power is continually appraised; power considerations continually come to the focus of attention and help determine power policy (especially, by the preceding hypothesis, in the case of power groups). But power is not always a considered value: the considerations brought forward are often unrealistic. A number of factors may be mentioned as contributing to this lack of realism.

First and foremost are the obstacles to social inquiry provided by the subject matter itself: the data are difficult to gather and often impossible to assess. A vast literature has been devoted to this point; it need not be enlarged on here.[7]

The intensity of the interests operative has an adverse effect on realism with regard to power facts. Where power is a value at all, it is likely to be an intense value; the consequent stress toward action interferes with warranted appraisals of the conditions. W. W. Willoughby (1911, viii) cites in this connection Hobbes's observation that the axioms of geometry would be disputed if they were objects of intense interest, "and if this be so," he concludes, "it cannot be a matter for surprise that the domain of political speculation should abound with varieties of opinions."

Moreover, politically important interests are usually sentimentalized. This structure of sentiment constitutes a more or less rigid predisposition largely determinative of the response to conditions. The policy arrived at is likely to be the most emotionally satisfying rather than the most realistic (for example, Hitler's order to hold at Stalingrad, contrary to a realistic appraisal of the military situation). Where the predisposition is intense and highly sentimentalized, the structure of sentiment is more likely to be replaced as a whole than modified piecemeal into realistic adaptation to conditions. If such a substitute structure is not readily available (for example, in a well propagandized utopia), unrealistic considerations are likely to be persisted in to the point of complete breakdown. Mosca says (1939, 175):

> A system of illusions [as he calls it] is not easily discredited until it can be replaced with a new system. When that is not possible, not even a sequence of sufferings, of terrible trials born of experience more terrible still, is enough to disenchant a people.[8]

Of particular importance is the effect of political symbols on the realism of power considerations. Monopolistic propa-

7. Jerome Frank's *Fate and Freedom* (Simon & Schuster, 1945) is a recent compendium of the difficulties of arriving at generalizations concerning social affairs which would make prediction possible.

8. On the effect of sentiment on power considerations see, in particular, Lasswell, 1930, 184–5 and throughout; and 1948.

ganda can effectively distort, conceal, and fabricate data concerning the power conditions.[9] The formalistic symbols of the political myth may obscure the facts of effective power. Such factors, as was pointed out in §6.1, are of less consequence for the considerations of power holders than for the considerations of those subject to power. On the latter their effect is considerable.

People always have been and they always will be stupid victims of deceit and self-deception in politics, until they learn behind every kind of moral, religious, political, social phrase, declaration and promise to seek out the interests of this or that class or classes.[10]

The formulation solely in terms of class interest is an unwarranted restriction; when generalized to apply to any groups with power interests, there is no doubt of the importance of this factor in interfering with realistic political considerations.

There are a number of factors, finally, resulting directly from the power situation. Thus power holders may limit access to the power facts. Again, relative power position distorts appraisal of conditions in characteristic ways. Tawney (1931, 230) has observed that "the strong are rarely as powerful as they are thought by the weak, or the weak as powerless as they are thought by themselves." Other features of the power situation may especially encourage excessive optimism or pessimism, as formulated in the hypothesis in §6.1. And so on. All these difficulties in the way of realistic power considerations add importance to the function of providing intelligence for policy makers.

DF. *Social planning* is the projection of considered decisions; *group planning*, of considered policy.

To plan is to formulate a pattern of value practices resulting from a realistic consideration of the conditions relevant to

9. The qualification "monopolistic" is important. It is unwarranted to assume that the circulation of much propaganda necessarily promotes error and confusion. Much depends on the content of the propaganda, and particularly on whether conflicting propagandas have equal access to the focus of attention. Compare Russell, 1938, 226: "Any useful purpose which is to be served by propaganda must be not that of causing an almost-certainly erroneous opinion to be dogmatically believed, but, on the contrary, that of promoting judgment, rational doubt, and the power of weighing opposing considerations; and this purpose it can only serve if there is competition among propagandas."

10. Lenin, *The Three Soures and Three Constituent Parts of Marxism*, 1913.

those practices.[11] We distinguish between social and group planning according to whether or not the plan is enforced by severe sanctions. Planning alone does not entail coercion: it may be voluntary. (It is therefore misleading to assert that liberalism *ipso facto* excludes planning.)

Planning becomes important wherever potential values remain unrealized (low degree of actualization), or where the practices in question are no longer integrated with one another. Thought must be taken, in other words, when action no longer proceeds smoothly to consummation of the goal values. (The familiar objection that taking thought interferes with action depends on a specific relation of planning to the process of decision making, and not to planning as such; there may be planning by fiat as well as discussion.)

DF. A *rational value practice* is one which is rationalized and planned.

That a value practice is rationalized (§4.4) involves two requirements: that the practice is economical with respect to all the values in the situation; and that it has been technicalized, that is, freed from sanctions unrelated to conditions.[12] We add, for the concept of rational conduct, that these results accrue, not adventitiously, but as a consequence of a process of taking thought. The concept coincides, therefore, with that developed by John Dewey in various writings:

> The difference between reasonable and unreasonable desires and interests is precisely the difference between those which arise casually and are not reconstituted through consideration of the conditions that will actually decide the outcome, and those which are formed on the basis of existing liabilities and potential resources.[13]

11. For a general discussion of planning, with an extensive bibliography, see Mannheim's *Man and Society in an Age of Reconstruction,* Harcourt, Brace, 1940.

12. On this application of the concept of the economical, compare Plutarch's remark in his life of Crassus: "Economy, which in things inanimate is but money-making, when exercised over men becomes policy."

13. It may be remarked that pragmatism is often misunderstood as being committed to the view that rationality of conduct may be brought about solely through the rigorous application of intelligence. This is a sheer mistake. Rationality consists in the use and implementation of intelligence, but whether or not this implementation occurs depends on the total personality structure (and in the case of a group, on the social structure as well). There is no commitment here to positions such as Laski's (1925, 114) that "in the long run power belongs to those who can formulate and grasp ideas."

An important derivative of the idea of rational power practices is the concept of *preventive politics*. Power practices have failed to maximize values when they have been directed solely toward the resolution, rather than prevention, of conflict situations. The problem of politics is conceived as that of coping with differences already sharply drawn. "But the problem of politics may be less to solve conflicts than to prevent them; less to serve as a safety valve for social protest than to apply social energy to the abolition of recurrent sources of strain in society." [14]

DF. Power is *self-conditioned* in the degree to which the conditions of its exercise result from practices of the self.

The concept has reference to the effect on power position of demands for power, and striving to satisfy the demands. Acquisition of power by a group may result from intense and well-organized activity, or bear little relation to the effort expended for its acquisition. The dominance of the Democratic party in the South today represents a low degree of self-conditioning; political power exercised, say, by a revolutionary party, a high degree.

Whether or not power which is not self-conditioned is stable depends on the situation of the self in question. A group may enjoy power with a low degree of self-conditioning either because power was obtained for it by some other group, or because power was easily obtainable with minimal striving. In the former case, its power position tends to be unstable, but not in the latter case. Power obtained by the cooperation of allied groups is unstable because with the development of internal power conflicts, conditions for the maintenance of power may no longer obtain. But where there is little self-conditioning because of the absence or weakness of *both* allies and rivals for power position, there is no necessity for continued striving to maintain the position.

14. Lasswell, 1930, 196 ff. The idea was a familiar one to the philosophy of the Enlightenment, but was subsequently neglected. Typical is the remark of Holbach in his *Système de la nature,* chap. viii: "Politics ought to be the art of regulating the passions of man, of directing them to the welfare of society, of directing them into a general current of happiness, of making them flow gently to the general benefit of all." The development of dynamic psychology has given new impetus to this conception, not on the optimistic basis of eighteenth-century rationalism, but in terms of a deeper understanding of human motivation.

§7.2 *Leaders and Bosses*

DF. The *leaders* of a group are its most active power holders, effectively and in the perspectives of the group. The *rank and file* are the nonleaders.

Leadership as here defined thus has reference to both formal and effective power. The leader exercises power, and that he does so accords with the identifications, demands, and expectations of the group. Where the latter are present but little effective power is actually exercised, we speak of formalistic authority and not leadership. In the converse case, where effective power has not been formalized by the perspectives of authority, we speak of *bosses*.

The differentiation between leaders and rank and file depends on personal characteristics as well as on the structure of interpersonal relationships. The qualities of leadership have been a subject of continued political interest since Plato's elaborate specification in the *Republic*. Emphasis has been put not only (as in Plato) on character and habit to be acquired by training, but also (as in Aristotle) on so-called natural endowments. "For that some should rule, and others be ruled," says Aristotle (*Politics*, I, 5), "is a thing not only necessary, but expedient; from the hour of their birth, some are marked out for subjection, others for rule." Whether by nature or nurture, there do exist differences among persons in their capacity for leadership.

In recent times, these differences have been given a racist formulation, and also made the ground of objection to the possibility of democratic political processes. But the existence of individual differences does not in itself provide the slightest warrant for generalizations about groups. Nor do differences in political aptitudes exclude a democratic recruitment of power holders: the group as a whole might share in the process of selecting those especially capable. And the differences in aptitude need not manifest themselves in the formation of closed castes: the degree of participation in decision making might correspond to the level of political aptitude, rather than be distributed on an all or none basis.[15] Calling attention to individual dif-

15. For a statement of the position being criticized see, for instance, Carl Murchison, *Social Psychology: the Psychology of Political Domination,* Clark University Press, 1929. An analysis of the democratic power process will be given in §9.4.

ferences in political aptitude, far from strengthening inequalities in distribution of power and other values, may in fact be implemented to lessen such inequalities, both among groups and within them.

The leader, then, has personal characteristics which differentiate him from the rank and file and which enter into their considerations as conditions of his leadership.[16] Among these qualities of leadership Michels mentions: "force of will," wide extent of knowledge, strength of conviction, self-sufficiency, and perhaps also moral qualities which "reawaken religious sentiments." Other writers call attention to similar personality traits; Machiavelli's *virtu*, for example, comprises such characteristics as courage, conviction, pride, and strength; similarly with the concept of the "hero" as developed in nineteenth-century thought; and so on. Needless to say, not all these qualities are to be found in all leaders, nor in equal degrees. The distinguishing trait of the political personality type, common to all leaders, is an emphatic demand for deference—chiefly in the forms of power and respect, and to lesser degrees of rectitude and affection. The leader, as personality type, is preeminently a politician: his conduct is directed by considerations of the acquisition and enjoyment of deference.

Within this general type various subtypes may be discriminated. The leader may be an *agitator* or *administrator*. He may place a high value on the sentimentalized response of the rank and file at large, or be more closely bound to particular individuals, concerned with coordinating the practices of the members of his immediate environment. He may rely upon the efficacy of symbols—formula and gesture, slogan and polemic—in transforming interpersonal relations, or place a corresponding emphasis on operations and organizational structures. And coordinate with these differences in identification and expectation may be differences in demand as well, the agitator orienting demands around remote and abstract goals,

16. On the role of such characteristics for leadership in primitive societies see, for example, Landtman's *Origin of the Inequality of the Social Classes*, University of Chicago Press, 1938, 318 and throughout: "The personal factor is of great importance not only in influencing a man's rise to chieftainship, but also in the maintenance of his power. There is abundance of statements expressing in varying terms that 'a chief's tenure of authority depends upon his ability to maintain it,' or that 'his influence is derived rather from his personal character than from any constitutional rule,' etc." On the general problem see especially Michels (1915), Lasswell (1930), and Weber (1925).

the administrator around the more immediate and concrete.

Other subtypes may be discriminated by focusing attention on the relations between leader and rank and file, rather than on the leader himself. For example, a suggestive distinction has been made between three types of leaders called "crowd compellers," "crowd exponents," and "crowd representatives." [17] The first, men of the type of Alexander and Napoleon, are described as "men who can conceive a great idea, mould a crowd big enough to carry it into effect and force the crowd to do it." The crowd exponents are those whose special skills lie in being able "to render articulate what is only vaguely or dimly felt or thought by the mass." The crowd representatives are leaders "who only express the known and settled opinion of the crowd."

However analyzed and discriminated, leadership exhibits the basic characteristics of a deference relationship. Power is being exercised: the dominance of the leader is not purely formal but effective, among the rank and file, at least, if not outside the group. The leader is respected: in part because of his personal qualities, in part because of the possession of power itself, he enjoys prestige. He is accorded rectitude, and, in varying degrees, affection: his power is not naked but appears in the group perspectives as right and proper.

PROP. Acquisition and maintenance of leadership is a function of the prestige of the leaders.

The hypothesis makes explicit the role of deference values other than power in the relationship between leader and rank and file. The leader is not only powerful but respected as well. Thus leaders are likely to be recruited from among the select within the group. The composition of the select varies, of course, with both conditions and considerations. Qualities and skills respected by some groups in some situations may be visited with contempt by other groups or in other situations. "In times of difficulty," Machiavelli observes (*Discourses*, III, 6), "men of merit are sought after, but in easy times it is not men of merit, but such as have riches and powerful relations, that are most in favor." The difference in the respect enjoyed by the military —and hence their likelihood to acquire leadership—in time of

17. M. Conway, *The Crowd in Peace and War,* Longmans, Green, 1915. See the discussion in M. Ginsberg's *The Psychology of Society,* E. P. Dutton, 1921, 156–7.

peace and of war is a striking example of the effect of conditions. Differences in considerations are illustrated in the transition from the feudal to the capitalist social structure by the changing respect status of, and recruitment of leadership from, commercial occupations.

Regardless of antecedent prestige, the leader enjoys respect as a direct consequence of his power position. Prestige accrues to leadership as such. Not only is the power of the leader "respected," the leader is himself respected for having it.[18] The appurtenances of leadership, the symbols and gestures appropriate to its exercise, contribute to this effect. Even "divinity" of a sort may be attributed to the leader by the rank and file. "The belief is frequent among the people," says Michels (1915, 63–4), "that their leaders belong to a higher order of humanity than themselves." It is of interest that even groups with prominent equalitarian demands exalt the leader in this way. "The phenomenon," Michels continues, "is, in fact, conspicuous in the history of the socialist parties during the last fifty years."

Thus maintenance of prestige is an important consideration for the leadership. If a prince must choose between incurring the hatred or contempt of his subjects, Machiavelli advises him to guard against contempt. For hatred is a threat to the leadership only if there is power to make it effective; but contempt in itself undermines leadership, which can thereafter be maintained only in the form of naked power. Such considerations are an important determinant of policy, giving rise to a principle which has been designated "the policy of prestige":

Having once commanded something, the rulers insist on the performance of the orders even though they may realize the command

18. As was already pointed out, however, there are cultures, like the Zuni, where assertiveness is frowned upon. "A man who thirsts for power or knowledge, who wishes to be as they scornfully phrase it 'a leader of his people,' receives nothing but censure . . ." (cited in Benedict, *Patterns of Culture,* Houghton Mifflin, 1934, 90). In our own culture, the history of the English Parliament also provides instances where office-holding was not particularly esteemed (compare also serving on selective service or rationing boards). In short, the hunger for power is not always dominant in all persons, groups, or cultures (on the general point see Margaret Mead, *Cooperation and Competition Among Primitive Peoples,* McGraw-Hill, 1937). In all such cases some measure of prestige may be conferred as a compensation for assuming the burdens which the exercise of power may involve.

was inexpedient. The nonperformance of B would cause decreasing obedience on the part of A, and thus would threaten the very existence of the power relationship; therefore rulers strive to prevent any case of disobedience.[19]

Prestige must be maintained at whatever cost in expediency.

PROP. The rank and file identifies with the leader and adopts his perspectives.

In an earlier section the hypothesis was formulated that there is a tendency to identify with those with whom the self cooperates. Identification is likely to occur also with those to whom prestige is accorded: the respected tend to be incorporated into the self. These tendencies are especially marked in the relations between the rank and file and their leader. Michels has called attention to the frequency with which political parties identify themselves with their leaders to the extent even of adopting the leaders' names. (The same may be noted with regard to the world's great religions.)

Certain features of the leadership relation itself contribute to the tendency toward identification resulting from the leader's prestige and from cooperation with him. The leader acts as representative of the group, and other groups and leaders react to him in that perspective. Symbols of identification make the relationship explicit. The leader acts in the name of the group: the group sees in him what Michels describes as "a magnified image of their own ego." The identification is thereby sentimentalized: the group is loyal to the leader. Thus leadership may be concisely characterized as the exercise of power with respect and loyalty from the domain.

As a result of the identification the perspectives of the leader permeate the rank and file. His demands and expectations, faiths and interests, are not so much "his" as "ours." Independently of this linkage by identification, the prestige of the leader adds weight to his opinions within the group. The leader is regarded as capable and informed, and these values are transferred by the group to his perspectives. Moreover, the leader's favorable power position enables him to impose his perspectives on the group by various forms of indoctrination.[20]

19. Timasheff, 1939, 184. Compare also Machiavelli, *Discourses*, I, 45: "There can be no worse example in a republic than to make a law and not to observe it; the more so when it is disregarded by the very parties who made it."

20. In the case of leaders of the type of "crowd exponents" and especially

PROP. Circulation of the leadership is less than that of the rank and file.

The hypothesis is twofold: members of the leadership are more likely to remain within the group than are members of the rank and file; and changes in the leadership occur less frequently than in the rest of the group. The first and weaker proposition results not only from the greater intensity of adherence to group perspectives likely to characterize leaders, but also from the fact that the leaders have more at stake in membership than do the rank and file—the prerogatives of leadership, and the potentiality of regaining leadership if it has been lost. (Exceptions may occur among groups of low accommodation, where loss of leadership is likely to imply loss of membership as well.)

The second proposition is the more important. Michels formulates it (1915, 79): "The leaders, when compared with the masses, whose composition varies from moment to moment, constitute a more stable and more constant element of the organized membership." A number of factors contributing to this stability are specified by Michels (1915, 98). For one thing,

> leadership is indefinitely retained . . . simply because it is already constituted. It is through gregarious idleness, or, if we may employ the euphuism, it is in virtue of the law of inertia, that the leaders are so often confirmed in their office as long as they like.

A second factor is constituted by the leadership's possession of power, which is implemented for the preservation of their position. The leaders may direct the procedures of nomination and election; control the channels of propaganda; engender or perpetuate crises in which their services are valuable to the group; and manipulate indulgences of the membership so as to maximize loyalty to the leadership.

A third factor making for stability of leadership is formulated in the following hypothesis.

PROP. The circulation of a leadership varies inversely with the disparity between its skills and those of the rank and file.

This is one of Michels' basic theses, elaborated throughout his study of *Political Parties:* "the leader's principal source

"crowd representatives," perspectives of leader and rank and file coincide as the result of a converse process of influence. It is the leader who adopts the perspectives of the rank and file; this choice of perspectives is in such cases a condition of leadership.

of power is found in his indispensability." Every organization rests on a division of labor, and hence specialization. And to the degree that distinctive skills are involved the specialist becomes indispensable. The leader is such a specialist.

> The leaders cannot be replaced at a moment's notice, since all the other members of the party [or other group] are absorbed in their everyday occupations and are strangers to the bureaucratic mechanism. This special competence, this expert knowledge, which the leader acquires in matters inaccessible, or almost inaccessible to the mass, gives him a security of tenure . . . (1915, 84).

What is fundamental is that the possession of certain values is a requisite of leadership, and that these values are nontransferable. (Leadership resting on a transferable value could be replaced by effecting the transfer.) Skill is the most striking of the nontransferable values; but there are others as well. Thus prestige is an important requisite of leadership not readily transferable. Hence stability of leadership will also vary with the disparity in the respect accorded the leaders and the rank and file. And the same will be true with regard to personal characteristics (for instance, prowess) on which leadership in a given case might be based.

As a consequence, the major threat to the leadership is provided, not by the rank and file itself, but by potential rivals for leadership with the requisite skills and other qualities.

> Whenever the power of the leaders is seriously threatened, it is in most cases because a new leader or a new group of leaders is on the point of becoming dominant, and is inculcating views opposed to those of the old rulers of the party. . . . It is not the masses which have devoured the leaders: the chiefs have devoured one another with the aid of the masses (1915, 164–5).

As a further consequence of the skill conditions, a leadership is rarely completely replaced by its rivals. In criticism of Pareto's "theory of the circulation of elites" Michels points out that "in most cases there is not a simple replacement of one group of élites by another, but a continuous process of intermixture, the old elements incessantly attracting, absorbing, and assimilating the new" (1915, 378). The rival leaderships are indispensable to one another as well as to the group. The new leadership cannot dispense altogether with the skills and experience of the old, nor can the old better maintain its favorable power position than by extending to rivals a restricted share in their own power. Hence

> very rarely does the struggle between the old leaders and the new end in the complete defeat of the former. The result of the process is not so much a "circulation des élites" as a "reunion des élites," an amalgam, that is to say, of the two elements (1915, 177).

Throughout even the most revolutionary changes a stable administration core remains, which is the more prominent the more specialized are the skills it possesses.

DF. A *boss* is an informal holder of effective power.

The power of the boss is not authoritative—though it is not necessarily contrary to authority. It may be compatible with, though not specified by, the political formula. But there are not, as in the case of the leader, group perspectives legitimizing and justifying his power position. There may be no respect or loyalty from his domain, and minimal identification with him. The power of the boss is often covert—that is, he may not appear as a power holder at all in the perspectives of a large part of the group. Where his exercise of power is overt, it is by definition naked power. But the element of coercion often takes the form of inducements rather than constraints: indulgence for submitting to his power often plays a more prominent part than deprivations for refusing to submit.

Various types of bosses may be distinguished in terms of the base value of their power. Designations are given in the following table.

TABLE 4

Informal Power

Base Value	*Type of Boss*
Power	Political Boss
Respect	Patriarch
Rectitude	The-arch
Affection	Favorite
Well-Being	Gangster
Wealth	Patron
Skill	Master
Enlightenment	Pundit

Most familiar, perhaps, is the boss whose position is based on power itself—the *political boss*. Other types of power holders are comprised under the concept, however, than the party or machine boss. The tyrant and usurper are also political bosses in the present sense in the degree that their power is not formalized and legitimized in the perspectives of their domain. They lack the respect and loyalty essential to leadership as here defined.

The *patriarch* exercises informal power based on his respect position. He is exemplified by the "elder statesman," a former leader, perhaps, no longer occupying a formal power position but still carrying weight in the process of decision making.

The *the-arch* in a similar way exercises power based on a high position with respect to moral values. The spiritual guide or father-confessor of the ruler is a boss of this type. Rasputin is perhaps the most familiar example.

The informal exercise of power based on affection yields a type of boss most conveniently designated a *favorite*. The king's mistress, for example, may participate to a considerable degree in the process of decision making, her power being nevertheless completely nonformal.

The *gangster* is the boss whose power is based directly on control over instruments of violence. The terrorist, bully, and war lord exemplify this form of nonauthoritative power. Such power is ordinarily naked, but it may also be exercised covertly. There is no identification; prestige accrues only in terms of the weight and scope of the violence.

We use the term *patron* to designate an informal power holder whose power is based on wealth. An important contributor to campaign funds, the financial backer of a revolutionary movement, the board of directors of a corporation in a "company town"—these are patrons in the present sense. Here power is more often covert; and though again identification is minimal, a boss of this type may enjoy considerable prestige.

The *master* is a boss whose power is based on special skills. These skills may be military, as in the case of Caesar and Napoleon, who were, in the early stages of their careers, bosses in this sense. The boss may owe his power to skills in the manipulation of symbols—the propagandist whose power is informal but of great weight, for example. Or they may be skills in negotiation—the "fixer." And so on.

A boss whose informal power is based on enlightenment is often termed a *pundit*. (Of course we use the term in a purely descriptive, nonnormative sense.) The ideologues and special advisers to the leadership exemplify this type. Though not themselves leaders, they may exercise power of great weight. The "brain trust" is a recent designation for this old and important type of informal power.

§7.3 *Representation*

DF. ***Responsibility*** is the formal commitment to practices in behalf of specified interests. The practices in question are the ***scope of responsibility***, and the standards to which they are to conform, the ***code of responsibility***.

Responsibility is a commitment—the projection of a course of action with the expectation of sanctions to be applied if that course is not followed. It is, moreover, a formal commitment, and the sanctions are formally applied. To accept responsibility is to submit to authority. Hence responsibility is always, ultimately, assumed rather than (merely) assigned. There is no authority, and therefore no responsibility, without consent. (Once responsibility has been accepted, however, release from it depends on the code of responsibility, not on the perspectives of the responsible.) The assigning of responsibility without consent is simply naked power; responsibility must be assumed in a situation of choice, not coercion.

Scope is involved in responsibility as in other power relations. In general, every relation of responsibility pertains only to certain practices and not others. A greater or lesser zone of privacy may be excluded from responsibility in the present sense. Various commitments may be made simultaneously, each with a different scope; and the corresponding practices may be integrated, congruous, or even in conflict.

The code of responsibility defines the fulfillment of the commitments made, and specifies the applicable sanctions. But like the political formula, this code need not be fully explicit and precise. Some degree of latitude is ordinarily connoted by the term "responsibility": the code may set limits to the practices, but within these limits might not specify the practices in complete detail. Responsibility confers a greater or lesser amount of discretion.

Responsibility as here defined may be applied to other interpersonal relations and values than those of power. In moral responsibility, for example, authority is internalized; the code of responsibility is part of the moral code; and the sanctions applied are deprivations and indulgences of such values as rectitude and respect.

PROP. Assumption of responsibility is accompanied by acquisition of privileges.

Privileges serve as compensating indulgences for the risk of deprivations entailed by the acceptance of responsibility. It is chiefly in this way that privileges function as expediency interests for the group: participation is inseparable from acceptance of responsibility, which must be compensated for if loyalty and solidarity are to be maintained. Thus, that every duty carries with it rights is not a logical truth but an empirical proposition, grounded in the conditions of group survival. (Indeed, it may not hold under special circumstances—slaves, for example, may have duties without corresponding rights.)

DF. The *agent* is the person or group responsible; the *principal*, those to whom he is responsible—those formulating and/or enforcing the code of responsibility.

We do not define the principal as the person or group the satisfaction of whose interests constitutes the scope of responsibility (and thus avoid the ambiguity of the phrase "acting on behalf of"). The king's minister may be committed to promoting the welfare of the king's subjects, as well as the king's, and yet be responsible only to the king, not the subjects. An elected representative is responsible to his constituency, but may be committed to promoting a more general, or more special, interest.

The principal is here defined by two functions: judging conformity of the agent's practices to the code of responsibility, and applying sanctions for nonconformity. The two functions may be exercised by the same or distinct authority structures. We may speak accordingly of the *judicial* and the *ministerial principal*. The agent is sometimes said to be responsible to the one, sometimes to the other; both are of course involved. Thus a cabinet may be said to be responsible to the legislature in being subject to its vote of confidence; and to the king in submitting its resignation to him. Where as single authority structure exercises both functions, we may refer to it as the *exclusive principal.*

PROP. Agents tend to identify with their principals.

The authority which shapes practices into conformity with the code of responsibility becomes internalized: it is incorporated into the self of the agent. The process is especially familiar in the child-parent relationship. The child becomes a "responsible" adult in the degree that the functions of externalized authority are taken over by the self. The identification here made constitutes the predispositional basis for later internalizations of authority; in the same way it may create predispositions for rebellion against authority.

Other factors may support or interfere with this predisposition. For example, an agent is more likely to identify with his principal the more prestige the principal enjoys. On the other hand, if a particular person is an agent for several different principals, the tendency to identify with any one of them is minimized. Again, the tendency to identification will vary with the degree of integration of the code of responsibility with the perspectives of the agent. Where the practices to which the agent is committed appear in his perspectives as, say, immoral, the authority enforcing responsibility is very largely externalized. And so on.

DF. *Primary power* is the power of a principal; *agency* (assigned power), of an agent. *Authorization* is the transfer of primary power to an agent.

Power is not always exercised directly by the power holder, but often by someone else made responsible for its exercise. An agent is authorized to exercise some or all of the primary power. This occurs normally as part of the division of labor in a power group: the primary power of the group may be exercised by a leader responsible to the group, or distributed in a hierarchy or other power structures. But the converse process of transfer may also occur: the primary power of an individual may be distributed among a group, often organized for that purpose. Authorization of agency does not *necessarily* result either in concentration or in dispersion of power: the resultant power pattern may have a higher *or* lower distribution index than that of primary power.

The doctrine of the social contract construed agency sometimes as a mechanism of concentration only (Hobbes), sometimes as a mechanism of dispersion only (Rousseau). In Hobbes, all give power to one; in Rousseau, each gives power to all. Both of these propositions, taken as allegations of fact, are false. There is no warrant for the assumption that the exercise of power by an individual or small group was always and everywhere preceded—or always and everywhere followed—by its exercise by the larger group constituting the domain of the power in question. Of course, this criticism has no bearing on the contract theory interpreted, as was originally intended, not as political science but as political doctrine. As such, it is concerned with the formal basis of power, not its real basis. And whether or not power rests formally on its authorization by its domain depends by definition on the political doctrine adhered to by the domain.

But the fact that authority is constituted by adherence to a political doctrine does not mean that power exercised under that doctrine is always agency authorized by its domain. The authority of the monarch—like all authority—is in fact constituted by the perspectives of his subjects. But he may appear in those very perspectives as a primary power holder, not an agent; or if an agent, an "agent of the Divine," not of his subjects. Agency, in short, is not identical with authority but is one form of it, depending for its power on a preexistent authority.

Authorization of agency is by *devolution* if the scope of the agent's power coincides with that of the principal except where specifically limited; and by *enumeration* if the scope comprises only what is specifically included therein by the authorization. Of course the scope of agency cannot exceed that of the primary power, and usually falls short of the latter; the same is true of the weight of primary and authorized power. But it is to be noted that power can increase its scope and weight by its own exercise: the agent may make use of his power position to replace his principal altogether.[21]

21. Hence in a chapter on conspiracy Machiavelli (*Discourses,* III, 6) warns the Prince against bestowing too much authority on his friends.

DF. *Representation* is agency formally exercised in the interest of the principal. A *constituency* is the principal of a representative.

A representative is thus an agent formally committed to the exercise of his power so as to satisfy the interests of his principal. (These may be either assumed or valid interests, according to the code of responsibility to which his agency must conform.) Not all agents are representatives: the criterion is whose interests the assigned power is formally to serve. The minister may be the king's agent, but he does not represent the king (in the present sense) except insofar as he formally serves the interests of the king himself, not the kingdom. Similarly, a military officer may be an agent of the commander-in-chief, but does not necessarily represent him.[22]

Since representation is a formal category, the degree of control exercised by the constituency over the representative is important. We may distinguish between *formal* and *effective representation*, and correspondingly between the *formal* and *effective constituency*. A representative may in fact be serving other interests than those of his constituency: not all representation is effective. The degree to which representation, like other political forms, coincides with patterns of effective control must be empirically determined. A government may be representative and in fact subserve the interests of special groups much narrower than those formally represented. To what degree this is true, and what groups constitute the effective constituency of the representative government must be determined by an investigation of the social structure, not the regime alone.[23]

22. The difference between agency and representation is clearly manifested in the concept of *trustee*. A trustee is an agent of X acting as the representative of Y.

23. The minimizing of this problem (if it is not to be dismissed as shrewd polemicizing) is one of the rare instances in the *Federalist*, of naïveté and shortsightedness. The discussion of the matter in No. XXXV, is summed up as follows: "It is said to be necessary, that all classes of citizens should have some of their own number in the representative body, in order that their feelings and interests may be the better understood and attended to. But we have seen that this will never happen under any arrangement that leaves the votes of the people free. Where this is the case, the representative body, with too few exceptions to have any influence on the spirit of the government, will be composed of landholders, merchants, and men of the learned professions. But where is the danger that the interests and feelings of the different classes of citizens will not be understood or attended to by these three descriptions of men?" It

PROP. Representation functions to stabilize the power structure.

Representation stabilizes power structure by providing a mean between the extremes of concentration and dispersion of power. The impracticability of the exercise of power distributed throughout a large domain is a familiar consideration. Equally important is the inexpediency of a concentration of power which cannot easily take account of the diverse and conflicting interests characterizing the domain. Representation of these interests serves to minimize threats to the power structure arising from a failure to fulfill intense and widespread demands and expectations. "Parliaments and parliamentarians," Friedrich points out (1937, 362), "appear as integrating agencies through which the plans of the central bureaucracy and the claims of the various interest groups are expounded to the larger public with a view to discovering a suitable balance."

The formalistic character of representation may also serve to stabilize the power structure of which it is a part. It does this in two ways. Positively, the forms of representation strengthen the bonds of interest, faith, and loyalty by which the power structure is sustained. The domain is indulgent to the power holders because the latter appear in their perspectives as part of, and acting in behalf of, the self.[24] Negatively, representation interferes with opposition to the power structure by dispersing responsibility. Animosity may be directed against some representatives among many rather than on the system of representation, or on the persons of the representatives as a whole rather than on the power structure. But authority is most forcibly challenged when it is concentrated. Its distribution makes possible the defense of the authority structure (and with it the structure of effective power) by localizing opposition, and, if necessary, satisfying the limited demands.

---

is of further interest that the problem of securing effective representation is discussed here in functional terms, though the constitution being defended provides only for territorial representation.

24. The point is not a discovery of the Marxists, though they have especially emphasized the formalistic character of representation. In his *German Philosophy and Politics* (Henry Holt, 1915, 117) Dewey calls attention to Hegel's thesis that "the chief function of parliament is to give the opinion of the social classes an opportunity to feel it is being considered. . . ."

DF. A *deputy* is a representative with a generalized code of responsibility (exercises maximal discretion); a *delegate* with a specialized code (minimal discretion).

A representative may be committed to a course of action specified in considerable detail, or left free to act within wide limits on behalf of his constituency. We distinguish on this basis between deputies and delegates. In particular, the deputy may attempt to discern and satisfy valid interests, while the delegate is restricted to the assumed interests of his constituency. "Your representative [deputy] owes you," Edmund Burke once declared, "not his industry only, but his judgment; and he betrays instead of serving you if he sacrifices it to your opinion." This concern with valid rather than assumed interests is often taken as the distinguishing mark of statesmanship. "The politician says, 'I will give you what you want.' The statesman say, 'What you think you want is this. What it is possible for you to get is that. What you really want, therefore, is the following.' "[25]

On the other hand, the generalized code of responsibility adds to the hazards of effective representation. The delegate at least acts in accord with the demands and expectations of his constituency, even though the latter may be mistaken as to its own best interests. The deputy, in his concern for valid interests, may be acting so often in opposition to the perspectives of his constituency that representation has ceased to be effective.[26]

DF. A *vote* is a unit expression of support or opposition to a proposed decision.

Voting as here defined is neither an operation only nor a merely formal act. The perspectives associated with the opera-

25. Walter Lippmann, *Preface to Morals*, Macmillan, 1929, 279–83.

26. Further objections to generalized representation have been formulated in terms of the absence of correspondingly general skills and enlightenment. "In proportion as the purposes for which the representative is chosen lose clarity and definiteness, representation passes into misrepresentation and the representative character of the acts resulting from association disappears. . . . It is chosen to deal with anything that may turn up quite irrespective of the fact that the different things that do turn up require different types of persons to deal with them. It is therefore peculiarly subject to corrupt, and especially to plutocratic influences and does everything badly because it is not chosen to do anything well" (G. D. H. Cole, *Social Theory*, Frederick A. Stokes, 1920, 108). See also the discussion in Ginsberg's *Psychology of Society*, E. P. Dutton, 1922, 162.

tion must be such as to make it in fact or symbolically an expression of support or opposition: the marking of a ballot under overt coercion does not constitute a vote. On the other hand, the vote is not limited to the formal acts set down in the political formula: voting may take place elsewhere than the polls, and in other ways than by a show of hands. The vote is an essential part of the political process regardless of the provisions made for it in the regime.

This general concept of the vote has been elaborated by G. E. G. Catlin (1927, 260–2) in a passage worth quoting at length:

Voting is not some rare and solemn function, but one taking place every day and every hour. Support, measurable as votes, is the condition of the performance of the supreme political act of "getting things done" by establishing a controlling relationship. We pay for the political goods of having custom and law on our side and meeting our demands, by always having behind us adequate support in voices which will favor our demands and uphold our rights and claims. And this wealth of support we earn by toiling to maintain, and submitting to the restrictions of, those conventions which are the political goods pleasing to those upon whose support we desire to count. It would be fantastic to imagine that we could state the voting units of every expression of will. But the study of the vote is very near to the heart of the political relationship. The vote is the money of politics; it provides the best unit of political calculation of what is and what is not feasible. The study of its fluctuations, in whatever place or occasion a vote is taken, is a study of the distribution of power and of the kind of policy to which men are at the moment prepared to submit, and the kind of control which they are willing to support.

DF. An *election* is a coordination of votes both formal and effective; a *plebiscite*, formal only.

By the formal coordination of voting is meant an authoritative specification of the time, place, and manner of voting. The distinction between formal and effective power practices is especially important in the case of voting. The suffrage (formal qualifications of voting) may extend to only part of the constituency; the vote may be coercively controlled; effective decisions may have been made in the selection of candidates independently of the electorate, or prior to the election in question; the issues to be voted on may have a bearing only on formal and not effective power practices.[27] Wherever such conditions obtain we have a plebiscite rather than a genuine election.

§7.4 *Parties and Factions*

DF. A *party* (political) is a group formulating comprehensive issues and submitting candidates in elections.

The term "party" is often used in a very wide sense to refer to any aggregate of persons sharing political perspectives. A party, in this wide use, is "a body of persons determined by a common choice of political convictions, and including all who share such convictions . . ." (Barker, 1942, 175). In this sense a party is indistinguishable from an unorganized and inactive segment of public opinion. On the present definition a party involves organization—it is a group; and it is characterized not merely by its perspectives but by distinctive practices as well. Burke's famous definition makes explicit these conditions: "A party is a body of men united, for promoting by their joint endeavours the national interest, upon some particular principle in which they are all agreed." [28]

The nature of these "joint endeavours" must, however, be further specified. Parties are distinguished from other demand groups in their concern with power—they attempt to exercise control over group decisions. A party, says Friedrich (1937, 297), is a "group of human beings, stably organized for the purpose of securing or maintaining the control of a corporate

27. For example, the Athenian democracy was only formally such in regard to the first condition: only about 3 per cent of the population were citizens with the right to vote. The plebiscites conducted by the Nazi regime are familiar examples of coercive control over voting. On the selection of candidates, for instance in the United States, Ostrogorski (1926, 42) quotes with approval the remark of a senator that the people have no more control over the selection of the man who is to be the president than the subjects of kings have over the birth of the child who is to be their ruler. For a discussion of the fourth condition of effective voting—significance of the issues voted on—see, for example, Beard, 1934, 89 and throughout.

28. *Speech to the Electors of Bristol.* Parties are not necessarily concerned with the national interest, but may be defined with regard to any group—there may be church parties, for example, or parties in local politics. However, the issues must be comprehensive in relation to the group in question. This is one basis for distinguishing parties from pressure groups, which are concerned with single issues and special interests.

body. . . ." And, it must be added, a "body" within which the group in question is already included. A group may exercise power over another without being contained in the other. It may be an *external power group*, exercising power by way of control over the leadership of the subject group, over the rank and file directly, or over some faction within the subject group. A party, on the contrary, is internal to the group over which it seeks power.

The present definition involves still another condition: a party is an internal power group whose status has been formalized—it functions as a part of the regime. There may be other internal power groups whose practices are not sanctioned by the political formula. Some of these groups may seek to affect decisions by the use of violence: private armies, guerrillas, "resistance" movements, revolutionary bands, and so on. We may refer to these generically as *private armies.* Other nonformal groups may affect decisions by means other than violence, for instance by persuasion or inducement. We call these *pressure groups.* Parties are neither pressure groups nor private armies, though they may engage in the corresponding practices in addition to those which characterize them as parties. They secure and exercise power through the formal coordination of votes.[29] (The distinction between private armies, pressure groups, and parties is, of course, a matter of degree.)

Like other groups, parties may have both principled and expediency interests in varying degrees (see §3.2). Formulation of issues—differences in policy—represents principled interests; submission of candidates without distinctive policy represents expediency interests. Of course, parties are usually associated to some degree with specific parts of the social structure. Occupational, religious, racial, and other groups give expression to their interests by means of the party. Interests which are principled for these subgroups may for the party itself be matters of expediency. A well-organized party in

29. Thus a party attempts to acquire power by occupying positions of authority. But these positions are not restricted to those of the established regime. A revolutionary party may seek to create offices as well as occupy them. But it is not a party in the present sense unless it attempts to strengthen its power position through the regime, even if it be for the purpose of overthrowing it. Thus many revolutionary groups loosely called "parties" are in present terms pressure groups and private armies.

which expediency interests are maximal and principled interests minimal is called a *political machine.*[30]

A regime is *uni-*, *bi-*, *pluri-*, or *multi-party* if one, two, a few, or many parties, respectively, are the major participants in elections. Pluri- and multi-party systems are likely to occur where there exist continuing differences within the group about the form which the regime should take—differences giving rise, for example, to monarchist, clericalist, republican, and socialist parties. (As such differencces become intense, private armies tend to emerge.) Where continuing differences concern only matters of policy within the framework of the regime, uni- and bi-party systems are more likely.

Where the regime authorizes only one party to formulate issues and submit candidates, we do not speak of a uniparty system (in which only one party is prominently active though others are authorized), but of a *political order.* "When the state not only regulates parties," Barker observes (1942, 39), "but so regulates them that it abolishes all parties other than the single party of the 'people' or 'nation' or 'proletariat,' it really abrogates the essence of party. . . ." The vote has become purely formal; and although the order may exercise effective power, it does so as the outcome of crisis and conflict, formally ratified by plebiscite, not as a result of the electoral process. The political order is "sectarian" rather than "denominational—it demands exclusive dominance, whereas a party assumes the existence of an opposition. It is likely, too, to exercise power of wider scope, particularly affecting the deference values. (Hence the designation "order": membership is a mark of distinction.)

DF. A *faction* of a decision-making group is a subgroup organized in relation to interests distinct from those of the rest of the group.

A faction is defined in relation to an interest, not a single act (for instance, a decision), so that it may be distinguished from a temporary grouping on some specific issue. Not all who vote in the same way on a particular question necessarily be-

30. Compare Michels, 1915, 376: "The term 'party' presupposes that among the individual components of the party there should exist a harmonious direction of the wills toward identical objectives and practical aims. Where this is lacking the party becomes a mere 'organization.' "

long to the same faction. We may refer to voting in the same way as *concurrence:* agreement in the making of a decision. Every alignment holds in relation only to a determinate scope of power: there is agreement and disagreement only on some kinds of decisions; for others, the pattern may be different. (Thus we can distinguish, for example, between commercial and military alignments.) A faction may be described then as a continuing alignment within a decision-making group: a subgroup concurring in all decisions relating to a specified interest. The interest may concern expediency only—for example, the faction may have been organized simply for the purpose of maintaining or increasing the power of the faction as such. Hence alignments need not always coincide with factional divisions: they will do so only in the degree that the faction interests are principled.

The faction interest is distinct from that of the rest of the group, but is not necessarily—as here defined—in conflict with the latter. In a famous passage the *Federalist* (No. X) defines a faction as a group "united and actuated by some common impulse of passion, or of interest, adverse to the rights of other citizens, or to the permanent and aggregate interests of the community." Factions *may* have this characteristic; but it is convenient to use the term in a more general sense, for any relatively stable subgroup with distinct interests, whether or not these conflict with the general welfare.

Of course, the characteristic interests of different factions within a group are likely to be in conflict *with one another*, for where they are congruous or integrated, circulation among the factions is likely to be high, to the detriment of their stability as factions. Such conflicts, however, are superimposed on basic agreements, since the factions are contained within the same group. (It may happen, however, that the factional interests exceed in intensity participation in the group, in which case secession—"splitting"—occurs.) Whether or not factions within a group interfere with the group interests depends, therefore, on the practices of resolving factional conflicts, and on the specific content of the factional and group interests. No generalizations can be made from the mere existence of diverse factions as here defined. That the interests of a group are best served by exclusion of diverse interests in its subgroups is a gratuitous assumption unless warranted in the specific case by empirical considerations.

Like a party, a faction is distinguished from a pressure group or private army by participating in decision making through formal mechanisms. But it is differentiated from a party, first, by being a subgroup of a decision-making body, and second by its more specialized and limited perspectives, so that factional interests often cut across party lines. The farm bloc in Congress exemplifies both these characteristics of a faction.[31]

The faction (if any) with most weight in the decision-making group is called the *dominant faction*, the others *opposition factions*. In the same way we distinguish between the *party in power* and *opposition parties*. Of course such designations cannot replace a configurational analysis of the actual distribution of power and influence among all the various parties and factions.

DF. A *clique* is an informal, impermeable, and highly personalized demigroup.

A clique is not as well-organized as a party or faction, nor does it like them formally participate in decision making. Again unlike both, access to membership (participation) in the clique is difficult—the members of the clique are in personalized relationship to one another. The clique ordinarily exercises its power conspiratively (behind the scenes), but it may organize a faction of which it then serves as the leadership. In this way, support may be recruited without violating the impermeability of the clique itself; and principled interests may be adopted (or at least avowed) by the faction, while the clique remains concerned chiefly with expediency interests.

31. In American political history, factions were most prominent in the eighteenth century, when decision making was concentrated in a small group, facing relatively few and simple issues. Parties were of maximal importance in the nineteenth century, with the growth of mass participation in at least the formal power process. In the twentieth century, with the proliferation of special interests conflicting with one another and often with the general interest, pressure groups have emerged into prominence.

PART THREE

The purposes served by political practices are the power *functions*, the comparatively stable arrangements by which these are carried out constituting the power *structures*. The power *process* is the pattern of all the political activities carried on in a given period.

VIII

FUNCTIONS

Institutions are integrated patterns of practice. The fundamental functions of political institutions are describable in terms of sovereignty and supremacy, the maxima of formal and effective power.

§8.1 *Sovereignty, State, and Government*

DF. *Sovereignty* is the highest degree of authority.

THE WHOLE notion of sovereignty has been objected to by many writers on the grounds of its formalistic character. Laski (1925, 44–5), for example, has urged:

It would be of lasting benefit to political science if the whole concept of sovereignty were surrendered. That in fact with which we are dealing is power; and what is important in the nature of power is the end it seeks to serve and the ways in which it serves that end. These are both questions of evidence which are related to, but independent of, the rights that are born of legal structure.

But it is precisely this relation of power to the "legal structure" (the regime, the structure of authority) which makes it necessary to invoke such concepts as sovereignty. It is this very concern with the ends and means of power which demands the inclusion of authority into the field of political inquiry. Though we emphasize the difference between formal authority and effective control, we do so not to reduce power to one or the other, but to explicate the roles which both play in the power process. If authority is to be taken into account in political science—and it is a political fact of the first importance—there must be considered as well the characteristics of supreme authority. And it is this that we mean by "sovereignty."

Nevertheless, the inclination to dispense with the term at least, if not the concept, is understandable. "It is safe to say that there exists no other term in political science," Willoughby observes (1911, 185), "regarding whose signification there exists such confusion and contradiction of thought, and in regard to which such an amount of dogmatism has been preached." In particular, the voluminous literature on sovereignty has frequently confused three quite distinct enterprises: (1) An empirical examination of the facts concerning certain features of the political process, on the assumption that the meaning of the term "sovereignty" is clear and distinct. (2) A logical analysis of the concept believed to be always designated by the term—an undertaking confused in turn by the fact that the concept occurs in the discourse of both political science and political philosophy, so that it, as well as its "analysis," sometimes functions descriptively and sometimes normatively. (3) An attempt to specify a clear meaning for the term which will be useful for inquiry into the political process, without regard to its functions in political philosophy. It is this last category to which the present definition is intended to belong.

Frequently the discussion has been formulated in terms of a search for the "locus of sovereignty"—the "ultimate source" of power. Here again there has been confusion as to whether "source" is meant in a genetic sense (whether historically or as a fiction like the social contract); or in the sense of the basis of power—the grounds on which the maintenance and exercise of power rests; or, finally, in the sense of the justification of power—what we have called its formal basis. The present definition deals again with the last alternative.

Further difficulties arise because of unwarranted assumptions concerning characteristics which it is supposed that sovereignty must always and everywhere exhibit, whereas sovereignty is as variable as the structure and basis of authority in general. It cannot even be assumed, for example, that there exists a sovereign for every group. While there is always some form and degree of authority, this may occur in a multiple structure no component of which is superior to the others, and such that even the structure as a whole cannot be said to be superior to each of its components.[1]

1. For examples of such societies see M. Fortes and E. E. Evans-Pritchard, eds., *African Political Systems,* Oxford University Press, 1940. Of their "Group B" societies they say (p. 14): "In the language of political philosophy, there is no individual or group in which sovereignty can be said to rest." It is possible, of course, to speak of the society as a whole as sovereign, but the concept loses its value if taken in this collective sense: political analysis is concerned with the *distribution* of control and authority. (The concept of "popular sovereignty"

Another common assumption concerning sovereignty is its "indivisibility." Willoughby, for example, asserts (1911, 195):

> The logical impossibility of conceiving of a divided sovereignty is apparent from the impossibility of predicating in the same body two powers each supreme. . . . In every political organization there must be one and only one source, whence all authority ultimately springs."

Of course, by invoking such empirically uncontrolled abstractions as "the will of the state" it is possible to ascribe to sovereignty any desired characteristic, especially an abstract unity. Empirically, the "source" of authority is that specified by the political formula—that is, that occurring in the perspectives of those accepting the authority as in fact authoritative. And the formula may specify several "sources," or at any rate, not make an unequivocal and precise specification of only one.[2]

The political forms described as a "system of checks and balances" constitute, in an empirical sense, a divided sovereignty—a concept which is not self-contradictory, but incompatible only with the assumption being discussed. The various "supreme authorities" may each be supreme with regard to different practices—their authority may be of different scope.[3] And where they are not of different scope, the situation is one of conflict, to be sure, but not of logical contradiction. Conflict is as much a feature of the political process as is integration or congruity.

---

is quite different, having reference to the relations between authority and its domain, not to the authority of the people collectively.)

2. Merriam, among others, has called attention to the existence and importance of such ambiguity and vagueness in the political formula: "While at times it may appear that the essence of the power situation is clearness and precision of arrangement and understanding, it is not infrequently found that political relations flow on most smoothly when juristic exactness hibernates, when the question as to the ultimate of authority is not too sharply raised. . . . And why should not political twilight be recognised as a useful reality as well as the sharper rays of high noon?" (1934, 54). This "twilight" zone may play an important part in other areas of interpersonal relations. It is involved to a significant degree, for example, in the pattern of relations which Tönnies calls a "Gemeinschaft": integration in such a pattern presupposes not a precise specification of mutual rights and obligations but, on the contrary, the refusal to make such a specification.

3. The United States Supreme Court, in the very case in which its right to veto Congressional legislation was established—*Marbury* vs. *Madison*—denied to itself jurisdiction over certain matters with regard to which it held that Congress is the supreme authority.

The oppositions of king and baron, church and state, represent facts of a kind that have played an important part in political affairs. Inquiry into such affairs cannot proceed from assumptions which deny the possibility of occurrence of some of the facts to be investigated.

A further common assumption concerning sovereignty is that, within its domain, it is "unlimited," "absolute," or "complete." This assumption, like the others, is an unwarranted universalization, and indeed can scarcely be asserted even of particular instances. Even the highest degree of authority may be limited in its scope, and subject to conditions set by the existence of lesser authorities and external powers.

> If perfect or complete independence be of the essence of sovereign power," Austin declared, "there is not in fact the human power to which it will apply. Every government, let it be ever so powerful, renders occasional obedience to the commands of other governments. And every government defers habitually to the opinions and sentiments of its sovereign subjects.[4]

Thus the definition of sovereignty simply as the highest degree of authority enables us to deal with it on the basis of observable practices and perspectives—those of "habitual obedience" (in terms of Austin's definition of sovereignty) or, more precisely, of habitual *formalized* obedience. But formal does not mean merely verbal; it comprises perspectives affecting conduct to a considerable degree. The empirical inquiry into the sovereignty of a particular group makes use of testimony from the members of the group, but verifies it by observations of externalized responses. Though authority has a normative character, such norms can be empirically described as patterns of perspectives and operations.[5] Consequently, "The sovereignty of the state is in no sense a sanctified metaphysical power; it is simply social pressure exerted through particular channels in support of existing political institutions and delegated agents of authority" (Barnes, 1924, 5).

In these terms particular indices can be specified to determine the persons and groups who are in fact sovereign in a given

4. John Austin, *Lectures on Jurisprudence,* 1867, I, 242.

5. For a more detailed account of the process, see Lasswell, 1939. Kelsen's theory of state (1945), though avoiding normative ambiguity, is nevertheless ambiguous as to the "naturalistic" (descriptive) characteristics of the state, about to be discussed.

political situation. For example, the sovereign has been characterized as the authority who decides the "exceptional" cases. Or, it is the authority which renders a final decision, so that there is no appeal to a higher authority.[6] And so on.

DF. A *state* is a sovereign territorial group.

It is an organized aggregate of persons inhabiting a common territory and containing within itself supreme authority. Everyone having authority over the group is in the group. It is to be emphasized again that only formal power is involved here; control over the state may be—and to some degree always is—exercised by external power groups. Authority also (in certain respects) may be exercised by other states through treaties; international agreements thus qualify sovereignty when external authority is relatively limited in scope, or may even transform a state into a province or some other subordinate political unit when external authority has a relatively large scope.

The concept of the state is a formal one, being defined in terms of sovereignty, hence authority—that is to say, formal power. Thus it is fundamentally the perspectives of the members of the state which constitute statehood.[7] Whenever a certain pattern of identifications, demands, and expectations with regard to power exceeds some selected critical frequency in the group, we may speak of the group as a state. But of course, though the state is defined in terms of formal power, its power is not *only* formalistic, or the perspectives on which its sovereignty rests would be highly unstable and its statehood correspondingly precarious.[8]

6. Carl Schmitt, "Soziologie des Souveränitätsbegriffes und politische Theologie," *Erinnerungsgabe für Max Weber,* 1923, II, 5; and J. K. Bluntschli, 1921, 493.

7. In general, it is the perspectives of the domain of authority, not of persons outside the domain, which is constitutive of the authority. Willoughby makes the point clear in relation to the legality of government (1911, 217): "The terms *de facto* and *de jure,* as applicable to governments, are purely relative. That is to say, their force depends upon the standpoint from which the given government is viewed. When a revolutionary government is termed illegal, it is such only as viewed from the standpoint of that political power from which its adherents have forcibly removed themselves. Viewed, however, from the standpoint of those who favor the establishment of such a political power, it possesses a legal character."

8. "The bonds of words are too weak to bridle men's ambition, avarice, anger, and other passions, without the fear of some coercive power" (Hobbes, *Leviathan,* chap. xiv).

Thus an observer undertaking to talk about the state may choose specific subjective experiences, such as a sense of loyalty to a community, and say that all who have this experience (and/or certain others) under specified conditions make up the state. The concept of the state may be amplified by searching for the external circumstances which precipitate the appearance of the subjective events which are characteristic of stateness . . . (Lasswell, 1930, 241–2).

Among such circumstances, perhaps the most important are those having to do with the use of coercion. The state is frequently defined by its monopoly over the instruments of violence. For example, Jhering defines the state as "the form of a regulated and assured exercise of the compulsory force of society." Lasson defines it as "a community of men which possesses an organized authority as the highest source of all force." Weber writes: "The state exists if the staff of a political union successfully displays the monopoly of a legitimate physical compulsion." Laski states more explicitly:

The state may legitimately be regarded as a method of organizing the public power of coercion so that, in all normal circumstances, the will of the government may prevail. It is the possession of this legal right to resort to coercion which distinguishes the government of the state from the government of all other associations.[9]

What is important here is not that the state exercises coercion, but that only it has the *authority* to do so. Other groups and individuals exercise violence in varying degrees, sometimes approaching that of the state itself. There are hired thugs, gangs, special police, and practices which we have designated generically as those of private armies. But such violence is not authoritative unless specifically commissioned or sanctioned by the state. Korkunov points out (1922, 342–3):

The state supposes always a fixed domination recognized by all. A mere fact of control, an establishment sustained by force alone, a military occupation, for example, over an enemy's territory is no state.

9. R. Jhering, *Der Zweck im Recht*, 1923, I, 307; A. Lasson, *System der Rechtsphilosophie*, J. Guttentag, 1882, 283; Weber, 1925, 19; Laski, 1935, 15.

Because of the superlative value attaching ordinarily to physical safety and well-being, the highest degree of authority may be ascribed to that over violence. The authoritative use of coercion by the state is thus comprised in its definition as a sovereign group.

Textbooks of political science often attempt to specify other differentia of the state. Garner, for example, lists eight differences between the state and other associations.[10] They are, roughly: (1) Membership in the state is compulsory; the citizen can throw off his membership only by expatriation. (2) A man cannot ordinarily be a recognized member of more than one state. (3) The state is confined within the circumscribed limits of a particular territory. (4) It is concerned with a great and ever-increasing variety of interests, and with general rather than special interests. (5) It is a permanent and enduring association. (6) It is a necessary association; men cannot live outside the state, but they can live without belonging to other associations. (7) voluntary associations lack the legal power of coercion. (8) Voluntary associations are subject to control and regulation by the state.

Of these differentia, (3), (7), and (8) are comprised in the present definition of the state as a soverign territorial group. Most of the others apply to other associations than the state as well, for example to a church: One can throw off membership only by "expatriation" (excommunication); a man cannot ordinarily be a recognized member of more than one church; the church may be concerned with a great and ever-increasing variety of interests, and be more permanent and enduring than many states. As for the state's being a necessary association, the same can be said with equal warrant for economic associations of some sort, as well as for such groupings as families. That the state is concerned with general rather than special interests is perhaps more important than the other differentia. The state maintains a framework of interpersonal relations with which particular interests can be expeditiously satisfied. This, as has been pointed out, is the essential function of au-

10. J. W. Garner, *Political Science and Government,* American Book, 1932, 63–4. His definition of the state includes the requirement that it be "independent or nearly so of external control"; this condition is rarely fulfilled. It is authority, not control, with regard to which the state is self-contained.

thority: a general pattern of decision making is adhered to in order to minimize conflict over each particular decision. Hence this characteristic, too, is comprised in the definition of the state in terms of authority.[11]

DF. The *governors* are the state authorities. The *government* is the pattern of governor practices.

Political science, as one of the sciences of interpersonal relations, deals not with "states" and "governments" but with concrete acts of human beings. The concept of the state has been defined as a group of persons whose practices and perspectives exhibit certain observable characteristics. Similarly here we define "government" in terms of the practices of specified persons—the state authorities. Every proposition about the abstraction "state" can be replaced by a set of propositions referring only to the concrete acts of certain persons and groups. And the same is true for the abstraction "government."

When state and government are conceived in purely abstract terms, they are easily hypostatized and confused with one another; and this confusion, says Willoughby (1911, 8), "has led directly or indirectly to a great majority of the erroneous results reached by political philosophers in the past." For acts ascribed to the state are in fact acts of its government and, more concretely, of a particular set of governors.

> Every act of the state that we encounter is, in truth, a governmental act. . . . Whenever a state acts in some given way it is invariably because those who act as its government decide to use its sovereign power in that given way. The state itself, in sober reality, never acts; it is acted for by those who have become competent to determine its policies (Laski, 1935, 12–13).

The confusion between state and government and its unfortunate consequences are well illustrated in the account frequently given of the "ends" of the state. The state is alleged to be always, "by its very nature," concerned with "general

11. The following are two representative definitions equivalent to that discussed in the present section. "Those who are united into one body, and have a common established law and judicature to appeal to, with authority to decide controversies between them and punish offenders, are in civil society one with another" (Locke, *Civil Government*, 87). "The state is an association which, acting through law promulgated by a government endowed to this end with coercive power, maintains within a community territorially demarcated the universal external conditions of social order" (MacIver, 1926, 22).

interests," the "common good," the "welfare of all," and so on. Failure to attain these ends is then ascribed to "defects of organization," "corrupt influences," or "selfish interests." The whole discussion becomes normatively ambiguous to a high degree, and the actual political process hopelessly obscured. The "ends" of the state—in a descriptive, not a normative sense—are what they are in fact found to be; and they are found to be the expression of the demands and expectations of a particular government, and of those of the governed to the degree that the latter exercise power and influence over their governors.

Some such influence is always exercised in that the maintenance of a government—like that of any authority—depends on the sentimentalized identifications, expectations, and demands of the governed. If the governed cease to adhere to the political formula whence the governing authority is derived, the regime collapses.[12] It may continue to exercise control, to be sure, but this control now has the form, not of government, but of naked power.

§8.2 *Supremacy, Body Politic, and Rule*

DF. *Supremacy* is the highest degree of effective power.

The concept of supremacy corresponds to that of sovereignty, with reference to control rather than authority, effective rather than formal power.[13] The two may or may not coincide in their application: the sovereign may be supreme, but it may also happen that the regime is highly formalistic, and supremacy be localized in other power structures than those exercising highest authority.

Just as with sovereignty, no assumptions are made here as to characteristics which supremacy must allegedly exhibit always and everywhere. The characteristics of supremacy derive from the practices of control actually found in specific cases. For instance, whether or not supremacy is "indivisible" depends, as with sovereignty, on the nature of the power pattern

12. Compare Thomas Paine, *Dissertation on First Principles of Government*: "The strength and permanent security of government is in proportion to the number of people interested in supporting it." In the classical discussions a similar point was often made by asserting the dependence of law on habit; see for example, Aristotle's *Politics*, Bk. II, and Machiavelli's *Discourses*, I, 18.

13. Bluntschli (1921, 494) makes a similar distinction between *Stätshoheit* and *Stätsgewalt* (the "dignity" and "power" of the state), but uses "sovereignty" to comprise both.

—here, the pattern of control. The highest degree of effective power may be localized in a single power holder, or in various organs and structures of control. Supremacy is "individual" or "divided" accordingly.

On the basis of this definition, various indices of supremacy may be specified. Control over the instruments of violence, or the power to exact tribute (formally: levy taxes) may be taken as such indices. More detailed specifications may be made where necessary: different forms of power may be compared in terms of their base values, control resting on the more intense values being closer to supremacy. (For example, in a society in which wealth is more highly valued than respect, power based on wealth is correspondingly more effective.) Supremacy with regard to a single form of power may be determined directly by a consideration of the weight of power over a given domain —the degree of participation in the making of decisions for that domain. And so on.

DF. *A body politic* is a supreme territorial group.

The definition is to be compared with that of a state as a sovereign territorial group. Here we are in the context of effective rather than formal power. Of course, every group organized with respect to power practices exhibits an authority as well as control structure. Indeed, a body politic exhibits an interpersonal process with regard to all values, not just power.[14]

A body politic is thus a politically organized society. (It constitutes a state only if this organization exhibits sovereignty.) Willoughby (1911, 11) refers to such a society as a "People"—"an aggregate of men living under a single political control." Whether it is a "nation" depends on additional ethnic factors. The present usage roughly coincides with that of Hobbes: "A body politic or civil society may be defined to be a multitude of men, united as one person by a common power, for their common peace, defense, and benefit." [15] But no speci-

14. Compare Willoughby, 1911, 2: "We distinguish between the conception of an aggregate of men as politically organized—as constituting a body politic—and the same community of men as forming merely a group of individuals with mutual economic and social interests. The body politic is the social body plus the political organization."

15. Hobbes, *Elements of Law,* I, 19. R. G. Collingwood in *The Three Laws of Politics* (Oxford University Press, 1941) notes that *"Lo Stato, etat, estate,* is a technical term in medieval politics for what we . . . have decided to call class. Among the classes or estates which together make up a body politic, medieval

fication is made here of the ends for which the supreme power is exercised.

Although sovereignty sometimes displays a formally complete and absolute character, supremacy is almost always limited and relative. Only the most insular body politic is completely independent of external control. The concept of supremacy need not be restricted to the cases (if any) of such complete independence, but may be applied to any relatively high degree of control. A set of continually warring tribes, for example, may be described as one body politic or many, according to whether the observational standpoint is directed toward the constant or variable features of the pattern of control. Of course, whether they constitute a single state or many depends on the political formula to which the tribes adhere. In any case, a body politic may remain constant throughout changes or dissolution of the state.

DF. The *rulers* are those supreme in the body politic.

The distinction between rulers and governors is thus again based on that between control and authority. And again, though the concepts are distinct, they may coincide to varying degrees in their application. The government may be more or less formalistic: the state may be ruled by a power behind the throne, or the king himself may rule as well as govern.[16]

The introduction of the concept of rulers may be regarded as a further step in the reduction of the abstract concepts of state and body politic to concrete observables. Previously it was pointed out that the acts of the state are reducible to acts of its government: the characteristics of the state at any given time are specifiable in terms of characteristics of its governor practices. Similarly, we may say that the acts of the body politic are acts of its rulers. When one state goes to war with another, for example, it is, concretely, the governors who de-

thinkers recognized one which enjoyed a monopoly of power and glory. By a not intolerable figure of speech, since this class did all the ruling, for political purposes you might refer solely to this class in discussing the body politic. Thus *Lo Stato*, the state, is occasionally used in the fourteenth century by synecdoche for the entire body politic. . . . The word 'state' as a designation of a body politic . . . disappeared from good Italian by about 1513. The fashion came back into use among the Germans of the late eighteenth century" (14–15).

16. The present usage of "rule" and "govern" is most convenient, though "govern" has the opposite sense in Thiers's formula "le roi règne et ne gouvèrne pas." See Bluntschli, 1921, 429.

clare war; and insofar as there is a genuine conflict between the bodies politic, it is the rulers who actively prosecute the war. Laski, previously quoted as insisting that the theory of the "state" is essentially the theory of the "governmental act," explains more concretely that "the state, at any given moment, means a body of men and women in possession of actual power" (1925, 96). It is clear that, in our terms, he is speaking of the body politic and its rulers as well as of states and their governors. As he puts it, then, the theory of the body politic is the theory of the act of rule: propositions about the acts of the body politic can be confirmed or disconfirmed only by inquiry into the acts of its rulers.[17]

The corresponding concepts introduced in this and the preceding section are given in the following table.

TABLE 5

Formal and Effective Power

Authority	Control
Sovereignty	Supremacy
State	Body Politic
Government	Rule
Governors	Rulers

PROP. Ruling practices remain independent of any but very large changes in the regime.

Governor practices as such are by definition determined by (and determinative of) the regime, but ruling practices are independent of it except insofar as they are limited by the necessity of avoiding open violation of the political formula. Changes in political forms, unless very thoroughgoing (if then) carry with them no necessary implication of change in control practices.

The position has even been maintained, and with some justification, that essential ruling practices have in fact remained constant throughout history.

17. Of course, this reduction of the concepts of state and body politic to governors and rulers respectively is logical rather than empirical. The statements are not to be construed as assertions about "what the state and body politic really are," but rather as operational definitions (coordinating definitions, semantical rules) for the terms in question.

The experience of all time shows that there has been little material alteration through the course of history as regards the essential practices of leaders and authorities in dealing with the masses; nor have there been vital changes in the techniques of summoning the masses to action or of preventing them from assertively taking over the control of events. . . . The attitude of those in power toward the masses and the part the masses ought to play in the scheme of things does not appear to have deviated greatly since the early stages of historic development.[18]

A partial basis for this position is formulated in the following hypothesis.

PROP. Ruling practices are determined chiefly by the expectations of the rulers as to the most economical means of maintaining and extending their power.

The most familiar exemplification of the hypothesis is in the case of the officeholder. It is a commonplace that "the procedure of an officeholder, if not his aims, in dealing with the problem of the masses is dictated by the exigencies of power holding and of continuance in office" (*ibid.*). And what is true of the relatively small weight of power which position of authority confers is all the more true of power in the hands of the rulers. In Treitschke's mordant phrase, "the state is no academy of arts; when it abandons power in favor of ideal strivings of mankind, it denies its own essential being and goes down."

It follows from the hypothesis that the activities of the body politic are such as are accepted by the rulers as being either advantageous to the shaping (production) of the values most esteemed in the society, or such as increase the share of available values, especially power, distributed to the rulers—in particular, by increasing the fighting effectiveness of the body politic in relation to others.

PROP. Ruling practices are limited by expectations as to resultant indulgences and deprivations from the domain of rule.

It was previously pointed out that conduct is by definition based on expectations as to the I:D ratio. What is empirical in the present proposition is its assertion that the conduct of

18. J. B. S. Hardman, article on "Masses" in *ESS*.

the domain of power is an important determinant of the I:D ratio for the power holders—especially in view of the concern of the rulers with maintaining and extending their power, as formulated in the preceding hypothesis. The rulers measure their indulgence, not merely by their power position, but by power potential as well. And the identifications, demands, and expectations of the domain are a significant factor in this potential. So much is this true that the limitation referred to in the hypothesis may be taken as a basic feature of the political process. The necessity of taking precautions against a withdrawal of favor on the part of the community at large is the core of the political way of thinking.[19]

As to the reason why the reactions of the domain must be taken account of by the rulers, the explanation often given is that of Hume: "Force is always on the side of the governed, so that the governors [rulers] have nothing to support them but opinion." This is not altogether true. A ruling minority may well have a complete monopoly on the exercise of violence, especially where complex instruments and materials are involved.

A more satisfactory formulation, perhaps, is in terms of the *potential* power of the domain in giving support to a rival leadership, so that the "principle of anticipated reaction" enables the rulers to meet the threat, not of the domain itself, but of rivals for its power. Also important is economy in maintenance of the rule, a factor which is sometimes crucial—for instance, when the rulers lack the resources (including the solidarity of the domain) to conduct a costly war in defense of their rule against rivals, especially if the latter are promulgating a utopia according with the demands and expectations of the domain. Thus the rulers depend on the adherence by the domain to the political doctrine, and find it necessary to avoid obvious violations of the political formula.

PROP. The rulers alter the regime whenever conformity to it is expected by them to constitute a significant deprivation.

The condition stated in this hypothesis is not easily satisfied. For first, as has been pointed out, apparent conformity is adequate—violations of the political formula are not themselves deprivational unless they are widely recognized as viola-

19. Friedrich, among others, has emphasized this principle; which he calls (1937, 16–17) "the rule of anticipated reaction."

tions. Moreover, it is the rulers themselves who largely determine the interpretation of the political formula, so that considerable latitude is available to it within the framework of the regime. And finally, the regime can be and constantly is being supplemented by practices not comprised within the political formula but not directly counter to it.

Nevertheless the situation does sometimes arise in which these various devices are inexpedient, more so, that is, than a change of the regime would be. And on the hypothesis, in such cases the regime *is* changed. Laski (1935, 293) puts the point clearly, though in a specialized way: "When the political forms have endangered the rights of ownership, the class in possession has always sought to adjust them to its needs." Here the proposition is in terms of an economic ruling class; but it applies to rulers of a different power base as well.

PROP. Ruling practices are limited by the social order.

Custom, morality, religion constitute effective limits to the exercise of power, even if they are not expressed in political doctrine or embodied in the regime. (There may be societal policy not dirctly implemented in decisions—as when, for example, the state is nonneutral with regard to religion without having a state-religion.) Laski (1925, 52–3) points out that

> in practice, legally unlimited power turns out to be power exercised under conditions fairly well known to each generation. Behind, that is, the legally omnipotent authority it is not very difficult to discern an electorate to whose opinions and desires increasing deference must be shown.

The most intense of these "opinions and desires" are those expressed in the social order. They limit not only authority but control as well. Rousseau (*Social Contract*, II, 12) rhapsodically refers to a law

> graven neither on marble nor on brass, but in the hearts of the citizens; a law which creates the real constitution of the state, which acquires new strength daily, which, when other laws grow obsolete or pass away, revives them or supplies their place, preserves a people in the spirit of their institutions, and imperceptibly substitutes the force of habit for that of authority. I speak of manner, customs, and above all of opinion.

However, the social order itself may be changed, or at any rate subjected to pressures, by those in power—as was done, for example, by Peter the Great and by Mustafa Kemal. But we cannot formulate here the analogue to the preceding hypothesis: the social order is not within the scope of power to anything like the degree to which the regime is subject to control.[20]

§8.3 *Political Functions*

DF. The *functional divisions* of a group are subgroups organized for distinctive practices in behalf of group interests.

A group is not simply an aggregate of persons engaged in the same activity. The practices are not simply parallel, but diversified and integrated in a more or less complex pattern of organization. The elements of this organization are ordinarily not individuals but again groups, organized for the performance of a particular function in the major pattern of organization. These subgroups are the functional divisions of the major group.

Certain types of functional divisions are common to all groups, regardless of variation in the principled interests of the groups, since they pertain to expediency interests—that is, to the maintenance of group activity, regardless of the goals to which that activity is directed. One such functional division has already been discussed: the *leadership*. In every group some subgroup performs the distinctive practices of decision making; the leadership is specialized to the exercise of power, and is organized for the fulfillment of that function. Of course, there is great variation in the forms which this organization takes: committees, councils, boards with chairmen, directors, managers. But in one form or another a leadership is one of the major functional divisions to be found in all groups.

A number of other such functional divisions may be specified. Not all groups, of course, exhibit articulation of function to the same degree; some of the divisions may be rudimentary; and a single division may be organized for the performance of more than one function. The following are some of the important functional divisions.

While one part of the leadership is specialized for power

20. See Pareto, 1935, 1009; and MacIver, 1926, 342.

practices within the group, another, the *diplomatist division* ("foreign service") is devoted to integrating these practices with those of other groups.[21] Unless the group be completely insular, the pattern of its relations to other groups is an important expediency if not principled interest. The diplomatist division specializes in power relations (negotiation and agreement) with other groups, rather than the manipulation of symbols, violence, or goods and services. The continuing direct interplay of offer, counteroffer, acceptance and rejection obviously differs from the addressing of symbols to large groups whose members are not all leaders. A *diplomat* is a diplomatist with formal status, and his function, as Talleyrand put it, is to negotiate: "Il faut negocier, negocier et toujours negocier." The diplomatist division includes more than a diplomatic corps: not all the practices of the division are formalized. The saboteur, spy, and agent provocateur may all be fulfilling diplomatist functions in the present wide sense.

An *internal diplomatist division* might also be distinguished as a part of the leadership. It has the function of making internal agreements in the name of the group, and includes various subleaders, representatives, mediators, arbitrators, conciliators, specialized negotiators. Among the last a particularly important function is carried out by the *fixer:* a nonformal negotiator in practices which, if exposed, would be countermores.

Several functional divisions of the group specialize in the use of symbols. The *intelligence division* is the subgroup making available to the leadership facts and analyses, and clarifying goals and alternatives. It provides expectations, that is, for the consideration of the policy makers of the group. The intelligence function may be distinguished from the *advisory function,* which recommends policy rather than merely presenting policy considerations; it provides demands as well as expectations. The intelligence function has been most fully developed in modern military organizations; but the same function is fulfilled with more or less adequacy in all groups. The advisory function is especially important where the power of the group is concentrated in the hands of a few individuals, or where the specialists in various skills do not themselves exercise power of corresponding scope.

21. The term is borrowed from Frederick S. Dunn and William T. R. Fox.

The *morale division* is the subgroup engaging in practices for the maintenance of morale, that is, intensity of group participation. Although such practices consist largely in the manipulation of symbols, morale considerations may enter into the selection of any group activities. A characteristic practice of the morale division is *ceremonialization:* the manipulation of group sentiment symbols in rigid patterns, in such a way that the practice, though of minimal externalization and reciprocity, appears in the perspectives of the group to be highly indulgent to it. Of course, ceremonialization accompanies the activity of other elements of the group organization, particularly, as has been seen, that of the leadership. But in addition to the ceremonial elaboration of other practices, there is likely to be a certain amount of purely ceremonial activity in the group.[22] Patterns of education of the young, including early training and subsequent initiation into the group, may also be taken as part of the work of the morale division, since an important component of it is the production of perspectives favorable to intense group paticipation.

The *propaganda division* may be distinguished from the morale division as another subgroup specializing in symbols, but concerned chiefly with demands and expectations rather than sentiments and identifications. Its function is to marshal public opinion in support of the policies of the leadership. It may deal, of course, with publics outside as well as within the group.

In every group some subgroup is concerned with the materials of group operations, dealing not with symbols or power practices but with goods and services. It may be called the *economic division.* The most familiar part of this division is the *supply corps*, and the related offices of treasurer and custodian. Like the others, the economic functions concern both the group itself and its relations with other groups. (In this latter aspect, the economic division is often grouped with the

22. From the standpoint of this functional analysis, religious institutions might be included in the morale division of the state. Whether or not religion is the opiate of the masses, it has certainly served, as Voltaire put it, to "keep mankind in order"—an order simultaneously moral and political. Religious practices, apart from any other significance they might have, contribute considerably to the maintenance of faith in and loyalty to the group at large. "There is not, there cannot be, a state without religion," M. A. Bakunin declared (*God and the State*, 1900, 84). At any rate, if the state be without religion, other institutions must take over the important morale functions which religion serves.

foreign diplomatist and propaganda services as carrying on "political warfare" as distinguished from the use of violence.)

A final functional division may be discriminated as specializing in instruments of violence: the *armed forces*. While this division is most familiar in the state, the military or "defense" function, as it is usually called, is important in lesser groups as well. (In the case of the state, a distinction is usually made between *army* and *police*, according to whether the violence is externally or internally directed.) The leadership may enjoy the protection of bodyguards; the group may engage in acts of terror of greater or lesser magnitude; private armies may be employed in behalf of group interests; and so on. The parliamentary sergeant at arms symbolizes the existence of this function in a vestigial form.

The following table lists the functional divisions just discriminated.

TABLE 6

Functional Divisions of a Group

Political Means	*Function*	*Subgroup*
Practices	Diplomatist	Leadership
Symbols	Intelligence	(Power Specialists)
Goods and Services	Advisory	Symbol Specialists
Violence	Morale	Economic Specialists
	Propaganda	Armed Forces
	Economic	(Violence Specialists)
	Police, Army	

DF. The *legislative function* is the formation of generalized policy.

The functions about to be discussed are ordinarily considered only in relation to the state as distinguished from other groups. Like most of the concepts introduced here, however, these are of more general application, and may be discriminated in the practices of the leadership of any group of sufficiently complex organization. What we are concerned with, in fact, are the phases of any complete act of decision making. Such generalization is important, not merely because of its usefulness in theoretical formulations, but more particularly because many of the concrete functions of government are coming to be carried on "outside of the pale and oversight of the state, under the supervision of specialized committees and functional associations, e.g., neighborhood groups and trade unions."[23] The legislature is not the only group enacting legislation; whoever makes policy is legislating. We are dealing here with functions, regardless of the structures—governmental or otherwise—which fulfill these functions. To what degree each function is being carried out by specific governmental structures must be empirically determined in each case.

We define the legislative function in terms of policy formation rather than decision making, which is one case only of policy (when policy is expected to be, and in fact is, supported by the application of sanctions. It is convenient to speak of "expected" and "completed" decisions). When legislation is both authoritative and effective, we refer to its outcome as a legislative *enactment.* In its purely formal aspect it constitutes a *statute;* and when it is effective without authorization it may be called a *fiat.*

DF. The *administrative function* is the specialization of policy in adaptation to particular cases.

General policy embodied in legislation is administratively applied to concrete situations. The specialized policy resulting must accord with legislation; to the degree that the administrator also forms general policy he engages in the legislative function as well. (It is not being assumed that these functions are ever completely separated in distinct authority structures.) When administration is both authoritative and effective, we refer to its outcome as an administrative *ruling.* In its purely formal aspect, administration issues *ordinances,* or even more specialized administrative *orders;* when it is effective without authorization we may speak of an administrative *edict* or more specialized *dictum.*

Law on this conception comprises both legislative enactment and administrative ruling. For it is clear that power resides in both the administrative and legislative functions—both are participations in the decision-making process. The attempt has been made, for instance by Goodnow (1900), to

23. Barnes, 1924, 3; and see also C. E. Merriam's *Public and Private Government,* Yale University Press, 1944, and Beardsley Ruml's *Tomorrow's Business,* Farrar & Rinehart, 1945, especially Pt. II.

set up a basic differentation between politics and administration, as though the latter were neutral with regard to policy, and simply selects means for the attainment of previously specified ends. But politics, in the sense of decision making, is a continuing process throughout the governmental act. Ends and means are here as elsewhere determined in conjugate relationships with one another. Indeed, so far from true is it that power resides only in the legislative function, with administration consisting only in the mechanical application of decisions already made, that administration has in recent times been acquiring more and more independence of legislative control altogether.[24]

The distinction between legislative and administrative functions is thus not intended as pointing to a strict demarcation between disparate practices, but as designative of discriminable phases in the process of decision making.[25] Concurrent with and permeating these phases of the governmental act are other moments of the decision-making process. Most familiar is the *judicial function:* that of authoritatively deciding the conformity of practices to the political formula. Others have already been discussed—the advisory and intelligence functions. And still others may be discriminated—*origination,* for example, the function of introducing policy to be decided on.[26] Table 7 gives the relations of the concepts discussed.

24. See, for example, L. D. White's article on "Public Administration" in *ESS.* "One of the paradoxes of modern administration," he writes, "consists precisely in that the more the legislature strains to control administration, the less it succeeds."

25. Compare the observation of the *Federalist,* No. XXXVII: "Experience has instructed us that no skill in the science of government has yet been able to discriminate and define, with sufficient certainty, its three great provinces—the legislative, executive and judiciary; or even the privileges and powers of the diffierent legislative branches. Questions daily occur in the course of practice which prove the obscurity which reigns in these subjects, and which puzzle the greatest adepts in political science."

26. Korkunov, among others, makes a similar analysis of the governmental act (1922, 356–7). Assigning primary status to the legislative function, he speaks of various "cooperating organs," which he divides into "the preparative, the consultive, and the executive. The preparative [intelligence function] procures the facts and materials from which the decision must be made; the consultive [advisory and originative functions] proposes a plan for the decision; the executive [administrative function] puts in actual realization the effect of the decision by material force." On the general theory, see also H. Lauterpacht, *Function of Law in the International Community,* Clarendon Press, 1933 (especially the last two chapters); E. Jordan, *Theory of Legislation,* Progress Publishing Co., 1937; and the writings of Hans Kelsen.

TABLE 7

The Decision-making Act

Phases	*Formal*	*Effective*	*Both*	
Legislative	Statute	Fiat	Enactment	Law
Administrative	Ordinance Order	Edict Dictum	Ruling	

DF. An *agency* is an authority structure; an *office*, a position of authority.

We may characterize agencies and offices in terms of their dominant functions as legislative, administrative, and so on. The distinction between agencies and functions facilitates the formulation of the question whether and to what degree a specified agency engages in functions other than the dominant one by which it is ordinarily characterized. An executive officer or agency of the government, for example, may be exercising some legislative as well as its dominant administrative functions.

Moreover, we may distinguish between agencies whose exercise of these functions is purely formal and those actually participating in that phase of the decision-making process (with or without authority). Thus we may distinguish between a *legislature* and an *assembly* according to whether the legislative power exercised is formal and effective or purely formal. And similarly, we may speak of the *formal* and *effective administration*.[27]

DF. *Jurisdiction* is the scope and domain of authority; *governmentalization* is increase in jurisdiction.

The jurisdiction of the various authority structures is among the most important specifications of the political formula, though the specification need not be—and indeed, rarely is—an exact one. The scope and domain of authority give the functional and territorial areas of jurisdiction. We may speak of *exclusive jurisdiction* over certain practices or persons if these

27. The study of the various political forms, both formal and effective, in which the functions discussed in this section are embodied, may be designated *political mechanics*. Inquiry into the machinery of government in this sense (cameralism, the initiative and referendum, the cabinet system, and so on), though important, is by no means the whole or the most basic part of political inquiry—contrary to the impression which many textbooks no doubt involuntarily give.

are subject to but one authority, and *concurrent jurisdiction* if several authority structures share formal power with the same scope and domain.

Interpersonal relations become governmentalized in the degree that they are subjected to regulation by authority. Formal power only is in question here: governmentalization of certain practices may even be accompanied by a decrease in the degree of control over them.

IX

STRUCTURES

The continuing arrangements—the structures—by which power is shaped and shared within the community can be described according to the form of rule (effective power) and, more generally, the form of polity (both formal and effective).

§9.1 *Elites, Hierarchies, and Ruling Class*

DF. The *power aggregate* of a given power relationship consists of those having power; the *subject aggregate*, those over whom power is had. *Power* and *subject groups* are organized power and subject aggregates, respectively.

It is convenient to be able to speak of the exercise of or subjection to power without specification of the degree of organization holding among the persons at either end of the power relationship. We designate such persons the power and subject aggregates, and we call them power and subject groups only when they are organized with reference to the power relation in question. Manufacturers constitute a power aggregate with regard to economic power, but they do not constitute a power group unless they are specifically organized as such. Similarly, the employees in a particular industry constitute a subject group or subject aggregate according to whether or not they are organized in a union.

PROP. The weight of power of a group varies with its degree of organization.

Of two groups both contained in a power aggregate, the more highly organized group is likely to participate more effectively in the making of decisions. And the same is true if we compare the weight of power exercised by the power group as a whole with that of the power holders outside the group. Conversely, the greater the weight of power exercised by a group, the higher the degree of organization the group is likely to have. There is more room for cooperation and solidarity, and these are the more important to the group the more it participates in the making of decisions. Thus a power group is almost always more highly organized than the corresponding subject group.

Because of organization, power cannot be conceived as a unilateral relationship. Both the subject and power groups participate in the making of decisions, though with different weights. The distinction between them is relative, being based on the comparatively greater power in the hands of one group; it is not a distinction between the group having all the power and the group having none. The mere fact that the subject group is organized as such gives it some share in the making of decisions—it being remembered that implementation of a decision is also part of the process of decision making: it helps determine whether or not a specific policy is in fact a decision. Solidarity and cooperation in the subject group make its acceptance of policy more important than in the case of an unorganized aggregate, and give it a corresponding weight of power. The effectiveness of even passive resistance is a clear indication of the power in the hands of the subject group.[1]

DF. The *elite* are those with most power in a group; the *mid-elite*, those with less power; the *mass*, least power.

The three terms correspond to 'elect," "mid-elect," and "reject," but in relation to power alone rather than influence in

1. As a consequence, both choice and coercion are, generally speaking, elements of the power situation. Choice is involved in that the decisions reached in the power process are partially determined by the policy of the subject group. But coercion is involved in that the weight of power in the two directions is by no means always the same: to deny that power is a unilateral relation is not to say that it is strictly symmetrical. Friedrich, among others, has directed attention to the implications for political theory of these considerations. "Power is neither simply a substance inhering in some agents, nor a relationship of a strictly mutual nature," he writes (1937, 14). "Where the substantive concept prevails, the thinker has been inclined to neglect the phenomena of genuine consent, interpreting them as propaganda, myths, symbols, etc. Where the relational concept has been emphasized, there has been a tendency to neglect the phenomena of conquest and government through force or constraint, to recognize their existence, but to stigmatize them as tyranny." Of course, "propaganda, myths, symbols, etc." *can* give rise to "genuine consent." (Saying that something is "mental" does not mean that it is not "real.") The point being made is that the unilateral conceptions of power tend to put undue emphasis on conditions at the expense of considerations, on operations at the expense of perspectives. Ideas are not literally weapons, but a theory of power must take account of the power of ideas as well as of weapons.

general. Whether the corresponding concepts coincide in their application is an empirical matter to be discussed shortly.[2]

The division into elite and mass can be made wherever there are any differences— whether as to weight, scope, or domain— in the amount of power enjoyed by various persons in the group. Nothing more is presupposed by the concept as here defined than the existence of some such differences. No more than this is contained in such assertions as Pareto's (1935, 246) that "every people is governed by an elite, by a chosen element in the population"; what is said, in effect, is that every people is ruled by—rulers.

The point is important in the light of the common supposition that to put the concept of elite to the fore in political science is to deny from the outset the possibility of democratic institutions. But whether a social structure is democratic depends not on whether or not there is an elite, but on the relations of the elite to the mass—how it is recruited and how it exercises its power. "It is not the existence of this limited group," says Friedrich, "but the method of its establishment which serves as the essential criterion of the several forms of government." [3]

The size of the elite is usually small compared with that of the mass.[4] The term "mass" itself connotes a multitude, but whether the mass as here defined is numerous in relation to the elite is

2. The phrase "in a group" is intended to emphasize the difference between the concepts of elite and power aggregate. The latter is applied to any specific power relation; the former, to the entire network of power relationships holding in the group. The elite consists of those who belong to the power aggregates of the most, or the most important, power relations. The rulers, as defined in the preceding section, may be regarded as the most active members of the elite, where the emphasis is on effective rather than formal power, and the group in question is a body politic.

3. Article on "Oligarchy" in *ESS*. Misunderstandings similar to that just discussed sometimes occur with regard to the concept of power. Philosophers have sometimes delineated societies in which "no person has power over any other." What is usually meant by such phrases can more clearly be expressed by describing certain characteristics of the power relations obtaining, rather than by speaking of the absence of such relations altogether. As Locke observed, "The great question which, in all ages, has disturbed mankind . . . has been, not whether there be power in the world, not whence it came, but who should have it" (*Treatises on Government,* I). And, it may be added, what kind and how much power, and to what ends it is directed. These questions will be discussed in later sections of this chapter.

4. Compare Laski, 1925, 21: "What, as a matter of history, can alone be predicted of the state is that it has always presented the striking phenomenon of a vast multitude owing allegiance to a comparatively small number of men."

an empirical question. Of course, where exactly to draw the lines between elite, mid-elite, and mass has not been indicated (nor can it be, without reference to a particular problem). But it is an empirical property of the power distribution that it ordinarily has a low distribution index, as compared with that for other important values.

PROP. Influence varies with power, the difference in influence of the elite and mass varying with the power of the elite.

The hypothesis formulates an empirical correspondence between elite, mid-elite, and mass on the one hand, and elect, mid-elect, and reject on the other. (It is not meant, of course, that the corresponding aggregates coincide person by person—it has already been pointed out that an individual may have a considerable amount of power without other forms of influence and conversely.) The hypothesis states, in other words, that the share of values received by an aggregate depends on its power, and that the differences in this share are greatest where the power of the elite is greatest.[5]

PROP. Upper elites tend to be skilled in the practices of interpersonal relations rather than of the area in which decisions are to be made.

The proposition rests on the fact that power practices are of a characteristic sort distinct from the nature of the practices over which power is exercised. (Administration of one type of enterprise is more like that of another than would be indicated by the differences in the characteristic practices of the two enterprises.) It must be emphasized that the hypothesis concerns upper elites only. Different elites considered as a whole may very well exhibit sharp differences in characteristic skills. In one society the elite may consist largely of military men, in another of lawyers. The hypothesis is that the upper elites of both will exhibit similar skills—in the practices of interper-

5. This hypothesis also has been enunciated by Laski (article on "Democracy" in *ESS*): "The benefits a man can obtain from the social process are, at least approximately and in general, a function of his power of effective demand . . ." —or, as we would say, of his degree of participation in the making of decisions. Laski holds further that this in turn depends upon the property owned, that is, that power is always a function of position in the economic value pattern. This more special proposition is to be distinguished from the hypothesis under consideration.

sonal relations. The composition of elites as a whole will be further discussed in the following section.

DF. A *hierarchy* is a structure of power relationships of varying amounts of power; a *co-archy* is a structure of equal power relationships.

A hierarchy is thus a coordinated aggregate of persons among whom power relationships hold so as to establish an order of superiors and subordinates. A section of this order may be called a *vertical echelon* in the hierarchy, as distinguished from a *horizontal echelon* constituted by power holders of equal rank in the hierarchy.[6] In a co-archy, the power exerted in one direction is the same as that of the converse: the members of the co-archy are equals in power status with regard to one another. Thus in a co-archy a horizontal rather than vertical echelon is most prominent. Such relations might characterize (at least formally) the power pattern in a league or confederation, for example. When two hierarchies share a domain of power, and are equal in power status, they are sometimes referred to as a *dyarchy*.

Hierarchies may be internally diversified with regard to weight, scope, or domain of power, and classified as *hegemonic*, *functional*, or *territorial*, respectively, according to the mode of distribution of power within the hierarchy. (Of course all three types are involved to some degree in almost all hierarchies.) The hierarchy of army officers is primarily hegemonic; the administrative hierarchy of the federal government is primarily functional; the hierarchy of a political party is often territorially diversified. Again, hierarchies may be classified by the base value of the power exercised. In these terms, the distinction is sometimes made between *genealogical* and *contractual hierarchies*, according to whether kinship or explicit commitment underlies the hierarchical relationship.[7] And so on.

6. Hierarchies are sometimes analyzed radically, rather than in terms of vertical and horizontal echelons. Here we speak of a *power center* and a *power periphery*. More detailed analyses may be made in terms of *subcenters*, the *radius of power*, and so on. See also chap. v, "The Pyramid of Power," in R. M. MacIver, 1947.

7. See, for instance, MacLeod, 1931, 103 ff., for a discussion of these structures. The present definition of hierarchy includes both "bureaucratic" and "pyramidal" structures in MacLeod's terms. See also R. H. Lowie's *Origin of the*

PROP. Power groups develop into hierarchies.

"Power is never a mere subordination of the many to the one," says MacIver (1926, 47). "It is, always, a hierarchy." A group exercising power diversifies its power practices in a coordinated structure of superiors and subordinates. This serves the principled interests of the power group in accord with the familiar advantages of the division of labor. (Accordingly, a hierarchy is the more complex the greater the scope and domain of the power exercised.)

An even more important factor making for hierarchy is the expediency interests of the group. The establishment of a hierarchy is a mode of resolving conflicts among power groups with overlapping domains and scope. As Timasheff explains (1939, 301–2):

> The tendency of power structures to form larger, complex systems is rooted in their very essence. Systems of domination which remained independent of one another and, at the same time, claimed obedience within the same social field, from the same individuals, would encounter conflicts. Conflicts among power structures result either in the destruction of all the conflicting units or in a combination of them into hierarchies.

Thus the formation of a hierarchy contributes to the stability of the power structure. It does so first by minimizing conflict—an order is established which assigns a specific and recognized place to each of the conflicting powers. And secondly, the structure enjoys the support of the entire hierarchy, each member of which now has a stake in the power distribution. When power is concentrated, support for the power structure is correspondingly limited; with the distribution of power, support becomes correspondingly widespread.

DF. A *bureaucracy* is a hierarchy of considerable power and diversification, and low circulation.

The term as here defined is descriptive, not normative. A bureaucracy is simply an impermeable and complex hierarchy. The preceding hypothesis is not to be misconstrued, therefore, as asserting that power groups always tend to constitute bu-

---

State, Harcourt, Brace, 1927, for a discussion of the kinship principle as one particular pattern of political organization.

reaucracies. The crucial question is the circulation occurring within the hierarchy. The members of the hierarchy might, for example, hold their positions for short elective terms, rather than constitute a hereditary bureaucracy.

DF. The *ruling class* is the class from which rulers are recruited and in whose interest they exercise power; a *dependent class* is one indulged by the power process, but not sharing in the rule; a *subject class* is one sharing least in both power and other values.

The rulers have been defined as those supreme in the body politic—the most active and powerful members of the elite. The ruling class is the effective constituency of the rulers, not necessarily formally but nonetheless effectively represented by the rulers. The rulers are recruited from this class, either on a hereditary principle or on the basis of skills or practices characteristic of the class. But the definition is of a social class, that is, a class specified with regard to both welfare and deference values. It enjoys a preferential share not only of power but of the other important values as well.

A dependent class is one sharing to a considerable degree the benefits of the rule, but not participating in it. Lacking power, it is dependent on the ruling class for the indulgences it enjoys. There may be some recruitment of rulers from dependent classes, but to no great extent, and such rulers usually exercise power of limited weight and scope. A dependent class constitutes an elect, therefore, but not an elite.

The concept of a dependent class is useful not only in its avoidance of the oversimplified dichotomy between ruling class and ruled, but also because there need not always be *a* ruling class. Several classes may participate in the rule and its benefits to varying degrees, and during a specified interval now one and now another may be dominant and the others dependent. This situation is especially characteristic of periods when new classes are rising to a dominant position. When a ruling class is no longer able to provide rulers, but must recruit them from other classes, its power potential is at a minimum. Its value position can be stabilized only as the locus of authority, and effective power passes into other hands. But there is rarely a sudden wholesale transfer of rule from one class to another (regardless of formal revolution). Rather, a dependent class comes to share more and more power till it finally quite displaces the old ruling class.

The subject class is least indulged in the distribution of values, and has least power. Again there may be several subject classes, with varying shares of influence. Some few individuals of the subject classes may even be recruited to participate in the rule. It must be emphasized that nothing is said in the definition about the relative permeability of ruling, dependent, and subject classes. In particular cases there may be a high degree of circulation among them. In others, the classes may be highly impermeable, and may be designated as *ruling* and *subject castes,* or *closed* rather than *open* classes.

PROP. A class acquires supremacy in the degree that it contributes to the more intense values of the society.

The hypothesis is that the class acquires a dominant position in the degree that the values which it shapes (creates, produces) are highly valued in the body politic. These values are not necessarily economic in the narrow sense. Societies ruled, for example, by a warrior class or priesthood confirm the hypothesis insofar as these classes owe their ruling position to the value put upon the activities characteristic of the class.[8]

Since values are agglutinative—those with a favorable share of some values are likely to acquire other values also—the supremacy of the class may often appear in the perspectives of the body politic to be based on values other than those characteristically shaped by the class. Tawney (1931, 231–2) points out, for example, that

> the class which, for the time being, is economically preponderant tends normally to be that which discharges the most conspicuous public obligations. Naturally, it often displays the graces of civilization in an exceptional degree. Naturally, again, the relations of cause and effect are commonly reversed, so that it is said to exercise power because it is educated and fit to govern, not to possess culture and influence because its economic position has brought exceptional opportunities of both within its reach.

8. There is a reciprocal effect as well: certain activities become valued because they are characteristically engaged in only by members of the ruling class—hunting and warfare, for example. The point is fully elaborated by Veblen, 1918. But the converse fact remains that hunters, for example, are likely to enjoy a favorable power position in societies that depend on them for sustenance, warriors in predatory groups, and so on.

The factor dealt with in the hypothesis is of course not the only one conditioning supremacy. In particular, the effectiveness of the utopia invoked for acquisition of power, and the ideology for its maintenance, is of great importance. It is not strictly true, as the *Communist Manifesto* asserts, that "the ruling ideas of each age have ever been the ideas of its ruling class." But where the "ruling ideas" are not those of the ruling class, the latter is correspondingly likely to lose its supremacy. The process by which one class supplants another in rule will be discussed in Chapter 10.

§9.2 *Forms of Rule*

DF. The *rule* is the pattern of ruler practices.

A description of the rule is thus a description of the way in which control is distributed and exercised in the body politic, just as the regime is constituted by the distribution and exercise of authority. But there is no simple correspondence between rule and regime: two states may exhibit the same regime but differ considerably in rule, or have the same rule under different regimes. Hence a comparison of the political institutions of two states, or of a pre- and postrevolutionary situation in a given state, must take account of both rule and regime—of effective as well as formal power.[9]

Most of the political, and many nonpolitical, characteristics of the state are a function of the patterns of effective rather than formal power. It is this which confers importance on the

9. "If it be borne in mind," says Goodnow (1900, 6), "that the political institutions of a people are to be found without, as well as within the law, and that the constitution cannot be understood without a knowledge of the administrative system, it is believed that the political institutions of different people will show a much greater similarity than would be thought to exist were the consideration confined to the formal provisions of the constitutional law." But a much greater difference as well, as other writers have pointed out. "Shifts of power can transform a state almost overnight . . . with no corresponding change in the actual form or constitution of government. So-called republican Rome made several rapid shifts from oligarchy to republicanism or democracy and back again without any serious change in the forms of its government, in its constitution. And when the republic became a monarchy, very few changes were necessary in the republican constitution. So, likewise, the French republic remained in form a republic when it became in fact an absolute monarchy under Napoleon in 1804; and, to use the language of the French Senate's proclamation of the monarchy, 'the republic is ruled by an emperor'!" (MacLeod, 1931, 107–8).

concept of rule.[10] The rule may be described by specifying the composition of the elite. Hence this has been one of the most important bases of differentiation among states since Aristotle: "States are characterized by differences in their governing [ruling] bodies—one of them has a government of the rich, another of the virtuous, etc." (*Politics*, III, 13).

In the following table, forms of rule are classified in terms of the composition of the elite.

TABLE 8

Forms of Rule by Composition of Elite

Base Value	*Elite*	*Rule*	*Rulers*
Power	Officials	Bureaucracy	Bureaucrats
Respect	Nobility	Aristocracy	Aristocrats
Rectitude	Righteous	Ethocracy	Ethocrats
Affection	Popular	Demosocracy	Demosocrats
Well-Being	Virile	Virocracy	Virocrats
Wealth	Wealthy	Plutocracy	Plutocrats
Skill	Skill Specialists	Technocracy	Technocrats
Enlightenment	Symbol Specialists	Ideocracy	Ideocrats

There are, of course, other ways in which rules may be classified; some of these will be considered in the following section. Here we distinguish rules according to the composition of the elite. Corresponding to the nature of the elite are characteristic forms of power. The base values of these forms are also given in the table. When other values are taken into account, other forms of power may be distinguished, hence other elites exercising such power, with corresponding forms of rule. Thus the table is not exhaustive even with this basis of classification.

Bureaucracy is the form of rule in which the elite is composed of officials; the rulers are known, of course, as bureaucrats. The term has previously been defined as a complex, impermeable hierarchy; and this sense coincides with its meaning as applied to a form of rule. Since the elite is composed of officials it is self-perpetuating: replacements are recruited

10. Compare Mosca, 1939, 51: "From the point of view of scientific research the real superiority of the concept of the ruling, or political class lies in the fact that the varying structure of ruling classes has a preponderant importance in determining the political type, and also the level of civilization, of the different peoples."

from within the hierarchy. Most often, this takes place on a hereditary principle. But a bureaucracy may also incorporate a technocratic element by recruiting replacements in part through a system of training for its civil service. In any case, the elite is characterized by its specifically political qualifications, associated with varying degrees of skill.

In using the term *aristocracy* to designate a particular form of rule, we are giving it a somewhat more special meaning than simply the etymological "rule of the best." In this wide sense, all rules could be called aristocracies, "best" being specified in terms of the values assumed to characterize the elite. We define aristocracy as the rule of the "best" in relation only to respect and derivative values (honor, glory). The elite in an aristocracy is composed of nobles, or, less formally, of the select groups in the society. (Specialists in the rituals of deference —those playing important roles with regard to ceremony— are also ordinarily included in this elite.) Nothing is said here, of course, as to what specific characteristics are in turn determinative of respect. One of the most common is age; the corresponding form of rule, a type of aristocracy, is known as *gerontocracy*. Where distribution of respect in the society takes account of sex differences, *gynocracy* (rule of women) may be a resultant form.

Ethocracy is the form of rule in which the elite is characterized by a particular status and function with regard to moral values. Of course, moral values may be—and usually are —associated with every elite, just as are respect and other values. But here the moral values serve as the distinguishing mark of the elite. Plato's *Republic*, for instance, describes a form of rule in which the elite is characterized largely in terms of moral excellence. The most familiar type of ethocracy is that in which the elite consists of a priesthood; the form is known, of course, as a *theocracy* (somewhat inaccurately, since the religion need not be markedly theistic).

A *demosocracy* is the form of rule in which the base value of the predominant form of power is affection. Since this must be widely dispersed to serve as a basis of power, demosocracy is rule by the popular, the favorites of the people.[11] The rulers

11. Thus the term is not to be misunderstood as designating a form of rule in which the mass itself directly exercises power. Rule is always by an elite; but the principle of elite recruitment, and the relations between elite and mass, differ

we refer to as *demosocrats*. When the favorite attains his status largely by manipulation of symbols of popular demands, identifications, and expectations he is known as a *demagogue*. But demosocrats may equally be recruited from among specialists in other skills—they may be popular military heroes, for instance. When the affection on which this form of power is based is not distributed throughout the group, but is most prominent among the reject, or when the acquisition and exercise of power is the externalization of crowd perspectives and practices, the form of rule has been called an *ochlocracy* (*mobocracy*).

The term *virocracy* is a coinage, there being no general designation for the form of rule in which the elite is recruited in terms of well-being (vigor, vitality, prowess). We call the rulers, in analogy to more familiar designations, *virocrats*. In many primitive tribes the chieftain is a virocrat in the present sense.

The most common types of virocracy are those in which the elite consists of specialists in violence. In the *predatory state* brigandage is the predominant form of power. *Praetorianism* is another type of virocracy, effective power being exercised by specialists in violence (the praetorian guard) whose office is to insure the safety of the formal center of power. In terms of the present definitions, a power structure resting on the institution of slavery is also a virocracy: the term *slavocracy* has been used in this connection. The *reign of terror* is also a type of virocracy, violence being implemented to secure respect for authority not forthcoming otherwise. The absence of a general term for such types of rule does not indicate that the type is unimportant, but reflects the fact that, because of the instability of naked power, forms of rule based on violence are likely to become associated with or transformed to some of the other forms.[12]

Plutocracy is the familiar form of rule in which the base values of the predominant forms of power are economic. The

---

considerably from one form to another. A demosocracy is constituted as such, not by its having no elite, but by the fact that the elite owes its position to popular affection.

12. On the importance of virocracy see, for example, Bagehot (1873, 49): "All European history has been the history of the superposition of the more military races over the less military—of the effort, sometimes successful, sometimes unsuccessful, of each race to get more military."

elite consists of the wealthy, and the rulers may be designated in a purely descriptive sense as *plutocrats.* They comprise those with a favorable position in the wealth pattern, whether as industrialists, financiers, or whatever. The predominant power is economic: subsistence power, ecopolitical power, and so on.

Where skill is the base value, we speak of the form of rule as *technocracy,* and the rulers as *technocrats.* We designate the elite as skill specialists; it comprises engineers, managers, experts, and so on. In the special case where power is dispersed throughout all skill groups, the type of rule is known as *ergatocracy* (literally, rule by the workers; to be clearly distinguished, of course, from the "dictatorship of the proletariat").

Any form of rule where the elite consists of symbol specialists we designate as an *ideocracy.* The term was introduced by Bluntschli (1921, 331), who gave it, however, a narrow sense for which another term ("theocracy") is already available. We apply it to any body politic in which the predominant forms of power are those resting on the manipulation of symbols. Among the special types may be mentioned the *lexocracy,* where the elite consists of those manipulating the symbols of the political formula.[13] Of the many meanings of "democracy," those which characterize it by the important role in the political process played by discussion call attention to its aspects as an ideocracy. Hobbes, for example, says (*De Corpore Politico,* II) that "a democracy in effect is no more than aristocracy of orators, interrupted sometimes with the temporary monarchy of one orator." Michels, too, characterizes democracy (1915, 60) by its recruitment of the elite from symbol specialists—orators and journalists. (Other elements in the concept of democracy will be discussed in §9.4.) [14]

13. See V. L. Parrington, *Main Currents in American Thought,* Harcourt, Brace, 1930, II, 118. Compare A. D. Lindsay's observation, in his *Modern Democratic State,* Oxford University Press, 1943, 113: "The moving speeches we make about the supremacy of law in the world would not sound so well if we had to say supremacy of lawyers."

14. Bluntschli, following the Aristotelian mode of classification, associates with ideocracy a "perverted form," which he calls *idolocracy.* (In Aristotle the basis of classification is the mode of distribution of the benefits of the rule, as well as the composition of the elite; this type of classification will be elaborated in the next section.) Bluntschli intended the distinction to correspond with that between religion and idolatry. It seems useful, however, to apply the term "idol-

Of course, these various forms of rule are not mutually exclusive; on the contrary, they rarely appear in pure form. A bureaucracy, for example, may also be plutocratic, officials being recruited from the economic elite; such a political structure is sometimes called a *business state*. A virocracy may be aristocratic, the elite consisting of lords, as in the *feudal state*. In the *garrison state* virocracy and bureaucracy are combined, the body politic being thoroughly militarized and bureaucratized.[15] The *party state* is both bureaucratic and ideocratic: power is exercised by party officials and symbol specialists. Plato's *Republic* describes a body politic which is not only ethocratic, but has important elements also of technocracy and ideocracy. And so on.

In short, the control process is not adequately described by being characterized simply as one form of rule or another. There must be specified all the forms of power entering in various degrees into the power process, and the relations and interactions among them. Nothing is gained by the spurious simplification in which all power structures are treated as instances of only two or three basic forms. The many forms thus far discriminated, moreover, have resulted from a classification only in terms of the composition of the elite. In the next section other discriminations will be made in terms of the relations between elite and mass.

PROP. The power order of elites in a society is correlated with the ordering of the values on which their power is based.

That is, the base values of the dominant forms of power are also the dominant values (as determined by total conduct, not merely symbols of demand). For example, wealth is the dominant value in plutocracies, respect (honor, glory) in aristocracies, and so on. The dominance of these values is embodied in the working conception of economy, that is, in the actual estimation in the I:D ratio in given situations or courses of action; it need not always coincide with the doctrines current.

---

ocracy" to any type of ideocracy in which the symbols manipulated are of a characteristically transempirical and antirational sort—those forms of rule in which the ruling position is occupied by what Barker (1942, 77) aptly calls the "mystagogue." Rules associated with religious institutions we have already classified as types of ethocracy, since not all religions are transempirical, while all are associated with particular moral doctrines.

15. See Lasswell, "The Garrison State," *American Journal of Sociology,* Vol. XLVI, No. 4, January, 1941 (reprinted in Lasswell, 1947).

(Choice of career by the young might also be mentioned as a significant index.)

Where the form of rule is "mixed"—as it usually is—several values may share the dominant position. In a plutocratic bureaucracy (business state), both power and wealth are deemed important, and each may often be exchanged for the other—the millionaire finds it worthwhile to buy an ambassadorship, the party boss foregoes the prestige of office to collect his graft. The purchase of titles is one measure of the degree to which a rule is still aristocratic: when aristocracy has fully given way to another form of rule, a title ceases to be of account. In other societies, rectitude and power are values of the same rank: it is a matter of indifference whether the ambitious young man enters the church or the army. And so on.

The proposition is formulated in terms of a co-relation—the relationship extends in both directions. High estimation of a particular value gives a high power potential to those enjoying a favorable position with regard to the value. In the preceding section the hypothesis was formulated that a class becomes a ruling class in proportion to its importance in the production of the important values. In the converse direction, the elite strengthens predispositions favorable to the value on which its power is based. And the very fact that power is based on that value has itself the effect of magnifying the importance of the value in the perspectives of the mass.

Symbols circulated by the elite may minimize the value on which its power is based if the elite is no longer important to the shaping of the value, or if its power potential is lowered in other ways. In a rising plutocracy wealth is extolled at the expense of other values (it has been taken as a mark of predestination to salvation, for instance). But as the position of the plutocrat comes to be challenged by a rival elite, values with a higher distribution index than wealth—such as rectitude and respect—may be brought to the fore, to limit and weaken in intensity demands for a redistribution of wealth, and thereby power.

§9.3 *Polity*

DF. The *polity* is the regime and the rule.

The polity is thus the political structure in the full sense, comprising both the authority and control structures. The whole value process in the society—its culture—is thereby characterized from the standpoint of power, and the society is from this standpoint a body politic. Any other value may serve as an analogous standpoint for social inquiry: where wealth is central, one speaks of the *economy* of the society; for skill, its *technology;* and so on. Thus in a sense all of the social sciences have an identical subject matter, but they adopt toward this subject matter varying observational standpoints (frames of reference) leading to different sets of problems. Hence, though political science as here conceived is characteristically concerned with polities, it is not limited to that concern ("science of government," "science of the state," and so on), but deals with the social process in its entirety, though always in its bearings on power.

The possibilities for the fruitful classification of power structures are inexhaustible, as indicated by the distinctions already made in this book, and in the history of scientific and popular usage. From a systematic standpoint, we look upon society as man seeking values through institutions. Power is one of the values, and our emphasis is upon the classification of power institutions according to the ways in which power is shaped and shared. The polities to be classified from this standpoint can also be related to whatever classifications prove useful in describing the institutions specialized to wealth, respect, and other values.

It should be emphasized that our categories refer to functional rather than conventional patterns. A pattern is conventionally designated when the term used to refer to it is the one locally prevailing, usually more significant in politics than in political science, and commonly emphasizing the formal rather than effective components of power. Thus the local community may speak of "business" policies where, from the standpoint of the scientific observer, the policies are actually decisions, and what is involved is not wealth but power. In the same way words like "property" may be used to refer to the "ownership" of the instruments of production (wealth); yet, from a systematic standpoint the relations may again, for the most part, constitute decisions (power), since choices made by the "owner" can be enforced against an objector by imposing severe deprivations (actual starvation, or mutilation by "company police").

For scientific purposes it is convenient to begin the investigation of concrete situations with "conventionally" named institutions, and gradually to determine the degree of severity that is expected to be used in coping with nonconformity to specific policies. In the absence of such studies—and partly as a stimulus to making them—it is often useful to classify "governments" (polities) according to prevalent terminology. These conventional terms are helpful guides to current policy thinking, and indicate the initial stages of scientific inquiries that aim at providing knowledge for which recognized categories are already in use.[16]

DF. The *constitution* is the basic pattern of the polity; the *formal constitution*, of the regime; the *effective constitution*, of the rule. The *charter* is the constitution authoritatively symbolized.

To describe the constitution is therefore to specify how the body politic is constituted as to both authority and control. The formal constitution is an embodiment of the political formula, or at any rate of the political doctrine from which the formula is elaborated. The formal constitution alone, however, is not an adequate description of the polity.[17] It is, in Burke's phrase, only "the vestment of the body politic." It is therefore important to extend the dual consideration of power —as authority and as control—to a distinction between the formal and effective constitution. The polity cannot be adequately characterized in either the one set of terms or the other, but only by applying them conjointly.[18]

16. An outstanding example of this type of well-timed classification is that of R. M. MacIver, 1947, 151. The terms are partly functional (systematic, scientific), and partly conventional (current usage in the political process itself). From our point of view many writers fail to clarify adequately not only the differences and relations between terms of these two kinds, but also between "value" and "institutional" categories. Nevertheless, mixed modes of classification are serviceable for science and policy in our historic period.

17. The importance of this proposition was already emphasized by Aristotle, who, defining the constitution as the "arrangement of magistracies in a state," makes it a point to distinguish between the constitution and the way in which power is in fact exercised: "In many states the constitution which is established by law, although not democratic, owing to education and habits of the people may be administered democratically, and conversely, in other states the established constitution may incline to democracy but may be administered in an oligarchical spirit" (*Politics*, IV, 5; and see also III, 6). Of course the disparity between rule and regime depends on more than the "education and habits of the people."

18. "The absence of a word to describe the type of society which combines the forms of political democracy with sharp economic and social divisions is

The distinction between "written" and "unwritten" constitutions is of less importance than whether a given set of constitutional symbols (that is, symbols purporting to be descriptive of the polity) is authoritative or not. The authoritative symbolization of the constitution we call the *charter* of the body politic. There is always a charter, save in the case of naked power, where control is exercised without recourse to authority.[19] But of course charters differ greatly as to elaborateness, systematization, and other stylistic characteristics. It is clear that the charter will not often describe the effective constitution: there is usually a disparity between authority and control. Rather, the charter describes the basic features of the formal constitution. Roughly speaking, the formal constitution is the legal structure of the body politic; the charter is the set of symbols (written constitution) by which the structure functions.

DF. The *allocation* of power is its distribution as to weight. *Citizens* are those in a body politic who share in the allocation of power; *subjects*, those who do not.

The allocation of power is, in particular, the distribution of the weight of power as between power and subject aggregates.

. . . unfortunate," Tawney has observed (1931, 98), "since it obscures the practical realities which it is essential to grasp. The conventional classification of communities by the character of their constitutional arrangements had its utility in an age when the principle objective of effort and speculation was the extension of political rights. It is economic and social forces, however, which are the most influential in determining the practical operation of political institutions, and it is economic and social relations that create the most urgent of the internal problems confronting industrial communities." The political taxonomy introduced in this chapter is intended to fill, in part, the lack to which Tawney refers. The "constitutional arrangements" in a formal sense must be accompanied by descriptions of the patterns of effective power.

19. But even here a charter tends to emerge as the patterns of effective power become stabilized, and expectations, demands, and identifications attach themselves to the symbols functioning in these patterns. Friedrich describes one form of this process as follows (1937, 111–12): "The total complex of effective restraints on governmental action which makes up the 'constitution' of a given community will necessarily crystallize into more or less familiar word patterns, such as 'legislative, executive and judicial power,' 'state's rights,' 'due process,' 'freedom of speech,' etc. These word patterns gradually become symbols of order, and thus the constitution as a political process emerges into the constitution as a political force." Friedrich is here concerned with patterns of limitation on effective power, but authoritative constitutional symbols emerge in a similar way for other patterns. (The phrase "constitutional government" implies the operation of a particular type of constitution, which will be considered in the next section.)

A subject is thus a member of the body politic who belongs only to subject aggregates. His share in decision making is minimal (consisting only in not rebelling against the decisions in the making of which he has not otherwise participated). The citizen, on the other hand, does have some weight of power: he may hold office, cast a vote, and participate in other ways in the exercise of power. (The present definition thus coincides with Aristotle's [III, 1]: "He who has the power to take part in the deliberative or judicial administration of any state is said by us to be a citizen of that state.") It is to be noted that the distinction between subject and citizen is not purely formal, but involves control as well as authority. It is possible to speak of citizens in a monarchy and of subjects in a representative government, if the allocation of effective power does not correspond to that formalized in the regime.

DF. *Autocracy* is the form of rule in which the weight of power is chiefly in the hands of one person; *oligarchy*, in the hands of a group of rulers; a *republic*, distributed throughout the domain.

In the preceding section rules were classified according to the composition of the elite. Here the classification is on the basis of the allocation of power—not to whom it is distributed, but whether and to what degree. In these terms we arrive at the classical distinction between rule by the one, the few, or the many—respectively, by an autocrat, by an oligarchy, or by the domain of power at large.[20]

20. See, for instance, Hobbes's classification (*Leviathan*, II, 19): "The difference of commonwealths consisteth in the difference of the sovereign, or the person representative of all and every one of the multitude. And because the sovereignty is either in one man, or in an assembly of more than one; and into that assembly either every man hath right to enter, or not everyone, but certain men distinguished from the rest; it is manifest, there can be but three kinds of commonwealth. For the representative must needs be one man, or more; and if more, then it is the assembly of all, or but of a part. When the representative is one man, then is the commonwealth a monarchy; when as assembly of all that will come together, then it is a democracy or popular commonwealth; when an assembly of a part only, then it is called an aristocracy. Other kind of commonwealth there can be none." It is interesting that in spite of Hobbes's nominalism, he seems to attach some absolute significance to this particular classification. But of course this basis of classification is important only where inquiry is concerned with political processes, structures, or functions empirically connected with the allocation of power (rather than, say, with the composition of the elite, or other bases of classification). Hobbes's terms have undergone considerable modification: "monarchy" is now generally recognized to be a classification of

The concepts both of autocracy and republic are idealizations: all rules are oligarchies to a greater or lesser degree. As previously put, the division into elite and mass is universal. The autocrat shares his power with subordinates, both to expedite the exercise of power and to stabilize the power structure. The citizens of a republic are not all equally active in their participation in the process of decision making; a few exercise a relatively great weight of power, and many exercise comparatively little. But that they are idealizations does not deprive the concepts of usefulness; we may speak of a rule as being more or less autocratic, more or less republican.

The present classification, it must be emphasized, is based on the allocation of power, not its scope. When autocracy is spoken of as having "absolute" rather than "limited" power, it is not entailed that all practices fall within its scope, but only that whatever decisions *are* made are made by the autocrat alone: within its scope his power is not limited by other power holders. A rule may be autocratic even if the effective constitution severely limits its scope; the point is that in such a rule there is no shared participation in the decision-making process. (Thus there might be in a society competing power holders, each limited in scope by the others, and at the same time autocratic within its own scope—for instance, "Church" and "State" in certain periods.) [21]

Oligarchy is the most common type of rule, with regard to allocation of power. The forms of rule distinguished in the preceding section apply most directly to oligarchies, since they arise from a classification of elites. But with modifications they could be applied to autocracies or republics as well; to the former by the base value of the autocrat's power, and to the latter by the composition of the politically most effective elements of the citizenry.

Intermediate between an oligarchy and a republic is a type of rule which might be called *stratarchy.* The ruling group proliferates into an extensive hierarchy, to such a degree that

---

formal power only; "aristocracy" has been found convenient to restrict to oligarchies based on respect; and "democracy" now designates a much more complicated notion to be discussed shortly.

21. It is often useful, however, to distinguish in another sense between *limited* and *total autocracy* (and correspondingly for oligarchies and republics), according to whether the allocated power includes within its scope the power to choose successors.

a high proportion of the body politic may be exercising some weight of power. The oligarchy has been stratified and considerably enlarged. Such a form of rule is closer to republicanism than autocracy in that considerable numbers of the domain of power participate in the process of decision making, although, to be sure, their participation may be limited to the administrative rather than legislative phase.

The term "republic" is here defined in a limited sense: power is allocated throughout the domain.[22] We include under republics both the "pure" form and the representational. But the representation in question must be more than merely formal; otherwise, the policy may be characterized as having a republican regime and an oligarchic or even autocratic rule.

PROP. Change in allocation in the direction of autocracy varies with the heterogeneity in perspective in the power holders.

The more heterogeneous the perspectives of those participating in the process of decision making, the more difficult it is to arrive at agreement in that process (concurrence). Continuity of the control process requires, however, a smooth flow of decisions. To this end, weight of power comes—by authorization or as the outcome of conflict—to the hands of a subgroup of the original oligarchy and, in the limit, to the hands of a single autocrat. This is the more likely to take place as concurrence assumes greater importance for the power holders, as in a war situation, for example. As Willoughby has pointed out (1911, 357–8),

22. A still frequent usage of the term is that insisted on by Thomas Paine (*Writings*, II, 421): "What is called a *republic* is not any *particular form* of government. . . . It is a word of good original referring to what ought to be the character and business of government. . . . Republican government is no other than government established and conducted for the interest of the public, as well individually as collectively." For this concept we shall shortly introduce the term "commonwealth." The present definition roughly coincides with that of the *Federalist* (No. XXXIX) as "a government which derives all its powers directly or indirectly from the great body of the people." (But elsewhere, so shifting and variable is usage in this area, the *Federalist* uses the term "republic" to distinguish the representational from the "pure" democracy [Nos. X and XIV].) Obviously, no single set of definitions can satisfy all the usages of these terms, nor is the present set intended in any sense to standardize usage. It is hoped only that the definitions given here will serve to make clear the various concepts involved, without any greater departure from common usage than is necessary.

The need of a unity of control and a full swing of power is then recognized by all as imperative; and once endowed with power, a commander with a victorious army at his back, and with a people already accustomed to autocratic rule, is easily able to retain his dominion after the necessity for its exercise is past.

Conversely, with a sharing of perspectives power tends to a wider allocation. For by hypothesis the decisions made will not vary significantly from those of a more autocratic rule. And the movement toward republicanism stabilizes the rule by strengthening solidarity: identification with and loyalty to the rule result from more widespread participation in it. (This is one function of coalition governments in the prosecution of a war; simultaneously with an increase in the autocracy of the rule there is an increase in the republicanism of the regime.) The matter is summed up by Friedrich (1937, 16) in the following formulation of the hypothesis: "A tendency toward concentration of power is the concomitant of a rather divided community, while a united community can function with rather dispersed powers."

PROP. As the power potential of the mass increases, allocation moves initially in the direction of autocracy.

Under such conditions concurrence is especially important to the elite. Failure to concur may result in loss of power to the mass (rather, to a counterelite supported by the mass). Hence, whatever increases the power potential of the mass will tend also to shift allocation in the direction of autocracy. Thus, a very low distribution index of important values (as in a depression), which sets up predispositions against the power structure; an increase in class consciousness of the subject classes; high organization of a counterelite; widespread criticism of the ideology, especially with the circulation of a utopia—all are factors making for a shift in the direction of autocracy.[23]

DF. *Regimentation* is increase in the scope of effective power, *voluntarization* is decrease. *Totalitarianism* is the form of rule

23. Compare Friedrich, article on "Oligarchy" in *ESS:* "This tendency of oligarchies to contract . . . seems to be inescapable under certain conditions, notably the threats to vested economic interests which usually attend radical democracies, particularly when they are aggravated by a narrowing field of foreign exploitation. This generalization is borne out not only by Periclean and post-Periclean Athens but by many of the Italian and German city-states as well as by contemporary developments."

with maximum regimentation; *liberalism*, with moderate regimentation; and *anarchy*, minimal.

Regimentation is the correlate at the level of control to governmentalization, increase in scope of authority. Practices are regimented when they are subjected to control, whether authoritative or not—that is, when policies concerning them are coercively sanctioned. Since the exercise of coercion is chiefly in the hands of the supreme power, the degree of regimentation is a measure of the scope of state control.

The term "regimentation" is sometimes extended to any organization of activity, whether or not the organization has a coercive base. The narrower sense of the term seems more useful, however: the politically significant difference is between the state and noncoercive associations, rather than between these private associations and the individual. The reason is that the individual is never free from subjection to influence, whether it is exercised in an organized or unorganized way; but he may be free in certain practices from subjection to power (coercive influence). Hence we define regimentation as a measure of the extent to which practices are coercively controlled, and not merely organized. Voluntarization of a particular practice does not mean that a person engaging in the practice does so without being influenced by others—all interpersonal relations constitute influence of some form or other—but only that the person is not being coerced to that practice.

A system of maximal regimentation is called totalitarian; the scope of power is all-inclusive—"everything for the state, nothing against the state, nothing outside the state." All practices are coercively controlled; in the familiar phrase, everything that isn't forbidden is obligatory. Although totalitarianism and autocracy are conceptually distinct, empirically they are closely associated. A totalitarian power tends to be autocratic, for no other (internal) power exists to oppose it; and conversely, autocratic power will tend to maximize its scope.[24] The distinction between the two emphasizes that their concurrence is a matter of fact, not logical necessity. Totalitarianism may emerge from a republican as well as an autocratic al-

24. Compare Barker, 1942, 289: "Any single authority is by its nature total. Having no other authority at its side, with which it must divide the exercise of power, it will equally leave no possible object (or subject) of power untouched: having no partners in power, it will leave no loop-holes and no exemptions from power."

location of power. The very fact that weight of power is widely dispersed may set up predispositions favorable to the inclusion of more and more practices within the scope of that power.

Liberalism includes some degree of coercive control, but considerable voluntarization as well. The term laissez faire is usually limited in its reference to the scope of polinomic power only—control over economic practices. (Discussions usually concern, moreover, only a part of the scope of polinomic power; other parts—for instance, taxation and the establishment and maintenance of property rights—are regarded as being perfectly compatible with a laissez-faire policy.) Thus a rule might be liberal, as here defined, without following a laissez-faire policy: economic practices might be subjected to the power process without necessarily a regimentation of practices with regard to other values. Whether this is a real possibility is of course an empirical question; the present point is that it is not excluded by the very meaning of the words.

As a rule approximates anarchy, it ceases to have the character of a rule at all. The scope of power shrinks to a minimum —in the limiting case, *no* coercion is exercised. Social control remains, of course, in the various forms of influence; but the control is noncoercive. Whether the weight of noncoercive influence is sufficient to maintain social organization cannot be settled a priori or in a general way. An anarchical society is by definition not a body politic, but it might conceivably retain its societal character. Because anarchy does not come within the range of political science, it cannot be said to be impossible; what does not exist for one observational standpoint might nevertheless be discoverable from other standpoints. We introduce the concept as specifying a limit; whether or not cases do or could exist at the limit falls outside the present inquiry.

PROP. Regimentation of specified practices increases with conflict with regard to those practices.

Practices come under the scope of power as conflicts involving them become (or are expected to become) more intense and widespread. Where integration or even congruity obtains, regimentation is unnecessary, although authority may come to be exercised because of its secondary values—for instance, prestige. Control may remain purely formal, and in the hands of an honorary official.

The conflicts may be of various kinds; in general, it is required that they be deprivational to the ruling class. Rulers, as was pointed out, do not exercise power as a general interest group but in behalf of that class, so that the degree of regimentation is a function of its I:D ratio for the ruling class. Thus regimentation may result from a conflict between opposing sections of the elite, sufficiently intense to threaten the stability of the rule. It may result from a conflict directly between the elite and the mass (or parts of the latter, especially when these are subject to the influence of a counterelite). There may be conflicts between special interest groups which may develop into either of the preceding two types. And finally, the conflict making for regimentation may be with an external power group. For example, religion may be regimented where the priesthood as an actual or potential elite conflicts with other elites; the strike-bound plant taken over by the state is an instance of conflict between elite and mass; laws compelling "fair trade practices" illustrate regimentation as a result of conflict among special interest groups; regimentation of industry in wartime is the case of conflict with external groups. In all these cases regimentation has the function of dealing with conflicts so as to preserve the value position and potential fixed in the rule.

DF. *Concentration* and *dispersion* of power is the degree to which diverse power functions are exercised by the same or distinct power structures. *Dictatorship* is rule by concentrated power; in *balanced rule* power functions are dispersed.

On the formal level, concentration-dispersion is the degree to which offices correspond with governmental functions—for instance, whether the executive agency performs legislative as well as administrative functions, or whether the same officials act as prosecutor, judge, and jury. Dispersion is here known as "separation of powers." The concepts are applicable to control as well as authority structures. The same or different power holders may formulate decisions, determine the conformity to them of specific cases, and apply sanctions to enforce them. In dictatorship these diverse functions are exercised by a single power structure; the separation of effective powers we designate a balanced rule.

The word "dictatorship" is frequently used synonymously with "autocracy" as referring to allocation of power. It is useful, however, to distinguish these two senses, and retain the term for its present definition.[25] Of course, autocracy is always dictatorial, but the converse need not be true. If there is only one ruler, he exercises all the power functions; but all of them might equally be exercised by some one oligarchical or even republican structure.

DF. *Centralization-decentralization* is the territorial and/or functional distribution of power. A *unitary* state is one in which the rule is centralized; a *federal* state, decentralized territorially; *syndicalist*, decentralized functionally.

As with the other categories of this section, the matter is one of degree. Formally, of course, the degree of centralization may be more or less precisely fixed, but on the level of effective power the distribution can be said only to approximate the one extreme or the other.[26]

The scope, weight, and domain of power are all three involved in centralization-decentralization. Different elements in the scope of power are, in general, differently distributed—some centralized, some decentralized. Again, centralization is of different degrees according to the allocation of the weight of power as between the state (the central power) and the subordinate groups. And the territorial and functional divisions pertain, of course, to the domain and scope of power, respectively.

§9.4 *Democracy*

DF. A rule is *equalitarian* in the degree to which elite recruitment is based on values to which there is equal access.

The definition concerns equality only in the political sense, that is, equality in power potential. The empirical relation between such equality and that with regard to other values has been dealt with in previous hypotheses. A high power position

25. The *Federalist* (No. XLVII) even uses the term "tyranny" here: "The accumulation of all powers, legislative, executive and judiciary, in the same hands, whether of one, a few, or many, and whether hereditary, self-appointed, or elective, may justly be pronounced the very definition of tyranny." "Dictatorship" is a somewhat less normatively ambiguous term; we intend it, of course, in a purely descriptive sense.

26. Such distinctions as that between federal states and confederacies have usually a formal reference only; see, for instance, Willoughby's discussion of this distinction in terms of sovereignty, 1911, 253–4.

is in general a necessary and sufficient condition for stable indulgence in relation to wealth, well-being, respect, and so on. Social and economic equality, even if attainable, cannot be maintained without political equality; and where the latter obtains, social and economic equality will result in the degree of its effectiveness.[27] It is equality in the wider sense, to be sure, which has entered into the conception of democracy from Plato to De Tocqueville. But we may restrict the present considerations to political equality, and treat the wider concept as its empirical condition and consequence.

A rule is defined to be equalitarian, not in the degree to which *power* is equally distributed, but rather *access* to power. Power is never equally distributed: there is always an elite, as has been previously emphasized. Theorists as divergent in their political perspectives as Bluntschli and Bryce have agreed on this point, and in almost the same unequivocal terms. Bluntschli writes (1921, 17):

In all states we find the distinction between governors and governed. . . . This distinction appears in the most manifold forms, but is always necessary. Even in the most extreme democracy in which it may seem to vanish it is nevertheless present.

Bryce puts it (1924, II, 542):

In all assemblies and groups and organized bodies of men, from a nation down to a committee of a club, direction and decisions rest in the hands of a small percentage, less and less in proportion to the larger size of the body, till in a great population it becomes an infinitesimally small proportion of the whole number. This is and always has been true of all forms of government, though in different degrees.

If political equality were defined so as to exclude the existence of an elite, the concept would be vacuous.

What is important, and what varies from one body politic to another, is the set of principles according to which the elite is recruited. Tawney says (1931, 87):

27. Compare Willoughby, 1911, 418: "History shows that the attainment of political equality leads inevitably to the demand for social and economic equality, for it does not take long for the lower classes to discover that equality in political rights is of but little value if they are not thereby able to raise their material condition to a comparative degree of equality with that of other members of society."

All forms of social organization are hierarchical. But these gradations may be based on differences of function and office, may relate only to those aspects of life which are relevant to such differences, and may be compatible with the easy movement of individuals, according to their capacity, from one point on the scale to another. Or they may have their source in differences of birth, or wealth, or social position, may embrace all sides of life, including the satisfaction of the elementary human needs which are common to men as men, and may correspond to distinctions, not of capacity, but of opportunity.[28]

The principles of elite recruitment may be such as provide equal opportunity for acquisition of power, or they may severely restrict its acquisition in various ways. The rule is equalitarian in the degree to which the elite is recruited in the one way rather than the other.

A republic is by definition an equalitarian form of rule, since power is not only potentially but actually shared by all in its domain; but this is not the only equalitarian form of rule. Oligarchy and even a limited autocracy might conceivably be equalitarian—for example, the autocrat might be chosen by lot. Political equality, as here defined, is a matter of equal eligibility to power status (of course, effective and not merely formal eligibility). Recruitment of the elite on the basis of skill (technocracy) is not in itself equalitarian unless there is equal access to the acquisition and exercise of skills. A plutocracy is not equalitarian unless there is equal access to wealth; nor an aristocracy unless the acquisition of respect is open to all. Thus nepotism and patronage in a bureaucracy, monopoly in a plutocracy, hereditary nobility in an aristocracy, an officer's caste in a virocracy—all are common institutions by which the respective forms fail of equalitarianism.

The classical discussions of political equality have included specifications of various practices required for such equality

28. Compare the remarks of Pericles on the Athenian democracy, as reported by Thucydides: "Because in the administration it hath respect not to the few, but to the multitude, our form of government is called a democracy. Wherein there is not only an equality amongst all men in point of law for their private controversies, but in election to public offices we consider neither class nor rank, but each man is preferred according to his virtue or to the esteem in which he is held for some special excellence: nor is any one put back even through poverty, because of the obscurity of his person, so long as he can do good service to the commonwealth."

—for instance, inheritance taxes in a plutocracy, or the anonymous training of children in an aristocracy (Plato, More). We may formulate all such requirements in general terms: Political equality requires that practices with regard to the values on which power is based be such that value potential is independent of value position. The effect of position on potential may be called the *transmissiveness* of the value (the value is in the form of "capital" rather than "consumption" goods). Equality requires not necessarily identical positions, but minimal transmissiveness. Not everyone exercises an equal amount of power, but the opportunity to exercise power is equally distributed.

DF. A rule is *libertarian* in the degree that responsibility is to the individual acting (the primary self); *authoritarian*, to others.

Liberty is here defined not in terms of the absence of responsibility but, on the contrary, presupposing it. (The absence of responsibility is usually designated "license.") Liberty is responsibility in which the self is both agent and principal: the self judges the conformity of its acts to the code of responsibility, and itself expects and demands sanctions for its violations. The code of responsibility is not coercively imposed, but is incorporated into the perspectives of the self. The authority entailed by responsibility is established by choice. Thus a rule is libertarian where initiative, individuality, and choice are widespread; authoritarian, if obedience, conformity, and coercion are characteristic.

The definition of liberty in terms of responsibility implies that we are here concerned, not with whether power is naked or not, but with the nature of the authority by which power is justified and the mode of acceptance of this authority. It will not do to say merely that liberty prevails wherever power is exercised "with the consent of the governed." Modern despotisms have made clear that the question turns on what is consented to and how consent is obtained. Slavery is not limited to the coercive deprivation of liberty; enslavement is even more profound when it is internalized, and not only consented to but even demanded by the self.[29]

29. See the elaboration and political application of this point in Fromm's *Escape from Freedom*, Farrar & Rinehart, 1941.

The crucial point is not whether power is clothed in authority—that is, consented to—but whether the consent does not involve a complete transfer of responsibility, and whether it is derived by a freely competitive manipulation of symbols. This conception of liberty is, in terms of the classical tradition, Spinoza's rather than Hobbes's. Spinoza declares (*Tractatus Politicus*, chap. xx):

> The last end of the state is not to dominate men, nor to restrain them by fear; rather it is so to free each man from fear that he may live and act with full security and without injury to himself or his neighbor. The end of the state, I repeat, is not to make rational beings into brute beasts and machines. It is to enable their bodies and their minds to function safely. It is to lead men to live by, and to exercise, a free reason; that they may not waste their strength in hatred, anger and guile, nor act unfairly toward one another. Thus the end of the state is really liberty.

On this conception, there is liberty in a state only when each individual has sufficient self-respect to respect others.

In terms of the way in which consent is arrived at, rather than by the content of what is consented to, liberty requires that an important role in the power process be played by persuasion.[30] It is not sufficient, of course, to say merely that consent is obtained by symbols rather than violence; it is essential that the symbols function with minimal external inducements and constraints. In terms of the distinctions of §5.3, the freely given consent to power which is constitutive of liberty presupposes education rather than indoctrination. Liberty is incompatible with both ignorance and bigotry.

Various types of liberty are sometimes distinguished in terms of the scope of self-responsibility. Thus political liberty is self-responsibility with regard to power, civil or individual liberty wth regard to respect. Political liberty entails either representative or direct self-rule; but the liberty is only formal if it is not effectively self-rule. Once representatives have been elected, it is still possible that practices be subjected to severe discipline, and obedience and conformity stressed at the expense of individual initiative. Thus, while effective representa-

30. Among the early and influential writers to emphasize this point was Bagehot (1873, 158): "A free state—a state with liberty—means a state, call it republic or call it monarchy, in which the sovereign power is divided among many persons, and in which there is discussion among those persons."

tion is a necessary condition of political liberty, it is not sufficient; other conditions will be discussed shortly in connection with the concept of a juridical rule.

Civil and individual liberty has reference to respect practices with regard to which there is self-responsibility. The individual has certain rights and immunities: the power process relegates to him alone the making of decisions (or determination of policy) with regard to certain practices (for instance, expression of opinion).[31] Civil liberty thus entails a voluntarization (rather than regimentation) of certain practices. But here again this is only a necessary but not a sufficient condition. Liberty may be lacking even though practices are not regimented: responsibility may rest neither with the state (rulers) nor the individual, but with private associations to whom the individual has resigned his responsibility. Barnes (1924, 5–6) has remarked that "probably less than a tenth of the limitations in the daily life of the individual, which constitute the real limitations upon personal liberty, are the product of law." Thus a liberal rule, as contrasted with a totalitarian one, is not *necessarily* libertarian (see, for instance, G. Myers's *History of Bigotry in the United States*, Random House, 1943); but, of course, the latter cannot be the case without the former.

DF. A rule is *impartial* in the degree to which there is an effective application of a formula distributing values on bases equally accessible to all. A *commonwealth* is an impartial rule; an *exploitative* rule, a partial one.

A rule is impartial when all values, and not only power, are distributed in terms of equal opportunity. (The definition is thus a generalization of the concept of equalitarian rule.) It is clear that the definition does not require strict equality of distribution. For instance, rewards may be proportionate to skill, provided that there is equal access to the acquisition and exercise of skill (educational opportunities, free choice of vocation, and so on). Indeed, a rule may be impartial even with great inequalities in distribution, if these result, for instance, from casting lots. Whether or not such a distribution is desira-

31. Doctrines of "natural rights" are normatively ambiguous formulations of such liberties. Demands are expressed as assertions of metaphysical fact; the "self-evident truths" of the Declaration of Independence were originally stated to be rather "sacred and undeniable."

ble is of no concern here; for that matter, there is no need to suppose that impartiality alone suffices to determine a satisfactory pattern of distribution. It is in any case useful to differentiate equality of value potential from equality of the value pattern.

The concept of impartiality corresponds in certain ways to the concepts of "justice" in the classical tradition. (The present term, however, is to be understood altogether in a descriptive, nonnormative sense.) An analysis of the various meanings of "justice" in the tradition is, of course, outside the scope of this inquiry. But one persistent element in these meanings is, without doubt, the impartiality of the value distribution. Value, in this connection as elsewhere, includes the negative as well as positive, so that impartiality as here defined includes such elements of justice as "equality before the law." [32]

A commonwealth is defined here in terms of its literal signification: a rule functioning for the *common weal*, enhancing the value position of all members of the society impartially, rather than that of some restricted class. Aristotle's distinction between "true" and "perverted" forms of government is in terms of their impartiality as here defined. All "true" forms are commonwealths:

> Governments which have a regard to the common interest are constituted in accordance with strict principles of justice [*sic*], and are therefore true forms; but those which regard only the interests of rulers are all defective and perverted forms, for they are despotic, whereas a state is a community of freemen (*Politics*, III, 6).

Aristotle's "perverted" forms we call exploitative rules.

Since the ruling class has been defined in terms of maximal benefits from the rule, a commonwealth has no clearly demarcated ruling, dependent, and subject classes. Classes in the sense of groups performing distinctive functions with regard to the various values still exist (the elite, for instance, is a power class), but they are impartially constituted and thus highly permeable. The exploitative society is replaced, not by a classless but a *casteless* society: class differentiations do not involve fixed

32. Other components of the traditional treatment of "justice" will be dealt with shortly in connection with juridical rule. We might mention here, however, the related concept of a *humanitarian rule*, as one in which indulgence exceeds that specified by the impartial rules of distribution. The quality of mercy has perhaps not received that attention in political philosophy which it deserves.

differences in status with regard to the various values of the society.

PROP. The impartiality of a rule varies with its republican character.

The proposition follows from previous hypotheses that the value distribution parallels that of power. Those with power are on the whole the chief beneficiaries of its exercise. The autocrats and oligarchs enjoy a more favorable share of values than do those over whom they have power. Only where power is distributed throughout its domain—that is, in a republic—is the rule impartial. As Aristotle put it (*Politics*, IV): "If liberty and equality, as is thought by some, are chiefly to be found in a democracy, they will be best attained when all persons alike share in the government to the utmost."

The existence of so-called "benevolent despotisms" cannot lightly be taken to be incompatible with this hypothesis. The "benevolence" in question is severely restricted in scope, both power and respect, for example, being ordinarily excluded. Moreover, as will be seen in Chapter 10, whatever the initial scope of "benevolence," it tends to contract till it coincides with the more restricted power pattern.

DF. A rule is *juridical* in the degree that the political formula provides opportunity for the effective challenge of decisions; and otherwise, *tyrannical*.

The present definition is an adaptation of Mosca's concept of "juridical defense." It may be compared also with Friedrich's definition of constitutional government (1937, 103) as "one with effective and regularized restraints on political, and especially, governmental action."[33] Timasheff makes a similar distinction (1939, 215) in terms of "legal order" and "despotic rule."

The juridical character does in fact correspond to a legal order, in that decisions are made in accord with specified rules (as set down in the political formula) rather than arbitrarily. That is, opportunity for challenge is provided for only when

33. Opportunity for challenge includes "restraints" but not conversely: power might be restrained—limited in scope—and yet tyrannical (arbitrary) within that scope.

conditions are set forth which decisions must meet, other than merely having been decided by certain persons (for instance, a divinely ordained king). The decision is challenged by an appraisal of it in terms of these conditions, which must be met by rulers as well as ruled.[34] The pattern of authority is thus describable, in the familiar phrase, as a "government of laws, not men."

Juridical control of decisions thus makes possible (though not necessary) the development of stable expectations with regard to the power process. Each particular decision is integrated with the whole pattern of decisions occurring in the society. Where such integration is lacking, we speak of tyranny: "Where law ends, tyranny begins." Tyranny is defined here as rule by decisions not open to authoritative challenge.

A rule is not juridical, of course, unless the opportunity for challenge is effective and not merely formal.[35] Such effectiveness requires that the rule be balanced, rather than dictatorial: different functions must be exercised by different organs. The "separation of powers" must hold, moreover, in terms of control, and not merely with regard to formal arrangements. Mosca says (1939, 138):

> If one political institution is to be an effective curb upon the activity of another, it must represent a political force—it must, that is, be the organized expression of a social influence and a social authority that has some standing in the community, as against the forces that are expressed in the political institution that is to be controlled.

The existence of a formal legal structure does not suffice, therefore, to make a rule juridical. A plurality of power centers is more important in this regard than formal limitations of authority. Friedrich puts the point very simply (1937, 499): "All political power is subject to abuse, no matter what the legal form of its exercise. But concentrated power is very much more easily abused than divided power." (There is, of course, an optimal degree of dispersion of power beyond which anarchy and thence tyranny is again more probable.)

Various political forms may be specified as adding to the op-

34. This last is taken as the essential requirement for legal order by R. v. Stammler, *Wirtschaft und Recht,* Veit, 1924, 483–500.

35. The challenge must be authoritative as well as effective: "despotism tempered by assassination" is still despotism.

portunity for effective challenge of decisions. Short tenures and removability from office, initiative and referendum, trial by jury and other such provisions are held to contribute in varying degrees to the juridical character of a rule. The scope of power, it might be mentioned, is not in itself directly related to juridical defense (though it may have an important bearing on whether the rule remains balanced rather than dictatorial). Indeed, it may well be that an enlarged scope of power is more favorable to the maintenance of juridical defense than a narrower scope, since conflicts *will* be resolved whether or not they fall within the formal scope of decision making, and the juridical character is less likely to be preserved in such nonformal decisions. As the *Federalist* has pointed out (No. XX), "Tyranny has perhaps oftener grown out of the assumptions of power, called for, on pressing exigencies, by a defective constitution, than out of the full exercise of the largest constitutional authorities."

DF. A *democracy* is a libertarian, juridical commonwealth; a *despotism* is a nondemocratic rule.

Democracy is thus defined here by three characteristics of the power process: (1) Power is exercised with a maximum of self-responsibility. Democracy is incompatible with any form of authoritarianism, regardless of the benefits accruing from such concentration of responsibility. (2) The power process is not absolute and self-contained: decisions are conditional and subject to challenge. Democracy is incompatible with arbitrary and uncontrolled exercise of power, regardless of the majorities by which it is exercised. (3) The benefits of the power process are distributed throughout the body politic. Democracy is incompatible with the existence of privileged castes, regardless of expectations concerning the assumed "common interest."

Other characteristics are related to these, both empirically and by definition. Thus a democracy is liberal rather than totalitarian (voluntarization is maximized, regimentation minimized), by the definition of libertarian in terms of self-responsibility. It is equalitarian (the elite constitutes an open class rather than a closed caste) by the definition of commonwealth in terms of impartiality. It is republican rather than autocratic (an inclusive rather than restricted oligarchy), as an empirical condition of impartiality. And the rule is balanced (dispersed) rather than dictatorial (concentrated) as an empirical condition of juridical defense. Thus an equivalent definition might have been formulated in terms of other combinations of characters, and indeed different characteristics or combinations of them have been taken by various writers as *the* definition of "democracy," all of them being in fact involved in one way or another. Similarly, the concept of despotism has various components, a rule being describable as despotic because it is autocratic, or totalitarian, or exploitative, and so on. The following table lists the various characteristics of democratic and despotic rule discussed in this chapter.

TABLE 9

Characteristics of Democratic and Despotic Rule

Characteristic	*Democratic Rule*	*Despotic Rule*
Allocation of Power	Republican (Inclusive Elite)	Autocratic (Restricted Elite)
Scope of Power	Liberal (Voluntarization)	Totalitarian (Regimentation)
Distribution of Power	Balance (Dispersion)	Dictatorial (Concentration)
Elite Recruitment	Equalitarian (Open Class)	Discriminatory (Closed Class-Caste)
Responsibility	Libertarian (Self)	Authoritarian (Other)
Value Distribution	Benefactive (Commonwealth)	Exploitative
	(Impartial)	(Partial)
Decisions	Juridical (Challengeable)	Tyrannical (Unchallengeable)

PROP. The stability of a democratic rule varies with the democratic features of the social order.

We have previously discussed the importance of the social order in setting limits to the exercise of power. Particularly is it relevant to the maintenance of juridical defense. Laski, among others, states categorically (1925, 85, 103–4):

> Governments are made responsible less by the laws they must obey than by the character they will encounter. . . . The maintenance of rights is much more a question of habit and tradition than of the

formality of legal enactment. It is the proud spirit of citizens, more than the letter of the law, that is their most real safeguard.

Maintenance of juridical defense requires, that is to say, the integration into the self of the perspectives described as "a democratic tradition."

Similarly, the maintenance of a libertarian rule requires a structure of character and habit capable of self-responsibility. As Bryce observes (1893, I, chap. 26), "It takes many centuries to form those habits of compromise, that love of order, and respect for public opinion, which makes democracy tolerable." Bryce formulates the matter in terms of servitude as a "natural state" of mankind; but the point he deals with has in recent decades been investigated in empirical psychological terms.[36]

The hypothesis must be qualified, however, by a recognition of the converse relationship between rule and social order: the rule itself has an important effect on character and habit.[37] The direction of the causal connection, however, is of less concern than the hypothesis of a co-relation between democratic rule and democratic social order. Democracy cannot, on this hypothesis, be established and maintained with attention only to matters of political mechanics—the organization and operation of the structures of authority and control. The personalities involved in these operations are of direct relevance.

PROP. The stability of democratic rule varies with the degree of politicization of conduct.

The politicization of the personality may be singled out as a trait of particular importance to the maintenance of democ-

36. See, for instance, R. Lippitt, "An Experimental Study of Authoritarian and Democratic Group Atmospheres," *Studies in Topological and Vector Psychology*, I, University of Iowa Press, 1940, under the direction of Kurt Lewin. That democratic rule rests on certain features of the "democratic character" is familiar in the tradition (for example, in the *Federalist*, No. LV); what is new in the present day is the body of empirical inquiry into the conditions and consequences of the development of such a character structure.

37. This converse relationship is discussed at length in Greek political philosophy, especially Plato. In the modern period, C. A. Helvetius makes this relationship fundamental. "The vices and virtues of a people are always a necessary effect of their legislation," he insists (*De l'esprit*, III, xxii). In this position he is followed by Dicey, among others: "The true importance of laws lies far less in their direct result than in their effect upon the sentiment or convictions of the public" (1926, 42).

racy, which rests on a widespread and intense concern with the distribution and exercise of power. Disinterest in political relations and practices is an abdication of self-responsibility. As Rousseau has declared (*Social Contract*, III, 15), "As soon as any man says of the state, 'What does it matter to me?' the state may be given up for lost." Similarly, maintenance of juridical defense requires constant consideration of the power consequences of policy. Eternal vigilance is the price of liberty because power tends to expand till limited by other power holders. Where the citizenry is not politicized, the power process will thus tend to shift in the direction of various despotic characteristics: oligarchy will contract, regimentation increase, power become more concentrated and less open to challenge, and so on.[38]

PROP. A democratic regime is a necessary condition for democratic rule.

While an appropriate character, habit, and tradition are necessary they are not in themselves sufficient conditions for the maintenance of democracy. The regime must conform to this character and habit. "The entire history of government," Friedrich argues (1937, 144), "shows that substantive restraints embodying the opinion and customs of the community, their way of life, rest upon a tenuous foundation, unless reinforced and backed up by procedural restraints of one sort or another." The sentimentalized expectations, demands, and identifications on which the regime rests are themselves components of the personality, and unless these are integrated with the other personality traits, the "democratic character" is ineffective.

For example, the habit of giving due consideration to divergent perspectives and opinions is of little political consequence in a state where only one party can legally function and a small elite controls the decisions of the party. The point has been generalized by Mosca, who warns (1939, 134, 147):

38. Here again the Athenian democracy, at least in its own perspectives, provides a useful example. "An Athenian citizen does not neglect the state because he takes care of his own household; and even those of us who are engaged in business have a very fair idea of politics. We alone regard a man who takes no interest in public affairs, not as a harmless, but as a useless character; and if few of us are originators, we are all sound judges of policy" (Pericles' Funeral Oration).

The absolute preponderance of a single political force, the predominance of any over-simplified concept in the organization of the state, the strictly logical application of any single principle in all public law are the essential elements in any type of despotism; for they enable anyone who is in power to exploit the advantages of a superior position more thoroughly for the benefit of his own interests and passions. . . . When a system of political organization is based upon a single absolute principle, so that the whole political class is organized after a single pattern, it is difficult for all social forces to participate in public life, and more difficult still for any one force to counterbalance another.

A particularly important characteristic of the regime is the degree of sentimentalization of the political doctrine on which it is based. For liberty includes freedom to challenge authority externally imposed in favor of the exercise of self-responsibility; and sentimentalization makes for intensity and rigidity in the perspectives of authority. Mosca has again put the matter clearly and forcefully (p. 139):

If a political organism is to progress in the direction of attaining greater and greater improvement in juridical defense, the prime and most essential requisite is that the principle on which the exercise of temporal authority is based shall have nothing sacred and immutable about it. When power rests on a system of ideas and beliefs outside of which it is felt that there can be neither truth nor justice, it is almost impossible that its acts should be debated and moderated in practice.

Of course, a democratic regime is in turn only a necessary but not a sufficient condition for democracy. The nature of the control process is fundamental. For one thing, as has been seen, the regime is changed when it conflicts inescapably with the interests of the ruling class. More important, the regime itself cannot guarantee liberty and equality because it is not determinative of the underlying control structures and functions. *Formally*, the peak of political equality is reached with universal suffrage: one man, one vote. But, as has been amply attested, "the democratic device of universal suffrage does not destroy economic classes or economic inequalities. It ignores them" (Beard, 1934, 3). The same is true of other classes and inequalities which have an important place in the control process. Similarly, a political form of "checks and balances" is ineffective unless the elements balanced against one another are in fact representative of different control groups.

In short, it is the entire social structure that must embody democracy, not merely the social order, the regime, or the rule alone. The problem of establishing and maintaining democracy is not a problem alone of character and education, or of suitable political forms, or of patterns and functions of control, but of all of these together.

The major points in the present treatment of the concept of democracy might be summarized as follows: (1) The formulations throughout are descriptive rather than normatively ambiguous. The question of how democracy is constituted and may be maintained is dealt with in terms which, it is hoped, lend themselves to the proliferation of empirical inquiries rather than the elaboration of metaphysical ideals and justifications. (2) The concept of democracy is analyzed so as to exhibit a content of great complexity, rather than in terms of some single characteristic like "self-government" or "freedom." (3) This is of particular significance as leading to a consideration of the complexity of conditions on which democracy rests. Democracy is not simply a matter of this or that feature of the social structure; the social order, the regime and the control structure are all involved. (4) Thus democracy is dealt with as a possible, though difficult, pattern of social organization.

If in recent years analysis of the power process has automatically been taken to be an obituary of democracy, this is due, we have tried to suggest, to the fact that democracy has often been unrealistically conceived in abstraction from the power process. The supposition that an analysis of the latter leads inevitably to a rejection of the democratic ideal indicates not loyalty to but suspicion of that ideal. It is a supposition which the present authors, at any rate, emphatically do not grant.

X

PROCESS

Among the prominent features of the political process are the rise and fall of political movements, and the occurrence and resolution of revolutionary and war crises.

§10.1 *Political Acts, Movements, and Cycles*

DF. A *political act* is one performed in power perspectives; a *political movement* is a continuing political act performed by an aggregate of persons in a power perspective of elaborated identifications, demands, and expectations.

We conclude our discussion of the political process, as we began, with a consideration of the *act* as the unit of which this process—and, indeed, all interpersonal relations—are composed. Like other acts, the political act passes through phases of "impulse," "subjectivity," and "expression." Conduct is goal-directed and hence implicates values; the impulsive phase of the act is constituted by the needs of or initial striving for those values. Every actor must take account of other actors in his environment as interfering with or supporting these strivings. Thus there emerge as further values, both instrumental and intrinsic, influence and power—control over others on the basis of lesser or greater sanctions. The political act takes its origin in a situation in which the actor strives for the attainment of various values for which power is a necessary (and perhaps also sufficient) condition.

Symbols of the ego in relation to others constitute the self of the actor, and provide identifications in the name of which the political act continues. Symbols of demand formulate the goals of the act (as well as the subsidiary goals of enlisting others in its support). Symbols of expectation present the self and environment in relation to the attainment of these goals. The phase of subjectivity is constituted by the workings of such symbols.

In these perspectives, the operations of power striving take shape as practices of various kinds, constituting the phase of expression of the act. Groups may be formed, articulated in complex structures, and performing a variety of functions transcending, transforming, or even reversing the original goals. Of course, the act may be interrupted in any of its phases, or it may terminate and give way to a new impulse without attainment of its goal.

A political movement is most simply characterized as a collective political act so conceived. It is performed by a large number of persons, exhibiting varying degrees of solidarity and organization (so that it is a wider concept than "a political act of a group"); engaged in a continuing pattern of practices (so that a single election is not a movement, though the campaign leading up to and including it may constitute one); and in a perspective which does not antecedently limit the goals, plans, and participants (so that a movement may change its direction or composition without losing its identity).[1]

As with the individual act, a political movement originates in a situation of need or tension. Insecurity and frustration (or contrariwise, highly indulgent expectations) produce a stress toward action. Initially, the experiences on which this stress is based are individual and private. Gradually, they are related to the experiences of others, and the private malaise or sense of unrealized opportunity ("if only things were different!") acquires a vaguely social formulation. Symbols of diagnosis and prescription multiply; symbols of identification emerge in relation to these, and the number of demands and expectations current is progressively limited. (This is the phase of subjectivity—public opinion, if the expectation of violence is relatively low.) The situation then becomes well defined, alignments take shape, and the movement passes into the phase of expression, with manipulation of directed symbols, goods, and services, and possibly violence, concurrently with such political practices as voting or legislating.

1. Since an act is defined as political in terms of its perspectives, its characterization as such may vary with changing observational standpoints. Thus a movement may appear to its participants as purely religious, say, and to outsiders as definitely political. The definition selected here takes the standpoint of the actor himself, and classifies the act as political only if power enters significantly into the perspectives of the actor as end or means for the act. Other definitions might emphasize the likelihood of later occurrence of such perspectives, or power consequences independent of perspective, and so on.

The situation is then transformed; *readjustment* is said to take place if the movement has had considerable effect on the environment, *catharsis* if its environmental impact has been minimal. In the former case, different patterns emerge according to whether or not violence is (or is expected to be) employed—we speak in this connection of crisis and its resolution. In the latter case, the needs with which the movement originated may or may not recur, and the conception of cyclical patterns becomes relevant.

DF. A *crisis* is a conflict situation of extreme intensity (high expectations of violence).

Intensity has been defined as stress toward action. When opposing powers conflict with one another, expectations of violence increase as the conflict becomes more severe, and the stress toward action to resolve the conflict correspondingly greater. Of course, the nature of the conflict, and of the acts stressing for completion, are not necessarily clear and explicit to the actors in the situation. The two major types of situation in which the expectation of violence is high are the war crisis and the revolutionary crisis. These will be discussed in the next sections. Here we will consider crisis briefly in general terms.

The development of a crisis situation from one of initially low intensity may be described from the side of perspectives in terms of the changing content of demands, expectations and identifications, and from the side of operations in terms of the manipulation of goods and services, instruments of violence, and symbols.

Sharp changes in the I:D ratio—sudden increase in deprivation without expectation of corresponding indulgence—increase intensity. A stress arises toward corrective action. However, it is the I:D ratio demanded, and not the deprivation itself, which is important: one may make sacrifices for future or symbolic indulgences. The increase of intensity is furthered by identification with others expected to be (or to have been) deprived; for such identifications increase the expectations of success in the corrective action, and moreover serve as a justification for it—it has more than a limited personal basis. A sudden deterioration in the general economic position of the group exemplifies this factor in the precipitation of crisis.

Changes with regard to the instruments of violence constitute a second factor making for crisis. Here it is the expectations which are fundamental. Shifts in the pattern of potential deprivation give rise to a stress toward action to forestall the threat. This is particularly so in the case of expectations of violence, since violence is exclusive of other practices of resolving conflicts: there can be no expectations of successful negotiation, for instance, without meeting this threat. Here an example is provided by naval maneuvers or the mobilization of reserves.

Similarly, manipulation by the other individual or group of symbols deprivational to the self increases intensity, setting up stress toward action to reaffirm the value of the self (see the next proposition). Here identifications constitute the important element of subjectivity: it is "we" against "them." The role of propaganda in the war crisis has been dealt with elsewhere at length.

Not every conflict, of course, eventuates in crisis: it may be resolved before the intensity of the situation mounts to an extreme. Whether or not such a resolution is possible depends, in general, on how easily the environment may be modified so as to eliminate the conflict, and on the flexibility of the predispositions leading to the conflicting acts. If to render the conflicting acts congruous the environment must be subjected to more thoroughgoing readjustment than the participants are willing or able to undertake, and the predispositions are too rigid to allow for modifications in the acts in question, crisis results.

Crisis is precipitated, therefore, not merely by conflict, but by the failure of available practices for the resolution of conflict. The matter is put in just this way by Friedrich (1937, 454–5): "Breakdown is not the result of special interests dividing the community, but rather of the particular maladjustments which prevent compromise between these interests."

Among such maladjustments, an especially important one is an erratic rate of change in conditions and considerations. Smooth adjustments can be made only with difficulty to fluctuating rates of change in the environment. The erratic tempo heightens uncertainty; frustration is generated by uncertainty, and destructiveness springs from frustration.

PROP. Conflicting political symbols increase in frequency and intensity with the intensity of the political situation.

The increasingly intense conflicts in the political arena are mirrored in the symbols reaching the focus of attention of the participants in the arena.[2] Such symbols are both a condition and consequence of power conflicts. Opposition grounded in conflicts of interest are solidified, and predispositional insecurities exacerbated by conflicting propagandas; and the incremental conflicts and insecurities thus generated in turn produce more, and more intense, symbols of the conflict. As the writer of Proverbs has it, "grievous words stir up anger."

Whether or not the proliferation of political symbols precipitates crisis depends, among other things, on the initial intensity of the situation. Where initial intensity is low, symbols may function to produce catharsis rather than crisis. The function of oppositional criticism as a safety valve is familiar. Again, the symbols may serve to maintain expectations of fulfillment of various demands when in fact the elite is unable or unwilling to satisfy these demands.[3] Or, more generally, manipulation of symbols may take the place of bread and circuses in "diverting, distracting, confusing and dissipating the insecurities of the mass."

PROP. As crisis continues, dominant power increases in both scope and weight.

The various fields of activity of the participants in the situation are brought under the scope of power so as to increase the expectations of a resolution of the crisis indulgent to those participants. The crisis tends to make itself felt in everything that is done in the situation: the more severe the crisis, the closer the approach to "total war."

Those over whom power is exercised relinquish what weight of power they have to the dominant power holders on the basis, first, of identifications with their leaders. The demand for

2. For a general discussion see Mannheim, 1936, and Lasswell and Blumenstock, 1939. See also L. P. Edwards, 1927, 112 ff.

3. Compare Bacon's essay on "Seditions and Troubles": "Certainly, the politic and artificial nourishing of hopes, is one of the best antidotes against the poison of discontentments; and it is a certain sign of a wise government and proceeding, when it can hold men's hearts by hopes, when it cannot by satisfaction."

resolution of the crisis acts on the predispositions set up by these identifications to strengthen, initially at least, faith in the leadership. (An element of charisma may come into play to offset insecurity: there is no limit to what the leader can accomplish with the weight of power in his hands.) This pressure is reinforced by the demands made by the self on the self: to relinquish the share of power is to acquit the self of responsibility. There are involved also expectations concerning expediency. Crisis is taken to impose restrictions on the process of decision making which necessitate more and more participation in the process by fewer and fewer power holders.

Hence, as the situation approaches crisis, the increase in scope and weight of dominant power makes itself felt within the elite as well. The elite contracts, power becoming concentrated in the hands of the initially most powerful segment of the elite. The lesser power holders relinquish their share in the expectation of a more expedient and indulgent resolution of the crisis, and more especially, to absolve themselves of responsibility, so as to prepare for a later favorable power position.

Further factors are operative within the elite. The crisis may be exploited by rival groups within the elite in the process of internal power striving. The threats implicit in the crisis situation for the elite as a whole provide a point of leverage for the dominant faction to improve its power position over against the opposition factions. Moreover, a section of the elite may be deprived of power (or other values) as a measure of resolution of the crisis. Such deprivation may make available goods and services, or increase the effectiveness of symbols in resolving the crisis, or strengthening fighting effectiveness (for instance, by improving morale.) Again, elite recruitment in a crisis situation tends to be based on skills appropriate to a resolution of the crisis favorable to the elite. Sections of the elite recruited on the basis of other skills (or other values than skill altogether) suffer a corresponding deprivation in power position.

The final outcome of the crisis situation, in spite of these factors making for contraction, may nevertheless be an expansion of the elite. The practices adopted may not suffice for a resolution of the crisis in which the elite as a whole can maintain its power position without incorporating new elements.

DF. *Political cycles* are sequences in which a given power relationship is regularly resumed after deviations from it.

The concept of a cycle is useful only if the recurring pattern can be described in sufficiently specific terms. The political process may be analyzed, as was pointed out, into a sequence of political acts; and since each act (if completed) runs through the same phases of impulse, subjectivity, and expression, one might be tempted to speak of a cycle of political needs, their symbolization, and their attainment or frustration, new needs thereupon arising and the process being repeated. Clearly, nothing is gained by speaking of cycles in such general terms. The pattern may fruitfully be conceived as cyclical only if closely similar needs continually recur and are continually dealt with in virtually the same ways.

Often, the attempt has been made to describe cyclical movements in terms of the so-called "law of the pendulum." [4] The "law" itself is only a restatement of the cyclical character of the pattern. The empirical problem is to isolate the conditions under which the pendulum movement in fact takes place. The assertion that every "extreme" political situation tends to develop into the "opposite extreme" is either a piece of metaphysical dialectic without empirical content, or a vague reference to one of the conditions of occurrence of cycles, requiring a fuller analysis of the concept of an "extreme." Among the cycles frequently alleged to occur are: war and peace, democracy and despotism, individualism and regimentation, centralization and decentralization, revolution and reaction. Rather than considering each of these explicitly, we shall formulate a general hypothesis on the occurence of cycles and describe in detail one or two examples.

PROP. Political cycles depend upon temporary differences in the I:D expectations of arena participants of equal power potential.

By definition, a political cycle exhibits two characteristics: an equilibrium pattern and a transitory disequilibrium. The hypothesis relates equilibrium to *equality* of potential, and pro-

4. See, for instance, G. E. G. Catlin's analysis of William B. Munro's paper in S. A. Rice, ed., *Methods in Social Science; a Case Book,* University of Chicago Press, 1931, Analysis 3.

vides for disequilibrium by reference to equality of *potential.* If potentials differ, the earlier state of equilibrium (if any) is not resumed, but the situation is permanently altered. Of course, the new equilibrium may in turn show transitory disequilibria.[5]

The hypothesis is, then, that cycles occur when there are differences in the degree of actualization of opposing powers potentially equal. If one participant or group of participants devotes itself to nonpolitical activities (or otherwise fails to maximize the impact of its power), decisions may be made that diverge from their preferences. With increasing divergence, there is increasing stress toward action on the part of the inactive participants, equality of potential then resulting in a redress of the balance, and the cycle is completed.

Obviously these conditions are very special, and cannot be assumed to hold throughout the political process. Potential depends to a considerable extent on power position, and power has usually a low distribution index. (Thus a ruling elite has today more nearly a monopoly over instruments of violence than ever before, whereas the gladiators of Spartacus, for instance, were as well armed, comparatively speaking, as the troops of Imperial Rome.) Again, even where potential is initially equal, it may not remain equal long enough for restoration of the equilibrium to get under way. (Here we have the familiar "too little and too late.") Or, conversely, the difference in potential may move so far in the other direction as again to prevent restoration of equilibrium. (Thus a successful revolution may profit from its own experience sufficiently to make counterrevolution vastly more difficult than the original political transformation.) Such considerations render dubious in the extreme any universalized form of the "law of the pendulum."

Nevertheless, some cycles do seem to occur; one of the most familiar is the *reform cycle* so often observed in American city politics. A prominent feature of the cycle is the "reform wave," in which citizens become extremely active in politics, protesting against "inefficiency" and "lawlessness," and adopting slogans about "business administration" and "law enforcement." The reform mayor and his officials may indeed restore

5. Some cyclical theories set up a number of positions of partial equilibrium within a recurring series, so there is movement through a series of stages rather than immediate return to the initial situation. The Aristotelian cycles are of this pattern. But ultimate recurrence of the original equilibrium is required in any case.

efficiency and reduce laxity in the police department and the courts. It is customary to say that the "good citizens" have been awakened to their "civic responsibilities." Evidently, in our terms, there has been a change in the I:D expectations that prevailed during the phase of the cycle in which "corruption" was spreading. Once more citizens are intensely interested in political news and comment; they finance campaigns, attend meetings, and canvass electors; pessimism about "dirty politics" has given way to optimistic expectations about the results of "throwing the rascals out."

Meanwhile the level of political participation on the part of certain elements in the community has remained relatively constant. The party politicians, the businesses requiring protection from the law (and the mores)—like prostitution and gambling, the businesses in search of franchises and government contracts, the individuals seeking patronage and sinecures—all remain politically alert. Clearly, they can be said to value power more steadily than do other citizens. They recognize that eternal vigilance is the price of their liberty to retain and extend their economic advantages. As individuals, their value position in society appears to them to depend upon power to a greater degree than is usual in the community.

Closer analysis of the reform cycle offers further illustration of the hypothesis here formulated. The voting behavior of electors living in different parts of the city conforms to the theory.

For many purposes it is convenient to classify a city into three zones, according to the income and mobility of its inhabitants. Zone One is an area of lodging houses and hotels; Zone Two includes middle-income residences; Zone Three, upper-income residences. (Often these zones approximate concentric circles, with Zone One adjacent to the centers of passenger transportation and retail shopping.) Politically significant demands are localized in these areas. The high mobility prevailing in Zone One is conducive to countermores conduct, such as sexual vice and gambling. Those with political power can increase their income by giving protection to these illicit activities. Furthermore, Zone One has a relatively high proportion of newcomers who want an economic foothold in the city, and give votes in return for jobs. Zones Two and Three include the more permanent residents who are raising families, and want protection from countermores conduct; moreover, they want adequate services, which involve property improvements like parks, lighted thoroughfares, and schools.

A rough political equilibrium is established among these zones. To some extent the demand for property improvement is integrated with the demand for jobs—jobs on the construction, maintenance, and operation of utilities, for instance. The demand in Zone One to escape the law, and the demand elsewhere for the law to be applied, can both be accommodated by laxity in Zone One and more rigid enforcement elsewhere.

But it is evident that the equilibrium is constantly threatened by the continuous influx of Zone One elements, who tend to extend countermores activities beyond their area. And although Zone One elements want the government to make larger expenditures on the improvement of property (affording jobs and contracts), they have no concern for efficient administration. Residents of Zones Two and Three, on the contrary, are torn between the demand for services and the demand to keep taxes at a minimum. Zone Three residents tend to concern themselves with social values, and to travel; hence they readily allow local political affairs to slip out of the focus of attention. It is only when cumulative encroachments by countermores activities and repeated scandals of inefficiency remind them once more of politics that Zone Three asserts its full weight. They go to the polls in relatively greater numbers; and they vote against proposed bond issues. Zone One, on the other hand, goes to the polls much as usual, and votes as usual for expenditures.[6]

It is apparent that the city reform cycle will subside in prominence if America becomes more actively threatened from without, and urban politics are subordinated to national interests. Power factors will arrange themselves in a new, and perhaps relatively more stable, equilibrium.

Another illustration of the political cycle is provided by the expansion-contraction sequence characteristic of monopolistic political parties (in our terms, political orders), to which we referred in a previous chapter. When the risks of party membership are high, especially during the struggle for the seizure of power, only persons strongly identified with the cause

6. See Robert E. Park and E. W. Burgess, *The City,* University of Chicago Press, 1925; and the ecological studies stimulated thereby.

(or its leaders) are likely to adhere to the organization. When the new order is established, the potential benefits of membership are attractive to opportunists of every kind. Party members are appealed to on grounds of kinship, friendship, and alleged conversion to endorse applications for the party rolls. Some members may endorse certain individuals in the hope of strengthening their own power position in a party local. Furthermore, when political crises are less intense, stress is laid upon other values than ideological purity. Skill in production or congeniality of temperament appear relatively more contributory to the daily tasks of the new order than they did before.

In consequence, party membership expands, and fanaticism correspondingly diminishes. But this process in turn sets up responses tending toward contraction. Many of the older party members have a strong vested interest in "fundamentalism," in keeping alive the ideological integrity of the movement. When they are in danger of being pushed to one side, perhaps on grounds that have little to do with doctrine, there is a disposition on their part to defend themselves by posing a doctrinal issue, and forcing the expulsion of the "unorthodox" from the political order. When such expulsions are attended by executions and other severely deprivational measures, they constitute a *purge*. Thereafter, the expectations that maintain crisis die down, as the victors feel more secure; and the factors making for dilution and expansion once more make headway. Thus is completed a cycle of expansion-contraction that is likened by Roberto Michels (*Italien von Heute*) to an "accordion rhythm." Here again we observe the important consequences that flow from differences in the timing of action by conflicting powers of equal potential.

§10.2 *Balancing of Power: the War Crisis*

DF. The *balancing of power* is the power process among the participants in an arena.

We have previously introduced various terms to designate characteristic phases of arena activity: encounter, determination, decision, alignment, ascendancy. For the entire process the historical term "balance of power" (or, more accurately, "balancing" of power) is available. A similar process can be defined for other values than power: it is the pattern of interaction with regard to the value in question (see §4.4 and Table 1). Thus "balance of trade" relates to wealth and the market, rather than power and the arena, the market including practices of exchange, production, transaction, and pricing. Similarly, in cultures in which respect is a value of great importance, the concept of "balance of face" has been found useful.[7]

Attention is being directed to this generality of the concept so as to bring out once more the perspectives in which the present framework is being developed. The subject matter of political science, as of any of the other social sciences, is the social process in its entirety; but for each science a particular value—here, power—is selected as the observational standpoint from which this process is considered. Military, economic, ideological, and diplomatic factors are not merely "relevant" to the balance of power, but constitute it.

It is to be noted that what has been defined here is a process, not a state of equilibrium. There is no assumption involved that an equilibrium always exists or can be brought about. Hence we speak of "balancing" rather than "balance" of power. The balancing of power is a component of every social process, not merely a characteristic of certain special conditions like those existing, say, in Europe during the last two centuries. (The term "balance" is to be construed more in the sense of "remainder" than in the sense of "equilibrium." Equilibrium holds only in the very special case where the "remainder"—the preponderance of power of a particular alignment compared with the others—is zero.)

Moreover, the power-balancing process must be sharply distinguished from particular "balance of power" doctrines. Such doctrines formulate policies (strategies) to be pursued by participants in the process, and are not to be confused with the

7. One of the first to use the term "balance of trade" was Francis Bacon, who also spoke of "balance of glory." See A. Wolf's *History of Science, Technology, and Philosophy in the 16th and 17th Centuries*, Macmillan, 1939, 614–15. An eighteenth-century comment on the balance of both trade and power is in Hume's *Political Discourses*, No. 6, 1752. On balance of face, see, for instance, A. H. Smith, *Chinese Characteristics*, Fleming H. Revell, 1894, 17: "In the adjustment of the incessant quarrels which distract every hamlet, it is necessary for the 'peace-talkers' to take as careful account of the balance of 'face' as European statesmen once did [*sic*] of the balance of power."

process itself. Typical doctrines are expressed in the familiar phrases: "no entangling alliances," "divide and conquer," "support the winning side," "unite against potential aggressors," and so on. Such phrases formulate perspectives within which power policy is to be determined. But the process may —and to some degree always does—take place without the elaboration of doctrines regarding it. The participants in the balancing do not necessarily think about or have a theory of the process as a whole. Power is not always a considered value, and power considerations, phrased in other terms, are often not recognized for what they are.

The balancing of power is particularly affected by the expectations that prevail about the probable mode by which conflicts will be settled.

DF. An arena is *military* when the expectation of violence is high; *civic*, when the expectation is low.

It is evident that the world as a whole constitutes a military arena, since the possibility of war is never completely out of consideration when major diplomatic issues are being negotiated. The internal life of a state constitutes a civic arena, save when the established order is under revolutionary attack (or in other periods of "martial law").

PROP. In a continued military arena participants tend to segregate into an encircled and an encircling group.

When the expectation of violence is high, participants in the arena continually group and regroup themselves into watchful and potentially belligerent combinations. World political history is a story of shifting alignments. Even on the eve of war, hostile powers may be cautiously feeling one another out with a view to a new combination, as was true of Germany and Britain in 1914, and of Germany and Russia in 1939.

The pattern of segregation is most clearly seen in a military arena in which there are several powers; but the pure pattern of encircled-encircling is seldom found. In World War I the Central Powers were almost completely encircled for a short time in 1917 before the collapse of Russia and after the entry of the United States. Even at that point the segregation was not complete, since some small neutral powers were permitted to exist.

PROP. In civic arenas participants tend to disperse (rather than segregate).

One premonitory sign of approaching war between North and South was the territorial segregation of opinion holders on hotly contested issues in large sectional regions. Since 1865, on the contrary, there has been a long attrition of the "solid South." In smaller localities segregation is not an unusual phenomenon. Especially familiar are the political cleavages between those who dwell in cities and the farmers, and, inside cities, the typical contrast in the political attitudes and perspectives of the residents of poor and of rich wards.

During noncrisis periods, persons of conflicting attitudes can live side by side. As antagonisms intensify, however, the dispersed pattern is broken up as fellow believers seek safety in segregation (the Loyalist families in the American colonies, for instance, sought refuge during the secession from the Empire by fleeing to the strongholds of imperial authority in New York and Canada).

PROP. The attention of a participant in an arena is focused on the sources of greatest expected deprivation, and greatest expected indulgence.

This proposition is a corollary of the earlier one that power holders strive to maximize their I:D ratio with regard to power. Statesmen pay attention to opportunities for power, putting pressure on the submissive portions of the environment, marshaling defenses against the dominant ones. If the statesmen of country A expect to be assaulted, or crucially supported, by B or C singly or in concert, B and C will be continually at the focus of attention. In the internal affairs of a state, party leaders concentrate on the elements within the party or outside that are assumed to be most promising for or most threatening against their power.

Discrepancies between the focus of attention and the facts measured the degree to which the intelligence function has failed to give decision makers what they require as a basis of realistic judgment. Probably no inquiries into the processes of politics are more rewarding than the study of factors that contribute to such discrepancies. We know that professional diplomats and soldiers sometimes make disastrous errors because of unrealistic perspectives. Imperial states have sometimes met unanticipated resistance, and party leaders notoriously are led into frequent error by depending upon optimistic reports from party hacks.

We must not, of course, attach exclusive importance to the breakdown of the intelligence function as a source of erroneous decisions. Often the foreign diplomatic and military missions have brought accurate reports which have been ignored because the elites were too sluggish, inefficient, or ignorant to use them.

It follows from the hypothesis under consideration that all participants in an arena group themselves in relation to the strongest. The strongest participants are the greatest sources of deprivation and (to a lesser degree) of indulgence. Smaller powers are particularly dependent for successful power striving on toleration or active support by strong powers. When the arena is organized around a single power, we speak of the pattern as *unipolar*, otherwise, *pluripolar* (including bi-, tri-, poly-, and multipolar patterns).

DF. A *universal state* (or *body politic*) is one including an overwhelming proportion of all peoples who are in significant interaction (contact) with one another.

There have been few universal states, states of such exceptional scope that they took in the "known world," and tapered off at the edges to a vague fringe of incompletely assimilated "barbarian" tribes. The present definition does not coincide with the meaning employed by Arnold J. Toynbee in *A Study of History*, who identifies the scope of a universal state with a "civilization." Some of Toynbee's examples do not include all the peoples or even states who are in active contact with one another; for instance, he calls the Napoleonic Empire (1797–1814) a universal state, despite the fact that neither Russia nor Britain were subdued.

For some purposes it is convenient to distinguish between a universal state—such as a "One World State"—and a power pattern in which a single state has overwhelming primacy, though not all-embracing authority. From this point of view we might call the Roman Empire, even at its greatest spread, an imperium rather than a universal state.

PROP. A unipolar pattern of power balancing is more likely with extremes of cultural disparity or homogeneity.

We mean by "disparity" not mere heterogeneity, but sharp discontinuities—gaps—in the distribution of cultural elements. The proposition is illustrated by the great empires that imposed themselves by force on people of a sharply contrasting level of culture. A note of caution is always in order when concepts like "level" of culture are introduced. The problem is to select a principle of classification that does not conceal a normative prejudice under the mantle of a supposedly descriptive category (like "civilization" when contrasted with "barbarism"). It is admissable to select criteria such as range of activities carried on and the complexity of their interrelationship, distinguishing in such specific ways between "civilizations" and "folk cultures," for instance. Where cultural disparities exist it is not always the most civilized group that organizes an imperium or universal state, as the Tartar invasion of China or the overrunning of the Roman Empire by Goths and Vandals bear witness. In recent times the civilizations have possessed great technical superiority to the folk cultures, and have been vastly superior in fighting effectiveness as a result.

At the opposite extreme from disparity as contributing to unipolarity is great similarity of culture. The universal states (or imperia) of the past have been aided, at least in many cases, by the spread of a homogeneous pattern of culture throughout a vast area far beyond the boundaries of a single state. This was followed by various power adjustments in the course of which a single state emerged, consolidating itself over an enormous region, thanks to the efficiency of cultural unity and the prestige of a rising civilization. Military dominion not preceded and accompanied by cultural homogeneity soon broke up (witness the Mongol or African empires).[8]

When we inquire into the prevalence of the pattern of unipolarity in the internal life of a body politic, we find much to support the hypothesis being discussed. In some polities

8. On questions of cultural classification, see A. L. Kroeber, *Configurations of Culture Growth,* University of California Press, 1944; P. A. Sorokin, *Social and Cultural Dynamics,* 4 vols., American Book, 1937–41; and Arnold J. Toynbee, *A Study of History,* 6 vols., Oxford University Press, 1934–39.

power is typically in the hands of an elite that includes a relatively small number of the elements of society. "White supremacy" in theory and practice exemplifies what is referred to in this connection. Not only is the elite narrowly based, but it may function through a political order with plebiscites, not through a party system with elections.

Unipolarity occurs in relation to homogeneity, not disparity, under such circumstances as a war crisis in a united democratic polity. Party differences are submerged and all-party coalitions come into being. (Strictly, these are not pure unipolar patterns, since the parties expect to resume their independence when the crisis is past.) A unipolar party system does not, however, depend exclusively upon the consensus arising from crisis. Unity may be made up of consensus tempered by indifference. In local politics, especially, an "opposition" party may wither away, leaving one party slate opposed by a few "no-party" independents who are regarded seriously by no one, including themselves.

PROP. A bipolar pattern of power balancing is more likely with a bipolar distribution of other values and institutions.

Universal states have sometimes been preceded or superseded by a bipolar system centered around two foci of economic strength and cultural prestige. At times in the history of China, for example, a northern center of dominance has stood over against a southern center. It is freely predicted at present that the dominant pattern of world power will soon be bipolar, if it is not already that, and that the dominant powers will be the United States and Russia. These are the two emerging poles of manpower, natural resources, and technology.[9]

A polypolar or multipolar pattern of power balancing is correspondingly favored by a polypolar or multipolar pattern of other values and institutions. After the disintegration of the Roman Empire in the West, power was characteristically dispersed in many impotent hands. The gradual emergence from this feudal (multipolar) system of a national (polypolar) system was connected with the growth of a few dominant trading and cultural centers.[10]

9. See, for example, Lasswell, *World Politics Faces Economics*, McGraw-Hill, 1945.

10. For details see, for instance, J. Kulischer, *Allgemeine Wirtschaftsgeschichte des Mittelalters und der Neuzeit*, R. Oldenbourg, 1929, II.

PROP. In the civic arena a biparty system is favored by the expectation that the effective executive will be elected by popular majority.

The two-party system in the United States owes much of its longevity to the constitutional practice, early established when the electoral college was transformed into a rubber stamp, of making the presidency depend upon a majority of the popular vote. The president is a chief executive in both the ceremonial and effective sense of the term. Hence the importance of the office is widely acknowledged; and since people do not, as a rule, "throw away their votes," alternatives are usually limited to two major candidates. Despite many factors working in the other direction, a strong factor making for a biparty system in British parliamentary government is the practice of changing the cabinet after an election, save in national emergencies. The effective executive is able to maintain discipline by the threat of forcing an election. (Note that the practice of proportional representation does not have the same effect on the party structure as single member constituencies do.) (Consult F. A. Hermens, *Democracy and Proportional Representation*, University of Chicago, 1940.)

A polyparty or multiparty system in the civic arena is favored, on the other hand, when the effective executive is expected to be chosen by procedures involving less than a majority vote of the electorate. The Third French Republic was well known for the number of parties and blocs in the chamber and senate. It was an unwritten rule of the constitution that the executive could not dissolve the legislature; hence the deputies could vote against the cabinet without running the risk of recontesting their seats.

DF. A *control area* is a domain not necessarily accompanied by authority. *Hegemony* is supremacy in a control area.

In world politics the control area of a power is a *sphere of influence* when control is not accompanied by authority. A hegemonic state is a *major power;* its *satellites* are the states within its sphere of influence. Where the total political arena consists of two or three powers with their satellites, we speak of the strongest powers as the *superpowers* (following William T. R. Fox, *The Super-Powers*, Harcourt, Brace, 1944). A *middle power* is a relatively strong power that has a narrow control area; a *small power* is a relatively weak power. Today the United States, Russia, and Britain may be considered to be superpowers; France exemplifies a major power; China is a middle power; Sweden, a small power.

It is convenient to distinguish between *neutral states* and *neutral powers*, the former being bound by formal agreement to refrain from taking sides, and the latter being expected to refrain in fact from taking sides. Switzerland has historically been at the same time a neutral state and a neutral power; the character of Belgium as a neutral power in 1914 was under suspicion.

Satellites have sovereignty, although they lack supremacy, since while preserving authority they are under external control. The maintenance of supremacy within the body politic is *self-determination;* when this is formalized we speak of *autonomy*. Every state is by definition autonomous; a satellite is a state lacking self-determination.

A more detailed analysis of the arena may be made in terms of control area patterns. Thus, a *buffer area* is a zone which is the concurrent domain of several powers, one of which may exercise hegemony. *Confrontation* is a balancing relation in which the control areas of two opposing powers are contiguous; *penetration*, a balancing relation in which the control area of one power extends beyond the outer bound of the control area of another power; *flanking* is a balancing relation in which one power adjusts its control area to further the encirclement of another.

The three patterns—confrontation, penetration, flanking—may involve any or all of the instrumentalities of power. The most intense level of each is *assault*. Given modern weapons, control areas are not only delimited along the surface of the land or sea; they involve control of the air, and even of subterranean space.[11]

DF. A *league* is a co-archy of states; a *confederation* is a league of maximal jurisdiction. A *concert of power* is a joint exercise of power by the participants in an arena.

Strictly speaking, any alliance based on formal equality might be called a league, but ordinarily the term is applied

11. On the history of military thought, consult *Makers of Modern Strategy*, ed., Edward Mead Earle, Princeton University Press, 1943.

where alliances are not narrowly circumscribed in scope, as in a customs union. The term "confederation" begins to be used when rather inclusive arrangements are expected to continue indefinitely. It is distinguished from a single state organized in a federal pattern by the fact that the decisions of the federal state are enforceable directly against individuals.

A concert of power is a special case of power balancing in which decisions are made by consensus, or by majority arrangement, and put into effect in a prevailingly military arena. The groups that act together retain their separate sense of identity, and expect to realign themselves outside of, or even in defiance of, the concert. Thus a concert is one kind of coalition, a "grand alliance." The "Concert of Europe" was sometimes able to cope peacefully with world political issues.

PROP. With increasing expectation of violence, the balancing process tends toward (territorial) expansion and (functional) generalization.

As crisis continues, and especially when it becomes more intense, each participant in the arena is drawn more and more actively into power balancing, searching for allies. The potential alignments become actualized, not only in the sense that a local conflict is broadened to include a region, and then the globe, but also in the sense that the functional groups in society are drawn in. Special efforts are made by contending elites to invoke racial, national, religious, economic, and other elements, so as to increase the fighting effectiveness of the conflicting powers.[12]

PROP. Necessary conditions for the balancing process to prevent violence are: (1) variations in power are measurable and visible in early stages; [13] (2) they are distributable among

12. In this connection it is particularly important to take into account the nature of the "self," since the participants in the political arena are not simply individuals, but groups, and groups depend upon the way in which selves are organized. The primary ego, as pointed out before, includes with the "I" or "me" a potentially wide range of symbols that include family, clique, neighborhood, economic class, and so on.

13. Note that our general account of the arena does not specify omniscience among participants, a postulate which has figured in the formal theory of the market. In the speculative model of the "perfect" market, the participants are assumed to have foreknowledge of the way in which their own alternatives of action will affect the situation. Morgenstern has shown, however, that the postulate of omniscience when taken in conjunction with other postulates of the

the participants in the balancing process; (3) the estimating process can be sentimentalized.

The underlying assumption, which follows from preceding hypotheses as to the exercise of power, is that violence will be avoided by the balancing process only (*if then*) when the expected I:D ratio for the power holders is less than unity. States do not go to war if their rulers expect a more favorable position by limiting diplomacy to negotiation and to the manipulation of symbols and goods and services. These will be the expectations only if the opposing alignment is judged to have equal or greater fighting effectiveness. (It is emphasized that the hypothesis deals only with necessary, not sufficient conditions.)

Hence the first condition that variations in power be measurable. Without this possibility there may be favorable expectations from the use of violence based on failure to judge correctly the fighting effectiveness of the conflicting alignments. And the variations in power must be visible in early stages, for expectations of violence contribute to war not only when they are very high but also when they are very low. War results not only from an exaggeration of the inevitability of war, but also from an exaggeration of the inevitability of peace.

For the balancing process to prevent violence, it is necessary, moreover, that variations in power lend themselves to equalization by redistribution among the participants in the process. Otherwise improvement in power position of one alignment will produce a stress toward violence to improve it still further, and in the opposing alignment a corresponding stress toward a compensating increase in power potential.[14] This process is most clearly exemplified in the armaments race, and the ineffec-

---

"pure" theory results in logical absurdities (*Zeitschrift für Nationalökonomie*, 1935, 337 ff.). The present hypothesis does not concern omniscience, but empirically warranted expectations. "Visibility," for instance, refers to the intelligence function and predispositions of elites with regard to the fighting potential of the environment. The likelihood of mistakes in the use of power are increased when the modes of estimate traditionally applied to the evaluation of fighting effectiveness are no longer adequate because of technological and social change. The scientific observer who seeks to describe these relations at any given time must make his own best estimate of potentials.

14. Wilson's position that "only a peace between equals can last" is thus derivable precisely from the "realistic" considerations emphasized by his critics.

tiveness of nondistributive preparedness as a preventive of violence. And it is exemplified further in the failure of any particular type of alignment pattern to attain more than a limited stability. All known systems of world politics have been "transitions" or "stages." Stability is not assured by the characteristics of any one political structure (the "unbeatable combination").

Finally, the process of measurement and redistribution must be sentimentalized, so as to enlist the loyalties of the mass. Violence may otherwise result from the necessity of the elite to maintain its position over against the mass. As the *Federalist* points out (No. VI),

> There have been . . . almost as many popular as royal wars. The cries of the nation and the importunities of their representatives have, upon various occasions, dragged their monarchs into war, or continued them in it contrary to their inclinations, and sometimes contrary to the real interests of the state.[15]

More generally, the balancing process cannot prevent violence unless widely circulating symbols and shared practices elaborate and implement the perspectives of peace rather than war. When identifications, demands, and expectations set up predispositions favorable to the exercise of violence, in the absence of practices adequate to the nonviolent resolution of conflict, the environment will not fail to act on those predispositions to produce a warlike response. In short, on this hypothesis the balancing of power process cannot prevent violence unless its outcome at any stage is conceived as being, in Wilson's terms, "not a balance of power, but a community of power; not organized rivalries, but an organized common peace."

§10.3 *Balancing of Power: the Revolutionary Crisis*

PROP. The stability of a rule varies with the intensity of perspectives (of both elite and mass) sustaining the elite.

15. The *Federalist* goes further, and feels "compelled to conclude that the fiery and destructive passions of war reign in the human breast with much more powerful sway than the mild and beneficent sentiments of peace . . ." (No. XXXIV). Contemporary psychology and anthropology tend rather to the view that war, in Malinowski's terms, is "not biologically impelled but culturally induced." In either case, symbols and practices may act on the predispositions in one direction or the other to produce contrary results.

Whether or not a rule is stable depends on the ability of the elite to recruit itself with a minimum of dissent. Such circulation of the elite can continue only so long as the ideology in the name of which it exercises its authority persists, and peaceful replacements in the elite are difficult in proportion as adherence to the ideology weakens in intensity. Thus this hypothesis is in substance another formulation of the previous proposition that maintenance of power depends on adherence to the political doctrine under which it is exercised.

The dependence of a power structure on the perspectives—identifications, expectations, and demands—of those in the domain of power was previously discussed, and has been repeatedly emphasized in the tradition. "No society is likely to endure," says Laski (1925, 193–4), "in which men cannot believe with passionate conviction." Machiavelli singles out as the most important cause of conspiracy against the sovereign his being hated by the mass of the people.[16] But even apathy undermines the stability of the structure, which requires continued support against the potential threat of rival elites. It must be recognized, however, that perspectives have their inertia just as do operations. Established patterns of thought and feeling—about the power structure as about everything else—tend to persist beyond their appropriateness to the environment.

Stability requires intense adherence to the political doctrine not only on the part of the mass, but of the elite as well. (This is not to say, however, that the elite must accept all the various ideological elaborations of the doctrine; on the contrary, some of these—in particular, those concerning formal power—may

16. *Discourses*, III, 6. Hence he says also that "princes should remember that they begin to lose their state from the moment when they begin to disregard the laws and ancient customs under which the people have lived contented for a length of time" (III, 5). An index of the weakening of the political myth, the breakdown of the structure of stable expectations with regard to established patterns of action, is the phenomenon of *distrust*, as described by Robert Warren, *The State in Society*, Oxford University Press, 1940, 58–9: "It seems to me that distrust is an underlying characteristic of our society and of our time. We distrust the concentration of power in the corporation; we distrust the concentration of wealth in the individual; we distrust the concentration of economic power in the national organization of labor; we distrust the attitude of concentrated economic power toward unorganized labor; we distrust the concentration of power in the state; we distrust other nations. Our social structure, national and international, is filled with mutual distrusts; our legislation is a composite of mutual distrusts; and our economy reflects the consequence of mutual distrusts. . . ." Warren is referring here especially to distrust of concentration of power; but it may take other forms as well.

Power is not strongest when it uses violence, but weakest. It is strongest when it employs the instruments of substitution and counter attraction, of allurement, of participation rather than of exclusion, of education rather than of annihilation. Rape is not evidence of irresistible power in politics or in sex.[18]

Exclusive reliance on violence for maintenance of rule is an index of weakness rather than of strength because in a crisis situation the instruments of violence may constitute a threat to the social structure as well as its major support. Defection of the instruments of violence—which can be brought about by means other than violence—would mean collapse. The strongest army is not proof against subversion by bribery, propaganda, or appeal to personal loyalties. Thus, as L. H. Jenks observes,

> In times of transition or instability the normal role of armed forces is likely to be greatly altered, augmented, or even reversed. . . . Most successful revolutions during the past century have been tolerated or even actively supported by important sections of the armed forces.[19]

DF. The *countermass* consists of those rejecting a given social structure; the *counterelite* are the leaders of the countermass.

We define these as aggregates, leaving open the possibility of varying degrees of organization. The countermass is not to be identified with the reject. Those at the very bottom of the scale of value positions lack politicized perspectives, and follow practices immediately indulgent, rather than those satisfying valid interests. The *lumpenproletariat*, as the Marxists have pointed out, rarely constitutes a significant opposition to the established rule. The countermass is largely drawn from the subject classes, to be sure, but may also contain segments of dependent classes (for instance, intellectuals), and in crisis situations even comprise parts of the ruling class. Similarly, the counterelite is recruited from even higher intervals on the scale of value positions.

18. Manifestations of violence within the group may also indicate, however, the intensity of an external rather than internal political situation. Catlin cites (1930, 119), a number of formulations of this point, for instance Spencer's dictum that "internal liberty varies inversely with external pressure" and Giddings' that "social pressure tends to increase when environmental pressure increases."

19. On the role of the army in revolutionary strategy, see K. C. Chorley, *Armies and the Art of Revolution,* Faber & Faber, 1943.

be recognized by the elite as not corresponding to the power facts.) Michels put the matter with characteristic emphasis (1915, 243):

> We may regard it as an established historical law that races, legal systems, institutions, and social classes, are inevitably doomed to destruction from the moment they or those who represent them have lost faith in their future.

For, among other reasons, this lack of faith on the part of the elite will be communicated to the mass, whose support for the power structure will thereupon diminish proportionately. Moreover, the political doctrine serves as a basis of solidarity for the elite; without faith in and loyalty to this doctrine, there is no basis for resolution of internal dissensions with minimum deprivation to the elite as a whole. And in turn, this lack of solidarity weakens resistance against the potential threat of rival elites.

Increasing intensity of the political situation is marked, therefore, by the elaboration of utopias alternative to the weakening political doctrine. Hence the transfer of the faiths and loyalties of the symbol specialists ("intellectuals") from the ideology to a utopia is an index of approaching revolutionary crisis (compare Edwards, 1927, 38). Generally speaking, symbols are the major political means available to the opponents of an established power structure. The inferiority of the opposition in relation to the elite is usually less marked with regard to symbols than with regard to violence or goods and services. When those specializing in the promulgation and elaboration of ideology turn instead to one or more utopias, the power structure has become unstable. While it may not be strictly true, as Wendell Phillips once declared, that "insurrection of thought always precedes insurrection of arms," it is at any rate an index of revolutionary crisis.

PROP. The stability of a rule varies with the degree to which those who make production policies make distribution policies (policies relating to value shaping and sharing are in the same hand).

The hypothesis thus embodies—and generalizes—the insistence of historical materialism on the role of modes of production and exchange in the power process. Large changes in the composition of the elite may be treated, on the hypothesis, as functions of large changes in the prevailing division of labor. Hence, in any given time interval, the probability of a transformation of the power structure will be increased if the processes of production have notably altered, so that those with power in these processes are without corresponding political power.

As was pointed out in §9.1, a class acquires supremacy in the degree that it contributes to esteemed values. The ruling class relies on its dominance in production for the acquisition of power; when its services in production become dispensable, or even no longer dominant, its power position is threatened. Mosca says (1939, 66),

> Ruling classes decline inevitably when they cease to find scope for the capacities through which they rose to power, when they can no longer render the social services which they once rendered, or when their talents and the services they render lose in importance in the social environment in which they live.

The following hypothesis is a further elaboration of this point.

PROP. The stability of a rule varies with the degree of actualization and realization of value for the mass.

Poverty has been held to be the parent of revolution since Aristotle (*Politics*, II, 6), and undoubtedly before. The predisposition to oppose the rule in most cases arises from continued deprivation under the rule. Those obtaining the smallest share of the values distributed are a permanent threat to the practices of control and distribution, making the threat effective as their value potential increases. Laski asserts (1925, 27), "The limitation in the number of those upon whom social good is conferred has always meant, in the end, an assault upon the foundations of the state by those excluded from its direction." That is, opposition to a rule varies with the degree to which the actual value position of the mass departs from its value potential.

The low degree of actualization becomes a serious threat in proportion as it enters into the demands, expectations, and identifications of the mass. It is a low degree of realization—disparity between value position and value demanded and expected—which is most directly effective. Technological developments or victorious wars, for instance, may raise expectations concerning the value distribution. It is the establishment of

identifications on the basis of such expectations, and the crystallization of demands in the name of these identifications, which constitute the important threat to the stability of the rule. Such perspectives set up certain practices of control and distribution as right and proper; opposition to the established patterns becomes morally justified and a duty to the identified group. "The impetus to reform or revolution," says Tawney (1926, 109), "springs in every age from the realization of the contrast between the external order of society and the moral standard recognized as valid by the conscience or reason of the individual." The standard of living may be "the highest in history" or "th highest in the world," but still not high enough when it is com pared with that of the elect, or with the demands made by th self on the self—basically, when it is compared with the valı potential.

PROP. The stability of a rule varies with the elite's conti over the instruments of violence.

"In the last analysis," writes Laski (1935, 13–14), "the st is built upon the ability of its government to operate succ fully its supreme coercive power." Clearly, control over the struments of violence is a necessary condition for the stabi of a rule, whether or not it be a sufficient condition. For reason, such power is least likely to vary with other variatior authority or control. Control over violence is the most fi entrenched, hedged about with the severest sanctions and rigid perspectives; in particular, it is the most tenaciously to by the elite, least subject to concessions.[17]

It is to be understood that the hypothesis does not imply the stability of the elite's power position varies with its *ex* of violence, but only with its ability to do so. The elite de predominantly on the exercise of violence only when first lished or just before collapse. "Only when it is crumblin about to give way to another does a hierarchy cease to be taneous through becoming preponderantly or exclusi matter of force," says Pareto (1935, 1154). This posi embodied in the earlier hypotheses that naked power tend transformed to authoritative power, and that acceptance political formula functions as an alternative to violence riam has pointed out (1934, 179–80):

17. See L. H. Jenks's article on "Armed Forces" in *ESS*.

PROP. The stability of a rule varies inversely with the degree of organization of a counterelite.

The importance of leadership during the actual course of revolution is among the oldest of political generalizations.[20] It is fundamental also in the prerevolutionary situation. On the other hand, the counterelite is relatively powerless unless it can rely on the support of the mass; and this support is not forthcoming so long as the elite preserves its authority. Hence the disintegration of an elite is a function of the emergence of a counterelite, in that the latter weakens the elite's authority by challenging it, and provides the mass with new symbols of authority and foci of identification.[21] It follows that prior to revolution itself the most intense conflict of the counterelite is with the dependent classes and those elements of the subject classes supporting the rule, rather than with the ruling class itself. Direct attack upon the ruling class must wait upon the undermining of its authority in the perspectives of the mass.

As the counterelite becomes more organized, and enjoys more widespread support, its demands may shift from supplanting the elite to sharing its rule. Revolutionary demands characterize the phases of minimal and maximal power of the counterelite; with an intermediate power position it seeks a place in the power structure. In this phase it bargains with and wrings concessions from the elite. Such concessions increase demands, bargaining raises expectations of success, and solidarity of the countermass and counterelite is continually strengthened by the identifications in whose name the demands have been made. Thus continuing concessions undermine more and more the position of the elite.[22]

20. It is stated explicitly, for instance, in Kautilya's *Arthaśāstra,* 277: "Disaffection or disloyalty can be got rid of by putting down the leaders; for in the absence of a leader or leaders, the people are easily governed and they will not take part in the intrigues of enemies."

21. See J. B. S. Hardman's article on "Masses" in *ESS:* "As a factor in hastening the disintegration of the power of the office holders the strength of the opposition is but of secondary significance as compared to the weakness of the authority itself. The masses are likely to perceive the trend of the contest and gravitate toward the stronger side."

22. See Pareto, 1935, 2059; and compare Clemenceau (cited in Sorel, *Reflections on Violence,* 1915, 71): "There is no better means [than the policy of perpetual concessions] of making the opposite party ask for more and more. Every man or every power whose action consists solely in surrender can only finish by self-annihilation. Everything that lives resists; that which does not resist allows itself to be cut up piecemeal."

The hypotheses of this section have thus indicated as factors in the stability of a rule symbols, goods and services, instruments of violence, and power practices—the major political methods. None of these singly is sufficient, each has been held to be necessary. Emphasis on all the factors is another expression of the present pluralistic observational standpoint (principle of interdetermination). The factors are not, of course, independent of one another. But no one of them can be singled out as always and everywhere *the* cause of changes in rule. In the analysis of any given situation, all of them must be explicitly taken into account.[23]

§10.4 *The Course of Revolution*

DF. A political change is a *transformation* or *reformation* according to the scope of practices involved and the degree to which they are modified; *moderate* or *radical*, according to whether or not the change is made in accordance with the political formula.

An important characteristic of the political process is the occurrence of novel perspectives and operations.[24] To a certain extent it is possible to anticipate the locus of innovation, to foresee, for example, that new political institutions are more likely to appear where new methods of production are coming into use than where established methods continue to be applied. More generally, we can expect that innovation is

23. The present emphasis on the multiplicity of factors entering into the precipitation of revolutionary crisis is neatly formulated in Hobbes (*Elements of Law,* II, 8): "To dispose men to sedition three things concur. The first is discontent [goods and services]; for as long as a man thinketh himself well, and that the present government standeth not in his way to hinder his proceeding from well to better, it is impossible for him to desire the change thereof. The second is pretence of right [symbols]; for though a man be discontent, yet if in his own opinion there be no just cause of stirring against, or resisting the government established, nor any pretence to justify this resistance, and to procure aid, he will never show it. The third is hope of success [instruments of violence and power practices]; for it were madness to attempt without hope, when to fail is to die the death of a traitor. Without these three: discontent, pretence, and hope, there can be no rebellion."

24. We mean novel in relation to antecedent practices, not in an absolute sense. Compare Bryce, 1893, I, 34: "There is wonderfully little genuine inventiveness in the world, and perhaps least of all has been shown in the sphere of political institutions."

the more likely to occur the greater the intensity of the continuing political situation.[25]

The definition concerns the extent of the innovation and the methods by which it is brought about. In both cases, of course, we are dealing with differences of degree, not absolute demarcations. Innovations consisting in changes in practices of limited scope, or in redistribution of power among top elites, or in purely formal rather than effective power practices, we call political reformations; and political transformations where the innovation effects a wide range of practices, replaces one elite by quite another, alters patterns of control as well as authority.

When the innovation is carried out in accord with the political formula, we speak of the means as moderate: the amendment of a constitution in the manner which it itself provides, the granting of concessions by an absolute monarch, or, in general, innovation through the normal legislative process. Radical methods are characterized by "direct action"—that is, action by others than duly constituted authorities, and usually by the exercise of violence. (Violence does not *necessarily* constitute a "radical" method; there may be cases, for instance, where the chief regularly defends his power position by a formalized test of his prowess.)

DF. A political *reform* is a reformation carried out by moderate methods.

Where the reform chiefly concerns the personnel of power, we refer to the innovation as a *succession;* where it concerns power practices, it is a *programmatic reform.* The election of a "reform administration" (United States) or a "Labor Government" (England) exemplify reform by succession; the adoption of the income tax amendment or repeal of the Corn Laws exemplify programmatic reform as here defined.[26] Such

25. The *anticipation* of a political innovation, even when correct, is to be distinguished from *making* it. On the one hand, a political prediction may function in the power process as well as in inquiry into that process, so that its enunciation may contribute to its own truth (as has been frequently pointed out with regard to Marxist predictions). On the other hand, political inventiveness requires a "foothold" in the political situation, so that the invention can be predicted without thereby occurring. See "The Self-fulfilling Prophecy" in Robert K. Merton, *Social Theory and Social Structure,* The Free Press of Glencoe, Illinois, 1949, chap. vii.

26. "Reform" is used here in a purely descriptive sense, and is not to be con-

changes are authoritatively sanctioned, and are superimposed on a continuity of authority and control patterns. By contrast, Hitler's coming to power under the political forms of the Weimar Republic is not merely a succession, nor the Nazi rule a merely programmatic reform: not only the authority but even the control patterns were radically altered when power was acquired.

DF. A *palace revolution* is a change in governors contrary to the political formula but retaining it.

A palace revolution is a nonauthoritative transfer of governmental authority which nevertheless retains the authority structures. It is a reformation by radical means. Assassination of the reigning monarch, but with continuation of the monarchy, exemplifies a palace revolution in the present sense. The term is usually limited to cases where the transfer of authority is effected by other members of the ruling group—a conspiracy by those inhabiting the "palace." [27] But here the meaning is more general: it includes any nonauthoritative change in government without corresponding changes in governmental policy.[28]

PROP. The likelihood of assassination varies (a) inversely with adherence to the political doctrine by the mass, (b) inversely with the actualization of power counterelites, and, (c)

strued as implying a preferential valuation of the new state of affairs. Both the passage and the repeal of the prohibition amendment, for instance, are reforms in the present sense. The concept is to be contrasted not with "reaction" but with "revolution," as is done, for instance, by Bluntschli, 1921, 507–8: "Reform implies (1) that the change is introduced in accordance with the constitution . . . the change must be constitutional in form. (2) The change must conform to the spirit of the constitution. . . . If either the form or the spirit of the constitution is violated, a change is no longer reform but revolution."

27. Compare Machiavelli, *Discourses*, III, 6: "Conspiracies formed by a number of persons have generally for their originators the great men of the state, or those on terms of familiar intercourse with the prince. None other, unless they are madmen, can engage in conspiracies; for men of low condition, who are not intimate with the prince, have no chance of success, not having the necessary conveniences for the execution of their plots." Nor, it may be added, are they likely to be afterward accepted as the bearers of authority, as would be the case with the "great men" of the state.

28. Palace revolution might be further distinguished from a *break in succession*, which is a transfer of authority not specified by the political formula, but not (directly) counter to it. For instance, when the king dies without heirs, the resultant conflict for the throne is not called a palace revolution, but neither is it the formal process of succession. It may, of course, provide the basis for revolution as well as reform.

directly with increasing concentration and narrowing allocation of authority or control.

The hypothesis has reference, of course, only to politicized assassination. The topic is introduced at this point because it is one of the characteristic practices by which a palace revolution is effected. But assassination has, of course, a more general significance as an index of a prerevolutionary situation; this aspect of assassination is formulated in part (b) of the hypothesis.[29]

Assassination increases, on the hypothesis, when the regime is acquiesced to without intense adherence by the mass to the political doctrine on which the regime rests. In the extreme case, assassination presents itself as a means, in the famous phrase, of "tempering despotism." And even short of such extremes, without intense adherence to the political doctrine, identification with (loyalty to) the bearers of authority is weakened; so that conspiracies and intrigues can readily purchase support and at any rate need fear no strong opposition. In a word, it is the perspectives of the mass which confer authority on the governors; when the latter are no longer cloaked in authority, the probability of assassination increases.

The second part of the hypothesis is that assassination is the more likely to occur when the regime stands in the way of rising power groups. The greater the disparity between the power position and potential of such groups the greater the stress toward enhancement of power position. And when the potential falls short of undisputed rule—because, for instance, of the strength of rival counterelites, or a too limited control over the instruments of violence—assassination is an increasingly probable practice. As Lerner puts it, "Assassination is an index of the gap between the driving political impulses of men and the limits for their attainment set up by the existing political forms." [29] Of course, if the potential of the rising counterelite were sufficiently great, these forms would be swept aside altogether.

From this standpoint, the significance of concentration of power is apparent. Clearly, little is to be expected from the assassination of individuals with only a small share in the decision-making process (except as a symbol of protest, as

29. See the article on "Assassination" by Max Lerner in *ESS*.

pointed out in the next paragraph). Conversely, Lerner observes, "Where power is centralized in a single person assassination recommends itself . . . as easily the best method for seizing it."[29]

In general, assassination functions as *propaganda of the deed* rather than as an instrument directly effecting changes in power practices. It is significant because of its effect on the perspectives of both elite and mass, rather than by its immediate consequences on the power process. What is important in the power process is usually not the particular individual, but the bases of elite recruitment, and the nature of the practices flowing from the resultant pattern of control. These are rarely changed directly by assassination. But the latter may bring certain demands prominently into the focus of attention, and alter by terror the structure of expectations of both rulers and ruled. Predispositions against violence, and initially intense faiths and loyalties may, however, give it a contrary effect; as is true of other forms of propaganda, propaganda of the deed can operate only on favorable predispositions.

DF. A *political revolution* is a radical change in the regime (authority structure); a *social revolution*, in the rule (control structure).

Revolution has often been regarded as a pathological process falling outside the "natural" course of political interaction. Such a viewpoint, having much in common with Aristotle's immanent teleology (but not his own political theory), is of course normatively ambiguous. The "natural" can be specified as such only by standards of valuation, which are rarely made explicit. From the observational standpoint of political science rather than political philosophy no such discrimination can be made. When political theory aims at the description and explanation of the political process rather than its justification, it must give to every part of this process the full weight and significance attaching to it by virtue of its empirical interconnections with the other parts of the process. From this standpoint, revolution and the expectation of revolution are to be considered as regular and important features of the political process.[30]

30. Compare Tawney, 1931, 288: "In a world where revolutions, carried out

be recognized by the elite as not corresponding to the power facts.) Michels put the matter with characteristic emphasis (1915, 243):

> We may regard it as an established historical law that races, legal systems, institutions, and social classes, are inevitably doomed to destruction from the moment they or those who represent them have lost faith in their future.

For, among other reasons, this lack of faith on the part of the elite will be communicated to the mass, whose support for the power structure will thereupon diminish proportionately. Moreover, the political doctrine serves as a basis of solidarity for the elite; without faith in and loyalty to this doctrine, there is no basis for resolution of internal dissensions with minimum deprivation to the elite as a whole. And in turn, this lack of solidarity weakens resistance against the potential threat of rival elites.

Increasing intensity of the political situation is marked, therefore, by the elaboration of utopias alternative to the weakening political doctrine. Hence the transfer of the faiths and loyalties of the symbol specialists ("intellectuals") from the ideology to a utopia is an index of approaching revolutionary crisis (compare Edwards, 1927, 38). Generally speaking, symbols are the major political means available to the opponents of an established power structure. The inferiority of the opposition in relation to the elite is usually less marked with regard to symbols than with regard to violence or goods and services. When those specializing in the promulgation and elaboration of ideology turn instead to one or more utopias, the power structure has become unstable. While it may not be strictly true, as Wendell Phillips once declared, that "insurrection of thought always precedes insurrection of arms," it is at any rate an index of revolutionary crisis.

PROP. The stability of a rule varies with the degree to which those who make production policies make distribution policies (policies relating to value shaping and sharing are in the same hand).

The hypothesis thus embodies—and generalizes—the insistence of historical materialism on the role of modes of production and exchange in the power process. Large changes in the composition of the elite may be treated, on the hypothesis, as functions of large changes in the prevailing division of labor. Hence, in any given time interval, the probability of a transformation of the power structure will be increased if the processes of production have notably altered, so that those with power in these processes are without corresponding political power.

As was pointed out in §9.1, a class acquires supremacy in the degree that it contributes to esteemed values. The ruling class relies on its dominance in production for the acquisition of power; when its services in production become dispensable, or even no longer dominant, its power position is threatened. Mosca says (1939, 66),

> Ruling classes decline inevitably when they cease to find scope for the capacities through which they rose to power, when they can no longer render the social services which they once rendered, or when their talents and the services they render lose in importance in the social environment in which they live.

The following hypothesis is a further elaboration of this point.

PROP. The stability of a rule varies with the degree of actualization and realization of value for the mass.

Poverty has been held to be the parent of revolution since Aristotle (*Politics*, II, 6), and undoubtedly before. The predisposition to oppose the rule in most cases arises from continued deprivation under the rule. Those obtaining the smallest share of the values distributed are a permanent threat to the practices of control and distribution, making the threat effective as their value potential increases. Laski asserts (1925, 27), "The limitation in the number of those upon whom social good is conferred has always meant, in the end, an assault upon the foundations of the state by those excluded from its direction." That is, opposition to a rule varies with the degree to which the actual value position of the mass departs from its value potential.

The low degree of actualization becomes a serious threat in proportion as it enters into the demands, expectations, and identifications of the mass. It is a low degree of realization—disparity between value position and value demanded and expected—which is most directly effective. Technological developments or victorious wars, for instance, may raise expectations concerning the value distribution. It is the establishment of identifications on the basis of such expectations, and the crystallization of demands in the name of these identifications, which constitute the important threat to the stability of the rule. Such perspectives set up certain practices of control and distribution as right and proper; opposition to the established patterns becomes morally justified and a duty to the identified group. "The impetus to reform or revolution," says Tawney (1926, 109), "springs in every age from the realization of the contrast between the external order of society and the moral standards recognized as valid by the conscience or reason of the individual." The standard of living may be "the highest in history" or "the highest in the world," but still not high enough when it is compared with that of the elect, or with the demands made by the self on the self—basically, when it is compared with the value potential.

PROP. The stability of a rule varies with the elite's control over the instruments of violence.

"In the last analysis," writes Laski (1935, 13–14), "the state is built upon the ability of its government to operate successfully its supreme coercive power." Clearly, control over the instruments of violence is a necessary condition for the stability of a rule, whether or not it be a sufficient condition. For this reason, such power is least likely to vary with other variations in authority or control. Control over violence is the most firmly entrenched, hedged about with the severest sanctions and most rigid perspectives; in particular, it is the most tenaciously held to by the elite, least subject to concessions.[17]

It is to be understood that the hypothesis does not imply that the stability of the elite's power position varies with its *exercise* of violence, but only with its ability to do so. The elite depends predominantly on the exercise of violence only when first established or just before collapse. "Only when it is crumbling and about to give way to another does a hierarchy cease to be spontaneous through becoming preponderantly or exclusively a matter of force," says Pareto (1935, 1154). This position is embodied in the earlier hypotheses that naked power tends to be transformed to authoritative power, and that acceptance of the political formula functions as an alternative to violence. Merriam has pointed out (1934, 179–80):

17. See L. H. Jenks's article on "Armed Forces" in *ESS*.

Power is not strongest when it uses violence, but weakest. It is strongest when it employs the instruments of substitution and counter attraction, of allurement, of participation rather than of exclusion, of education rather than of annihilation. Rape is not evidence of irresistible power in politics or in sex.[18]

Exclusive reliance on violence for maintenance of rule is an index of weakness rather than of strength because in a crisis situation the instruments of violence may constitute a threat to the social structure as well as its major support. Defection of the instruments of violence—which can be brought about by means other than violence—would mean collapse. The strongest army is not proof against subversion by bribery, propaganda, or appeal to personal loyalties. Thus, as L. H. Jenks observes,

> In times of transition or instability the normal role of armed forces is likely to be greatly altered, augmented, or even reversed. . . . Most successful revolutions during the past century have been tolerated or even actively supported by important sections of the armed forces.[19]

DF. The *countermass* consists of those rejecting a given social structure; the *counterelite* are the leaders of the countermass.

We define these as aggregates, leaving open the possibility of varying degrees of organization. The countermass is not to be identified with the reject. Those at the very bottom of the scale of value positions lack politicized perspectives, and follow practices immediately indulgent, rather than those satisfying valid interests. The *lumpenproletariat*, as the Marxists have pointed out, rarely constitutes a significant opposition to the established rule. The countermass is largely drawn from the subject classes, to be sure, but may also contain segments of dependent classes (for instance, intellectuals), and in crisis situations even comprise parts of the ruling class. Similarly, the counterelite is recruited from even higher intervals on the scale of value positions.

18. Manifestations of violence within the group may also indicate, however, the intensity of an external rather than internal political situation. Catlin cites (1930, 119), a number of formulations of this point, for instance Spencer's dictum that "internal liberty varies inversely with external pressure" and Giddings' that "social pressure tends to increase when environmental pressure increases."

19. On the role of the army in revolutionary strategy, see K. C. Chorley, *Armies and the Art of Revolution,* Faber & Faber, 1943.

PROP. The stability of a rule varies inversely with the degree of organization of a counterelite.

The importance of leadership during the actual course of revolution is among the oldest of political generalizations.[20] It is fundamental also in the prerevolutionary situation. On the other hand, the counterelite is relatively powerless unless it can rely on the support of the mass; and this support is not forthcoming so long as the elite preserves its authority. Hence the disintegration of an elite is a function of the emergence of a counterelite, in that the latter weakens the elite's authority by challenging it, and provides the mass with new symbols of authority and foci of identification.[21] It follows that prior to revolution itself the most intense conflict of the counterelite is with the dependent classes and those elements of the subject classes supporting the rule, rather than with the ruling class itself. Direct attack upon the ruling class must wait upon the undermining of its authority in the perspectives of the mass.

As the counterelite becomes more organized, and enjoys more widespread support, its demands may shift from supplanting the elite to sharing its rule. Revolutionary demands characterize the phases of minimal and maximal power of the counterelite; with an intermediate power position it seeks a place in the power structure. In this phase it bargains with and wrings concessions from the elite. Such concessions increase demands, bargaining raises expectations of success, and solidarity of the countermass and counterelite is continually strengthened by the identifications in whose name the demands have been made. Thus continuing concessions undermine more and more the position of the elite.[22]

20. It is stated explicitly, for instance, in Kautilya's *Arthaśāstra,* 277: "Disaffection or disloyalty can be got rid of by putting down the leaders; for in the absence of a leader or leaders, the people are easily governed and they will not take part in the intrigues of enemies."

21. See J. B. S. Hardman's article on "Masses" in *ESS:* "As a factor in hastening the disintegration of the power of the office holders the strength of the opposition is but of secondary significance as compared to the weakness of the authority itself. The masses are likely to perceive the trend of the contest and gravitate toward the stronger side."

22. See Pareto, 1935, 2059; and compare Clemenceau (cited in Sorel, *Reflections on Violence,* 1915, 71): "There is no better means [than the policy of perpetual concessions] of making the opposite party ask for more and more. Every man or every power whose action consists solely in surrender can only finish by self-annihilation. Everything that lives resists; that which does not resist allows itself to be cut up piecemeal."

The hypotheses of this section have thus indicated as factors in the stability of a rule symbols, goods and services, instruments of violence, and power practices—the major political methods. None of these singly is sufficient, each has been held to be necessary. Emphasis on all the factors is another expression of the present pluralistic observational standpoint (principle of interdetermination). The factors are not, of course, independent of one another. But no one of them can be singled out as always and everywhere *the* cause of changes in rule. In the analysis of any given situation, all of them must be explicitly taken into account.[23]

§10.4 *The Course of Revolution*

DF. A political change is a *transformation* or *reformation* according to the scope of practices involved and the degree to which they are modified; *moderate* or *radical*, according to whether or not the change is made in accordance with the political formula.

An important characteristic of the political process is the occurrence of novel perspectives and operations.[24] To a certain extent it is possible to anticipate the locus of innovation, to foresee, for example, that new political institutions are more likely to appear where new methods of production are coming into use than where established methods continue to be applied. More generally, we can expect that innovation is

23. The present emphasis on the multiplicity of factors entering into the precipitation of revolutionary crisis is neatly formulated in Hobbes (*Elements of Law,* II, 8): "To dispose men to sedition three things concur. The first is discontent [goods and services]; for as long as a man thinketh himself well, and that the present government standeth not in his way to hinder his proceeding from well to better, it is impossible for him to desire the change thereof. The second is pretence of right [symbols]; for though a man be discontent, yet if in his own opinion there be no just cause of stirring against, or resisting the government established, nor any pretence to justify this resistance, and to procure aid, he will never show it. The third is hope of success [instruments of violence and power practices]; for it were madness to attempt without hope, when to fail is to die the death of a traitor. Without these three: discontent, pretence, and hope, there can be no rebellion."

24. We mean novel in relation to antecedent practices, not in an absolute sense. Compare Bryce, 1893, I, 34: "There is wonderfully little genuine inventiveness in the world, and perhaps least of all has been shown in the sphere of political institutions."

the more likely to occur the greater the intensity of the continuing political situation.[25]

The definition concerns the extent of the innovation and the methods by which it is brought about. In both cases, of course, we are dealing with differences of degree, not absolute demarcations. Innovations consisting in changes in practices of limited scope, or in redistribution of power among top elites, or in purely formal rather than effective power practices, we call political reformations; and political transformations where the innovation effects a wide range of practices, replaces one elite by quite another, alters patterns of control as well as authority.

When the innovation is carried out in accord with the political formula, we speak of the means as moderate: the amendment of a constitution in the manner which it itself provides, the granting of concessions by an absolute monarch, or, in general, innovation through the normal legislative process. Radical methods are characterized by "direct action"—that is, action by others than duly constituted authorities, and usually by the exercise of violence. (Violence does not *necessarily* constitute a "radical" method; there may be cases, for instance, where the chief regularly defends his power position by a formalized test of his prowess.)

DF. A political *reform* is a reformation carried out by moderate methods.

Where the reform chiefly concerns the personnel of power, we refer to the innovation as a *succession;* where it concerns power practices, it is a *programmatic reform.* The election of a "reform administration" (United States) or a "Labor Government" (England) exemplify reform by succession; the adoption of the income tax amendment or repeal of the Corn Laws exemplify programmatic reform as here defined.[26] Such

25. The *anticipation* of a political innovation, even when correct, is to be distinguished from *making* it. On the one hand, a political prediction may function in the power process as well as in inquiry into that process, so that its enunciation may contribute to its own truth (as has been frequently pointed out with regard to Marxist predictions). On the other hand, political inventiveness requires a "foothold" in the political situation, so that the invention can be predicted without thereby occurring. See "The Self-fulfilling Prophecy" in Robert K. Merton, *Social Theory and Social Structure,* The Free Press of Glencoe, Illinois, 1949, chap. vii.

26. "Reform" is used here in a purely descriptive sense, and is not to be con-

changes are authoritatively sanctioned, and are superimposed on a continuity of authority and control patterns. By contrast, Hitler's coming to power under the political forms of the Weimar Republic is not merely a succession, nor the Nazi rule a merely programmatic reform: not only the authority but even the control patterns were radically altered when power was acquired.

DF. A *palace revolution* is a change in governors contrary to the political formula but retaining it.

A palace revolution is a nonauthoritative transfer of governmental authority which nevertheless retains the authority structures. It is a reformation by radical means. Assassination of the reigning monarch, but with continuation of the monarchy, exemplifies a palace revolution in the present sense. The term is usually limited to cases where the transfer of authority is effected by other members of the ruling group—a conspiracy by those inhabiting the "palace." [27] But here the meaning is more general: it includes any nonauthoritative change in government without corresponding changes in governmental policy.[28]

PROP. The likelihood of assassination varies (a) inversely with adherence to the political doctrine by the mass, (b) inversely with the actualization of power counterelites, and, (c)

strued as implying a preferential valuation of the new state of affairs. Both the passage and the repeal of the prohibition amendment, for instance, are reforms in the present sense. The concept is to be contrasted not with "reaction" but with "revolution," as is done, for instance, by Bluntschli, 1921, 507–8: "Reform implies (1) that the change is introduced in accordance with the constitution . . . the change must be constitutional in form. (2) The change must conform to the spirit of the constitution. . . . If either the form or the spirit of the constitution is violated, a change is no longer reform but revolution."

27. Compare Machiavelli, *Discourses,* III, 6: "Conspiracies formed by a number of persons have generally for their originators the great men of the state, or those on terms of familiar intercourse with the prince. None other, unless they are madmen, can engage in conspiracies; for men of low condition, who are not intimate with the prince, have no chance of success, not having the necessary conveniences for the execution of their plots." Nor, it may be added, are they likely to be afterward accepted as the bearers of authority, as would be the case with the "great men" of the state.

28. Palace revolution might be further distinguished from a *break in succession,* which is a transfer of authority not specified by the political formula, but not (directly) counter to it. For instance, when the king dies without heirs, the resultant conflict for the throne is not called a palace revolution, but neither is it the formal process of succession. It may, of course, provide the basis for revolution as well as reform.

directly with increasing concentration and narrowing allocation of authority or control.

The hypothesis has reference, of course, only to politicized assassination. The topic is introduced at this point because it is one of the characteristic practices by which a palace revolution is effected. But assassination has, of course, a more general significance as an index of a prerevolutionary situation; this aspect of assassination is formulated in part (b) of the hypothesis.[29]

Assassination increases, on the hypothesis, when the regime is acquiesced to without intense adherence by the mass to the political doctrine on which the regime rests. In the extreme case, assassination presents itself as a means, in the famous phrase, of "tempering despotism." And even short of such extremes, without intense adherence to the political doctrine, identification with (loyalty to) the bearers of authority is weakened; so that conspiracies and intrigues can readily purchase support and at any rate need fear no strong opposition. In a word, it is the perspectives of the mass which confer authority on the governors; when the latter are no longer cloaked in authority, the probability of assassination increases.

The second part of the hypothesis is that assassination is the more likely to occur when the regime stands in the way of rising power groups. The greater the disparity between the power position and potential of such groups the greater the stress toward enhancement of power position. And when the potential falls short of undisputed rule—because, for instance, of the strength of rival counterelites, or a too limited control over the instruments of violence—assassination is an increasingly probable practice. As Lerner puts it, "Assassination is an index of the gap between the driving political impulses of men and the limits for their attainment set up by the existing political forms." [29] Of course, if the potential of the rising counterelite were sufficiently great, these forms would be swept aside altogether.

From this standpoint, the significance of concentration of power is apparent. Clearly, little is to be expected from the assassination of individuals with only a small share in the decision-making process (except as a symbol of protest, as

29. See the article on "Assassination" by Max Lerner in *ESS*.

pointed out in the next paragraph). Conversely, Lerner observes, "Where power is centralized in a single person assassination recommends itself . . . as easily the best method for seizing it." [29]

In general, assassination functions as *propaganda of the deed* rather than as an instrument directly effecting changes in power practices. It is significant because of its effect on the perspectives of both elite and mass, rather than by its immediate consequences on the power process. What is important in the power process is usually not the particular individual, but the bases of elite recruitment, and the nature of the practices flowing from the resultant pattern of control. These are rarely changed directly by assassination. But the latter may bring certain demands prominently into the focus of attention, and alter by terror the structure of expectations of both rulers and ruled. Predispositions against violence, and initially intense faiths and loyalties may, however, give it a contrary effect; as is true of other forms of propaganda, propaganda of the deed can operate only on favorable predispositions.

DF. A *political revolution* is a radical change in the regime (authority structure); a *social revolution*, in the rule (control structure).

Revolution has often been regarded as a pathological process falling outside the "natural" course of political interaction. Such a viewpoint, having much in common with Aristotle's immanent teleology (but not his own political theory), is of course normatively ambiguous. The "natural" can be specified as such only by standards of valuation, which are rarely made explicit. From the observational standpoint of political science rather than political philosophy no such discrimination can be made. When political theory aims at the description and explanation of the political process rather than its justification, it must give to every part of this process the full weight and significance attaching to it by virtue of its empirical interconnections with the other parts of the process. From this standpoint, revolution and the expectation of revolution are to be considered as regular and important features of the political process.[30]

30. Compare Tawney, 1931, 288: "In a world where revolutions, carried out

Revolution is characterized by radical methods of political innovation, whether on the level of formal or effective power. Nothing is said in the definition concerning the specific content of these changes (their direction); only the extent and method of the change determine whether or not it is revolutionary.[31] In a political revolution the authority structures alone are changed, the underlying pattern of control remaining unaltered. An example is the replacement of a monarchy by a republic with the same ruling class and the same basis of elite recruitment—for instance, the American Revolution. In social revolution it is the patterns of control which are changed, as for instance in the Russian revolution. A social revolution is ordinarily a political revolution as well: basic changes in the control structure cannot be brought about easily within the framework of the old regime. The regime operates, as we have seen, to sustain the control structure with which it is associated; the new patterns of control also require, therefore, new political forms.[32]

Changes in the social process sometimes extend beyond

---

with varying degrees of violence, treachery, and heroism are the source whence the most respectable of states derive their title, to greet with cries of scandalized propriety a diagnosis which refers to them is obviously . . . either naif or insincere."

31. Compare Michels, 1915, 3–4 n.: "The expression 'revolutionary' is frequently applied simply to the struggle for liberty conducted by inferior classes of the population against superior, if this struggle assumes a violent form, whereas logically [that is, by the definition chosen] revolution implies nothing but a fundamental transformation, and the use of the term cannot be restricted to describe the acts of any particular class, nor should it be associated with any definite external form of violence. . . . From this outlook, the concepts 'revolutionary' and 'reactionary' ('reactionary' as contrasted with conservative), 'revolution' and 'counter-revolution,' fuse into a single whole. It is moreover utterly unscientific to associate with these terms moral ideas whose theoretical bearing is purely evolutionary [*sic*]. Yet we have to remember that in political matters such judgments of value may be effective means of struggle towards political and sometimes also towards moral ends; but they are apt to lead us astray if we use them to aid us in defining historical tendencies or conceptions."

32. When, however, a counterelite acquires power without mass support, it may preserve the forms to disguise changes in the control patterns. Compare Machiavelli, *Discourses*, I, 25: "He who desires or attempts to reform the government of a state, and wishes to have it accepted and capable of maintaining itself to the satisfaction of everybody, must at least retain the semblance of the old forms; so that it may seem to the people that there has been no change in the institutions, even though in fact they are entirely different from the old ones. For the great majority of mankind are satisfied with appearances, as though they were realities, and are often even more influenced by the things that seem than by those that are."

power practices to other values as well. The patterns with regard to all the basic values of the culture may change; we may then speak of *total revolution.* This takes place, for instance, when a "primitive" culture is abandoned for the Western European. There is, of course, a continuous gradation between all these types of political innovation.

PROP. Social revolution occurs within a short time span only by the exercise of violence.

None of the other political changes—succession, programmatic reform, palace revolution, political revolution—necessarily deprives the elite of power; indeed, many of them even strengthen the power position of the elite. In social revolution, the power position is directly threatened, and the elite meets the threat with every available means. When symbols, goods and services, and diplomacy are exhausted or no longer effective, violence ensues. Voluntary relinquishment of power —"revolution by consent"—is excluded by this hypothesis; as indeed it was by the earlier hypothesis that power is always exercised in the manner accepted by the power group as the most economical way of maintaining and increasing its power. Michels observes (1915, 245),

> A class considered as a whole never spontaneously surrenders its position of advantage. It never recognizes any moral reason sufficiently powerful to compel it to abdicate in favor of its "poorer brethren."

A political transformation can be brought about only by radical means.

The time factor enters into the hypothesis because changes in the control patterns may be so gradual that there is no stage at which violence is expected by the elite to be more economical than further alteration in these patterns. And even with this expectation on the part of the elite, it may be difficult in the given situation for it to enlist the support of a sufficiently large part of the dependent classes and the mass.

Thus the instruments of violence play a particularly important role in the revolutionary transformation. This role, however, is not that of directly supporting social revolution. For the fighting strength of the armed forces of the old regime is more or less seriously impaired—with regard to both predispositions and environmental factors—by the recurrent crises of the prerevolutionary situation. The revolutionary service which the army renders, as A. Meusel points out (article on Revolution in the *ESS*), is "not the active one of supplying the revolution with a military instrument, but the purely passive one of leaving the tottering regime [rule] defenseless." [33]

Social revolution, then, occurs only with direct action by the mass. This is the essence of its "radical" character. The typical pattern of palace revolution is action by a clique; and political revolution may be carried out by a relatively small power group in a coup d'état. Social revolution, on the other hand, entails a much more thoroughgoing reconstruction of the political situation than could be carried out by any such group, however well organized, without the active participation of the mass. A powerful counterelite is a necessary but not a sufficient condition for social revolution. On this hypothesis, revolution occurs not when the value position of the mass is at its lowest point but at a relatively high one (compare Edwards, 1927, 33–4).

Direct participation of the mass in social revolution has been repeatedly emphasized in Marxist theory. Trotsky, for instance, writes (1936, I, xvii),

> The most indubitable feature of a revolution is the direct interference of the masses in historic events. . . . The history of a revolution is for us first of all a history of the forcible entrance of the masses into the realm of rulership over their own destiny.

This is not to say that mass action in revolution is in accord with explicitly formulated plans and programs; neither, on the other hand, is it merely a response to agitation. The mass follows the leadership of a counterelite on the basis of predispositionally intense perspectives of opposition to the established power pattern. For brief periods, it may act independently of

33. Where the army does retain its fighting effectiveness, it often constitutes itself an autonomous power, and plays an independent role in the revolutionary process. The point is made by L. H. Jenks ("Armed Forces," *ESS*): "When the authority nominally in control of the army does not or cannot actually exercise its power, such control may lapse into other hands and the army may play the part of an independent and often deciding political factor." This is clearly exemplified, for instance, in the history of the late Roman Empire.

such leadership; but some leadership—rank-and-file consellation appears as action continues.

The continuation of a social revolution, once initiated, depends on continued participation by the mass (the revolution is not "complete" till the counterelite has is fact sufficient power to maintain itself). Such continued participation presents greater difficulties for the counterelite than the initial acts of revolutionary opposition. As Machiavelli tersely puts it (*The Prince*, VI, 5),

> The nature of the people is mutable; it is easy to persuade them of anything, but difficult to keep them in that persuasion. Hence the prophet should be so well prepared that when they no longer believe he can make them believe by force.

In particular, therefore, the revolution must proceed (or be symbolized to the mass as proceeding) from one success to another. The mass is far less favorably predisposed to withstanding even temporary setbacks than is the counterelite. Thus the counterelite as well as the elite strives to set limits for mass action; for, as was pointed out in the preceding paragraph, the mass may break away from the leadership of the counterelite, and it is the more likely to do so as deprivations multiply in the course of the revolution. The counterelite cannot attain power without the instrumentality of the mass, but the instrument is a threat to its own position as well as to that of the elite it seeks to supplant.[34]

PROP. Succession, programmatic reform, and palace revolution function as substitutes for political and social revolution.

The hypothesis is twofold: first, that the less fundamental changes have the (proximate) consequence of reducing the intensity of predispositions favorable to the more fundamental ones; and second, that the changes occur because of expectations of this consequence.

Every succession, programmatic reform, or palace revolution alters the structures of the mass's expectations, identifications, and demands simply because of the overt change in the political situation. Opposition perspectives in the mass are not ordinarily directed to the adoption of fully specified pol-

34. See, on this point, J. B. S. Hardman on "Masses" in *ESS*.

icies, but toward a more or less unspecified "change in policy." (This is exemplified, for instance, in the American electorate's voting for the "outs" in periods of deprivation and for the "ins" in periods of indulgence regardless of the absence of significant principled differences between the two major parties.) Thus the less fundamental changes weaken demands for the more fundamental ones because the latter are in considerable degree simply demands for "a change." The process is reinforced by the elite's symbolization of the less fundamental changes as being more fundamental than in fact they are. A palace revolution is almost invariably symbolized as a change not merely in governors but in power practices and value distribution; reform is always represented as "sweeping" and permanent; even a succession with continuity of policy may nevertheless also be designated as a "New Deal." (In the same way political revolution may have the proximate consequences of weakening demands for social revolution, and may be symbolized as such; this is exemplified, to a degree, by the February revolution in Russia.)

On the hypothesis, it is because of these considerations that the less fundamental changes are brought about by the elite. Of course reforms occur in response to intense demands by the mass; but these demands are effective only as threats—however implicit and indirect—to the power position of the elite. Bismarck's policy of social reform, for instance, resulted from explicit considerations of this kind. Trotsky states the point in general terms (1936, I, 246):

> It is indubitable that under pressure from the popular mass, ruling classes have more than once in history made concessions. But "pressure" means, in the last analysis, a threat to crowd the ruling class out of the power and occupy its place.

It may be repeated that on the present view the threat does not stem directly from the mass, but is constituted by the possibility of mass support for a counterelite.

Political theorists (for instance, Friedrich) sometimes speak of *constituent power* as the "residuary power of a not inconsiderable part of the community to change or replace an established order by a new constitution." If this power is understood in a formal sense, it is by no means characteristic of every body politic. The subjects of a king ruling by divine right, for instance, do not have the formal power of abolishing the monarchy, or even replacing the king by one of their own choice. In general, the formal constitution may or may not make proviso for its own abolition or even amendment. On the level of control rather than authority, constituent power is in fact the power of making revolution. This power is, indeed, universal (though not, to be sure, the power of making successful revolution), and this fact is thus an important consideration for every elite. As Willoughby declares (1911, 282–3):

> The fact is, as must be apparent to all, that there are limits to the endurance of any people, however patient, unenlightened, and submissive, and when oppressed beyond this limit they will prefer the evils of open resistance to those of submission; and if this oppression be carried so far as to excite the opposition of the entire people, or a large portion of them, the ruling powers will be overthrown. These are facts that are necessarily recognized by every ruler.

The present hypothesis is that such recognition enters as a consideration in every extensive reform.

It is to be added that the hypothesis deals only with the proximate consequences of succession, programmatic reform, and palace revolution. Their more remote consequences may nevertheless be to increase the likelihood of political and social revolution. They increase the politicization of the mass, strengthen expectations of changes in the control structure and value distribution, and weaken the old symbols of authority. And they may also enhance the value position and thus power potential both of the mass and of various counterelites.

PROP. The course of revolution is sought to be limited by each participant group to the attainment of a favorable power position for itself.

This hypothesis rejects the conception of revolution as carried out by a coalition of opposition groups "working together for the common good," the allocation of power among these groups to be determined after the elite is overthrown. It asserts, on the contrary, that revolution is a process of internal power striving among revolutionary groups as much as a conflict between these groups and the elite. There is power balancing among the various counterelites, as well as between them and the elite they seek to supplant.

In particular, the social revolutionary movement comprises always more limited opposition groups, seeking only a palace revolution (change in governors), or only a political revolution. As the more limited aims are attained, support will be withdrawn by the groups having those aims, and they may in fact actively oppose the further course of the revolution.[35]

Even a social revolution falls short of totality. It is limited to changes in the control structure, and does not necessarily extend to other values than power except as these are directly affected by that structure. Hence it comes about that sections of the old elite continue to belong to the elect (with regard to wealth and well-being, for example).[36] Such sections of the elite may be prepared even to support the initial stages of the revolution in the expectation of being able to limit its further development by the power accruing from their support. Similar considerations arise from the fact that even the control structure is not completely transformed. Techniques are retained, and with them specialists in the appropriate skills. Thus partial control remains in the same hands, those of a relatively permanent subelite (civil servants, specialists in production, and so on). This subelite, too, may give limited support to the revolutionary movement.

PROP. The counterelite constitutes the initial elite of the new power structure.

"The members of the first following," says R. Schmidt ("Leadership," in *ESS*), "are destined to constitute the leading class of the reorganized state, of which they are the nucleus." This is due to the fact that, as Schmidt observes, "the reconstruction of a state presupposes the existence of a trained hierarchy to replace the nucleus of the old state." Such a hierarchy is provided by the counterelite.

35. Compare A. Meusel, article on "Revolution" in *ESS:* "The closer a social group is to its goal, the less likely it is to undertake revolutionary action and the more eagerly it will exploit a revolution for its exclusive benefit. After the first concessions have been gained, the groups which have thereby achieved emancipation . . . tend to withdraw from the revolutionary struggle and to constitute themselves a new party of law and order." One of the techniques by which such groups strive to limit the course of revolution, Meusel points out, is to symbolize its further progress as deprivational to those intermediate between them and the most aggressive counterelite.

36. Compare Catlin, 1930, 116: "Change in history has usually involved the displacement from power of those who held rule and wealth under an earlier regime, and who remain wealthy, but not powerful under the new regime."

The point to the hypothesis is that revolution does not in general diminish the total amount of control or authority, nor necessarily decentralize or disperse it, but transfers it from one elite to another. The mass is directly active in revolution, to be sure, and the resultant power practices may therefore be more indulgent to it, but a power structure remains, and it remains roughly pyramidal. (The universality of the differentiation between elite and mass has already been discussed.) The aim of revolution is not to widen the distribution of power—formal aims elaborated in the utopia are not in question here—but, for the mass, the aim is to improve its value position with regard to other values than power and, for the counterelite, to put power in its own hands. (Compare the popular slogan in the opening phases of theh Russian revolution, "Bread and Peace!" with the Bolshevik slogan, "All Power to the Soviets!"). Far from always decentralizing and dispersing power, revolution may have the contrary tendency.

This tendency becomes stronger in the degree of prior organization of the revolutionary process. The revolution involves an internal power striving, as well as conflict with the old elite, and organization increases the potential of the striving groups. The new-won power will thereby be effectively applied against rivals within the counterelite, with the justification of "defense of the revolution." This has been an important element in the anarchist position. Bakunin would have "the revolution" occur as a spontaneous outburst of the masses; its direction by a well-organized counterelite would "inevitably lead to a class dictatorship under an organized oligarchy." Similarly, G. Sorel points out (***Reflections on Violence***, B. W. Huebsch, 1915, 118):

> Experience has always shown us hitherto that revolutionaries plead "reasons of State" as soon as they get into power, that they employ police methods and look upon justice as a weapon which they may use unfairly against their enemies.

It is, no doubt, with this phenomenon in mind that Ambrose Bierce devilishly defined revolution as "an abrupt change in the form of misgovernment."

The present hypothesis refers to the counterelite as only initially constituting the elite of the new rule. As was pointed out in the preceding hypothesis, the course of revolution brings to the fore not one but several counterelites. Continued internal power striving may significantly alter the composition of the ruling group. In general, as the revolution becomes stabilized new skills become important, and the bases of elite recruitment shift accordingly. The agitator, for example, may give way to the administrator, and the specialists in symbols and violence to those skilled in diplomacy and the organization of production.

PROP. Symbols of a successful utopia continue to function as ideology.

In the prerevolutionary situation, the utopia marshals support for the counterelite by symbolizing it as representing the mass and, particularly, the valid interests of the mass. It provides, moreover, rival symbols of authority, and new principles justifying the proposed redistribution of power. When the transfer of power occurs, the utopian symbols of identification, demand, and expectation replace the ideology of the supplanted rule and function in turn as the new ideology. Every new elite speaks a new vocabulary.

As the revolution becomes solidified, effective power practices may deviate more and more from the formal patterns elaborated in the erstwhile utopia. The disparity between formal and effective power, between principled and expediency interests of the new elite does not, however, reflect itself immediately in the political symbols invoked. The new power structure continues to be symbolized as the realization of the revolutionary perspectives. As Pareto bitingly observes (1935, 1555),

> Burning today the idols they worshipped yesterday, emulating the "reactionary" governments which they were wont of yore to vilify, they are concerned to create an impression that they still cherish the principle which they found so convenient when they were fighting those governments.

Symbols effective enough to bring revolution to culmination cannot easily be abandoned when the revolution is won. New counterelites are continually brought forward by the power process; support of the mass remains a necessary condition for the stability of any rule.

DF. The patterns of *diffusion* and *restriction* of revolution are the practices by which revolution is territorially extended or limited.

Revolution may have an effect in the world arena as well as in the body politic in which the transformation originates. Where this effect is marked, and the symbols of identification invoked are worldwide rather than parochial in scope, we may speak of the area of origination as a *world revolutionary center*. France—and more particularly Paris—was the center of a world revolutionary upheaval in 1789 and the years following. The "rights of man" were opposed to the privileges of the king and nobility; and presently these rights were sought by radical means, and claimed for all men everywhere, not only in France. In 1917 Russia was the seat of another world revolutionary transformation, this time in the name of the world "proletariat" against the world "bourgeoisie" (and feudality).

If *total diffusion* occurred, the world revolutionary pattern would become the pattern of a universal state. Both the French and Russian patterns stopped short of universality; they were *partially diffused* and *partially restricted*. If there had been total restriction, the pattern would have disappeared (as effective in the world arena).

Various patterns of restriction may be invoked. *Restriction by revival* is the modification of the revolutionary pattern by reactivation of earlier patterns. (Such revivals may occur either within or outside the center.) The pattern of strong executive power was rejuvenated in France after the initial phases of supremacy of the assembly. In Russia, the institution of money was only one of the many former practices incorporated after the early period of experiment with "war communism." The sentiments connected with nationalism and patriotism were reactivated in the Russian pattern after the dogmatic phase of revolutionary internationalism and antipatriotism. Some of the revivals outside Russia and France were extremely reactionary, ancient institutions being given renewed support in opposition to the threat presented by the revolutionary center. In Hungary, for instance, the failure of the brief Soviet regime was followed by many efforts to do away with liberalism and to reinstate the feudal past.

Restriction by partial incorporation consists in limiting the scope of the revolutionary center by adopting some features of the center pattern. In struggling against France older elites found it expedient to make many concessions, such as adopting the appeal to mass patriotism and nationalism. Often the recruiting base of the elite was enlarged, and such institutions were copied as universal suffrage, written constitutions, and bills of rights. The vocabulary of the "Great Revolution" was no doubt more widely diffused by partial incorporation than the operations originally linked with the words. Elites protected themselves in the same way from the inroads of the Russian Revolution, often increasing the frequency with which terms like "Socialist" or "Socialism" were invoked, and multiplying the social security functions of the state.

Restriction by functional differentiation consists in rejecting the initial world revolutionary pattern in the name of new key symbols. The "liberal" revolution was not functionally differentiated until the Communists (Socialists) began to attack its basic claims, to declare that the plutocrats were the winners, not the "people," and to incite against the "plutocracy" in the name of the "proletariat." The first great challenge confronting the Russian Revolution was in the name of "race." (Actually the concept of "race" was given modern form parallel with, and to some extent derivative from, the economic class analysis of Marx.) In the name of achieving political conditions that would make possible the breeding of an "Aryan" elite, the Nazi racists scorned the economic materialism of the Communists and put forward an equally sweeping version of human destiny. Another challenge—but one that has not yet made itself as potent as the racial myth—rejects the claim of the Russians to speak in the name of the whole working class, declaring that the proletariat has been betrayed into yielding power to a new ruling class of "bureaucratic collectivists."

The process of diffusion, on the other hand, is not limited to the adoption of the *initial world revolutionary pattern*, the institutions proclaimed and put into effect during the early phases of revolution. It is convenient to distinguish from this initial pattern the world revolutionary *pattern of the epoch*, the institutions, deriving from the revolution, common to the major states of the world after the revolutionary process has gone forward for some time.

Although the revolution in France did not keep to the initial form, nor did it bring about a world state, the new institutions contributed to and shared in the new adjustment of institutional life among the major powers of the nineteenth century. There was a general liquidation of feudal perspectives and operations, and a rise of nationalism, industrialization, and democratic ideologies. A parallel development may occur in our period as the movements given so much impetus by the Russian Revolution come to rest, and common institutions are approximated throughout the globe.

However, the outlines of the world revolutionary pattern of our epoch are far from clear. In a bipolarizing world of continuing crisis, considerations of fighting effectiveness may favor the rise to power of elites which are recruited in the main from the military and the political police. One or more garrison-prison states may eventually encompass the globe. If the factors sustaining these developments persist, the direction of recent history will be reversed. Instead of enlarging the domain of mobile societies, the trend will be toward the restriction of mobility and the restoration of caste. But it is not "inevitable" that this "developmental construct" will be corroborated by the course of future events. If the factors supporting the intensity of crisis are reduced in strength, the factors carrying the world equilibrium in the direction of world commonwealth can assert themselves once more.

FREQUENT CITATIONS

Aristotle. *Politics.*

Bagehot, W. *Physics and Politics.* D. Appleton, 1873.

Barker, E. *Reflections on Government.* Oxford University Press, 1942.

Barnes, H. E. *Sociology and Political Theory.* Alfred A. Knopf, 1924.

Beard, C. A. *Economic Basis of Politics.* Alfred A. Knopf, 1934.

Bentham, J. *Principles of Morals and Legislation.*

Bluntschli, J. K. *Theory of the State.* Clarendon Press, 1921.

Bryce, J. *American Commonwealth.* Macmillan, 1893.

——— *Modern Democracies.* Macmillan, 1924.

Catlin, G. E. G. *Science and Method of Politics.* Alfred A. Knopf, 1927.

——— *A Study of the Principles of Politics.* Macmillan, 1930.

Dicey, A. V. *Law and Public Opinion.* Macmillan, 1926.

Edwards, L. P. *Natural History of Revolution.* University of Chicago Press, 1927.

ESS. Encyclopedia of the Social Sciences.

The Federalist.

Friedrich, C. J. *Constitutional Government and Politics.* Harper, 1937.

Goodnow, F. J. *Politics and Administration.* Macmillan, 1900.

Hobbes. *Leviathan.*

Kelsen, H. *General Theory of Law and State.* Harvard University Press, 1945.

Korkunov, N. M. *General Theory of Law.* Macmillan, 1922.

Laski, H. J. *Grammar of Politics.* G. Allen & Unwin, 1925.

——— *State in Theory and Practice.* Viking Press, 1935.

Lasswell, H. D. *Psychopathology and Politics.* University of Chicago Press, 1930.

——— *World Politics and Personal Insecurity.* McGraw-Hill, 1935.

——— *Politics: Who Gets What, When, How.* McGraw-Hill, 1936.

——— and Blumenstock, D. *World Revolutionary Propaganda.* Alfred A. Knopf, 1939.

——— *The Analysis of Political Behaviour.* K. Paul, Trench, Trubner, 1947.

——— *Power and Personality.* W. W. Norton, 1948.

——— Leites, N., and Associates. *Language of Politics; Studies in Quantitative Semantics.* G. W. Stewart, 1949.

Lippmann, W. *Public Opinion.* Harcourt, Brace, 1922.

Locke. *Two Treatises on Civil Government.*

Lowell, A. L. *Public Opinion and Popular Government.* Longmans, Green, 1913.

Lowell, A. L. *Public Opinion in War and Peace.* Harvard University Press, 1926.

Machiavelli. *Discourses.*

——— *The Prince.*

MacIver, R. M. *Modern State.* Clarendon Press, 1926.

——— *Web of Government.* Macmillan, 1947.

MacLeod, W. C. *Origin and History of Politics.* J. Wiley, 1931.

Mannheim, K. *Ideology and Utopia.* Harcourt, Brace, 1936.

Marx and Engels. *Communist Manifesto.*

Merriam, C. E. *New Aspects of Politics.* 2d ed., University of Chicago Press, 1931.

——— *Political Power.* McGraw-Hill, 1934.

——— *Systematic Politics.* University of Chicago Press, 1945.

Michels, R. *Political Parties.* Hearst's International Library, 1915.

Mosca, G. *Ruling Class.* McGraw-Hill, 1939.

Ostrogorski, M. *Democracy and the Party System.* Macmillan, 1926.

Pareto, V. *Mind and Society.* Harcourt, Brace, 1935.

Rousseau. *Social Contract.*

Russell, B. *Power.* W. W. Norton, 1938.

Tawney, R. H. *Equality.* Harcourt, Brace, 1931.

Timasheff, N. S. *Introduction to Sociology of Law.* Harvard University Press, 1939.

Trotsky, L. *History of the Russian Revolution.* Simon & Schuster, 1936.

Veblen, T. *The Theory of the Leisure Class.* Macmillan, 1918.

Wallas, G. *Human Nature in Politics.* A. Constable, 1908.

Weber, M. *Wirtschaft und Gesellschaft.* J. C. B. Mohr (P. Siebeck), 1925.

Willoughby, W. W. *An Examination of the Nature of the State.* Macmillan, 1911.

INDEX